W.D. MACKINTOSH

July 1937

EUROPE IN ARMS

by the same author

EUROPE IN ARMS

by

LIDDELL HART

FABER AND FABER LIMITED
24 Russell Square
London

First Published in March Mcmxxxvii
by Faber and Faber Limited
24 Russell Square London W.C.1
Printed in Great Britain by
Latimer Trend & Co Ltd Plymouth

Tribute from a Sassenach
to
IAN HAMILTON
and
JOHN KENNEDY
leaders of men
and men of imagination

Foreword

========

The rearmament of Europe, as well as the technical development which affects it, is moving so fast that anyone who attempts to write a book on the subject is like a man trying to jump on a bus along a road that has no halting places. If he were to set out to write an entirely fresh book, allowing the time needed to study each aspect of the question, he would almost certainly have to rewrite it by the time he had finished it. In these circumstances, it has seemed wiser to make use of material already written, after studies of the various problems, revising and adding to this as required. The original material thus utilized consists partly of articles contributed to *The Times* during the past two years, as its Military Correspondent and adviser on defence in general; partly of articles contributed to various British and American reviews, military and general, or to *The New York Times*. This material has been selected for its bearing on the general theme of the book, and composed in chapters, some of them merely revised, others freshly woven, with new material. I offer the product in full recognition of its faults and deficiencies. With more time a much better book could have been written on

Foreword

the subject. But for that it would be necessary to call a halt in the ever-accelerating process of rearmament and progress of invention. And the onlooker, although he may see most of the game, is not allowed a whistle.

In treating such a subject there are many aspects which call for attention and invite discussion. I realize that those covered here are by no means exhaustive. The arrangement, too, has been a difficulty because so many of the aspects blend into others. The idea which has guided the grouping ultimately adopted is made clear by the titles given to the four parts of the book; but these parts are not watertight compartments—they merely represent the predominant nature of the chapters in each. Thus the chapters in Part I are mainly concerned with the present state of the forces of the Great Powers; those in Part II with some of the chief problems of warfare and current defence policy; those in Part III with the new measures that are being taken or, in the writer's view, might be taken; those in Part IV with an analysis from different angles, and in the light of past experience, of the process of forecasting the nature, course, and effects of future wars. The opening chapter is a reminder of the purpose of defence, lest we forget that it is only a means to an end.

Contents

Contents

x

CHAPTER I

The Defence of Freedom

The war to exhaustion has had as its sequel a generation of revolutions in reverse. One by one the nations of the Continent have been engulfed in civil strife, from which they have emerged with a form of government and an attitude to the rights of the individual that is essentially alien to our tradition. This island, if now less of an island strategically—because the air has bridged the sea—is more than ever an island politically. That situation calls for serious reflection. Will England stand rocklike amid the totalitarian tide until that tide ebbs? Our constitution for several centuries has had its roots in the growing idea of individual liberty. Our history rests on the reconciliation of that idea with order. In the modern world we have sought, instinctively rather than of plan, to combine the legacies of Greece and Rome. For a time, in the last century, our example had an ever-widening influence; it was embraced, with more enthusiasm than understanding, by nations where the tradition of freedom had no roots. They adopted the form of what they conceived to be our constitution without being infused by its spirit. They tried to pin down to a formula what we, with a practical wisdom born of experience,

I

The Defence of Freedom

have never attempted to formulate. The war of 1914-18 interrupted this liberal expansion. Even here it imposed a check on the process of growth. Abroad, its first effect was, naturally, to strengthen the position of all autocratic governments, and thus stiffen their resistance to reform; ultimately, it produced a cataclysm so disruptive that even those who desired to introduce the rule of right were compelled to maintain their rule by might. Recourse to such means endangered the end, while a just repugnance to them hindered their effectiveness even in preserving the newly established democracies. These conditions were the opportunity of more positive and less scrupulous men, for whom the use of force needed no apology, and a further series of upheavals raised to power a new set of rulers whose revival of authoritarianism was the more intense because authority was fresh to them. Their political gospels might show many different facets, but they had a fundamental similarity of attitude—in their deification of the State as represented by themselves, and their extremely positive negation of the individual's freedom of thought and expression. Alike to Communism and Fascism, uniformity is an ideal, and nonconformity a crime. Moreover, the ideal is expressed by a practice of putting the people into military uniform. This invests with doubt any assertion that a gospel is for home consumption, and makes it inevitably the concern of other peoples.

But for this factor there would be little cause to raise the question of England's power to resist the totalitarian tide. Her tradition of ordered freedom has an older and a deeper foundation than any regime of compulsory order. It is true that since the war there has been some erosion of the rights of the individual through the legacy of war legislation, the intensive growth of social legislation, and the

The Defence of Freedom

accompanying tendency to bureaucratic development. But among our people in general the impulses that lead to revolution, and thereby provide opportunity for those who crave autocratic power, seem to be a diminishing element. Toleration has never been so widespread, nor violence so widely disfavoured. The decline of the Liberal party, and the consequent loosening of that sectional label, has helped the spread of liberal ideas through all parties. And they are strongest of all among the growing number who find consistent allegiance to a particular party inconsistent with truth: with that scientific study of conditions which offers the surest basis of progress. Thus, internally, this country's situation to-day offers a better assurance than at any time since the war of evolution in accord with our tradition. The only serious danger to-day lies outside our borders. And the external danger is also the most probable agent towards any revival of internal danger. War is a compound menace. It threatens not only our national existence but all that makes existence worth while.

Events abroad have brought this menace to the fore, and its implications must be faced. At present we are not facing them squarely. One section looks to the repair of our own arms—and looks no further: the need of arms is asserted with little regard to whether they will be effective, and still less to where they may lead. Another section, forswearing arms, looks so far ahead that it overlooks the reality of immediate risks: contemplating a world of common ideals it ignores the destructive power of force exercised by neighbours who have different ideals. 'Pacifism' and 'patriotism' are hurled from side to side as opposed terms of reproach. Meantime a large part of the public, confused by the counter-cries, tends to take the line of least resistance to the danger. Such passive acceptance of

3

fate does not even promise the fragile hope that a policy of passive resistance holds out, while it jeopardizes the building of actual defences. The dangers of this national division, and confusion, in the present critical situation ought to be realized. Without sacrificing the natural diversity which is the source of vitality it should be possible to reach some common basis of co-operation among men of good will. They must combine in building a bridge, unless what each holds dear is to slip into the chasm.

The first need is to achieve a clearer idea of differing points of view. The ardent believer in defence by arms must try to understand the intellectual position of the pacifist, instead of hurling denunciations which miss the mark while marring the atmosphere. The ardent lover of peace must respond, by giving due weight to the practical case for armed defence. Perhaps the difficulty is greater for the former, the 'instinctive patriots' who are accustomed to accept unquestioningly so much that thoughtful men are bound to submit to the test of reason. They are apt to regard as blasphemy, against the tribal gods, an attitude that is essentially a searching for truth and a fervent desire for a true basis of national faith. But they should be able to see the danger of splitting the nation, and should realize that any persecution of pacifism is the surest way to strengthen it. The problem of reconciling pacifists to the necessity of defence is more complex. The arguments for abjuring force have so clear a moral basis that, in a Christian country, they start with a moral advantage over the arguments for rearmament. In theory, they must command the assent of all decent men, while their simplicity strengthens their appeal. And even on practical grounds there is a stronger case for pure pacifism than is generally realized. The power of non-violent resistance has been

4

demonstrated on occasions, and in spite of its experimental nature it has achieved some notable successes. Its advocates, however, are inclined to overlook the fact that these have been obtained against opponents whose code of morality was fundamentally similar, and whose ruthlessness was thereby restrained. Moreover, its employment against a government, by the spiritually minded members of a religious or political movement, is quite a different matter to its employment in the conflict of nations. To offer any chance of success here, it not only demands a higher collective morale than any army has attained, but requires this fortitude to be shown by a whole people. The effectiveness of an army can be maintained by strong leaders supported by an adequate nucleus of staunch and highly trained troops, since it is the well-aimed shots which mainly count, whereas the effectiveness of non-violent resistance is undermined if a fair proportion of members can be induced, by weakness or self-interest, to serve the opponent's purpose. Comparatively, an army is more dependent on its strongest elements, an unarmed force more dependent on its weakest.

Facing these difficulties honestly, and taking account of prevailing conditions, can any reasonable man hold out the expectation that the nation as a whole could be persuaded to try the tremendous experiment of pure pacifism? If not, its advocacy can only weaken the power of this nation to resist the forces of hostile nations, where pacifism is suppressed. The breakdown of our defences might spell the end of our tradition of freedom as well as of the pacifist aim. The issue cannot be shirked. Those who prize peace for the sake of ideals, not merely peace at any price, have a grave responsibility. If the need of defence be admitted as a practical necessity, it largely lies with them whether the defence is adequate. Their support is essential. By withholding it, they invite the downfall of the home of their ideal. In return for their support, however, they may justly expect guarantees that it shall not be abused; that measures of defence shall not lead to militarization or the curtailment of freedom. Here the Government, the services, and the vocally patriotic have a duty: to avoid offence. Denunciations of pacifism inevitably excite suspicion of the speakers' ultimate aims, and thus stiffen opposition. Propaganda for defence too often fails to convey any idea beyond arming because others are doing it. None but the unthinking and those whose patriotism is mere self-interest would regard defence as worth while if, in the process of defence, the spirit of this country were to be extinguished and only the husk remain.

But something more than a working agreement on actual measures is needed. This is too passive—and passive defence will not suffice against a vigorous challenge. There is overflowing vigour in the foreign nationalisms, even though it be obtained by a contraction of spirit which tends to ultimate exhaustion. Men who are infused with a faith, even a false one, will beat men who have no faith; only a good one can withstand the impact. Those who complain of the younger generation's lack of patriotism should, rather, reproach themselves for their failure to define and teach patriotism in higher terms than the mere preservation of a geographical area, its inhabitants and their material interests. Such a material appeal offers no adequate inspiration, nor cause for sacrifice, to the young. Those who are concerned with practical questions of defence ought to realize the practical importance of ideals, especially in arousing the British people. Again and again it has been found that the economic appeal had little power to overcome their characteristic inertia until something stirred their latent idealism. The man who does not take due account of this element is a fool. Its prevalence, as well as its purity, would seem to have increased in recent times. The significance of repeated demonstrations of its power is the greater because it has had no prophet to express it adequately. The professed patriots have concentrated on a doctrine of national self-preservation, and their appeals have had a metallic ring. This marks a relapse. Two generations back, Kipling provided the British people with a gospel of Empire which raised Imperialism above mere materialism: to-day its crudity jars, but it has found no replacement. There is need for a new vision—one bigger than Kipling's, and better. Need, also, for the sense of a mission—not so much to rule as to influence by example. To gain this we must grasp the elements that matter in our tradition—above all, the spirit of freedom. In freedom, truth is perceived and justice promised. From the trinity, vitality springs. If Fascism and Communism can raise enthusiasm among the young, how much better sources have we from which to generate it. At the same time it requires, not a diminished but an intensified self-criticism. For in such self-criticism is the foundation of a faith that can alone assure secure progress. The interests of the State should never demand injustice to the individual, nor any restriction of freedom save where it is used for active interference with others' freedom—justice and freedom are the true interests of the State. Fear and suspicion poison the well-springs of a people—their absence from the atmosphere is the test of whether the State is fitted to fulfil its end. Once aware of the essential elements of our tradition, we betray it if we commit or condone a breach of them within our own land. In upholding them

The Defence of Freedom

against external threats we have a cause worth defence, and sacrifice. It offers a common rallying ground for all parties, and classes. For here patriotism and pacifism are combined in a positive form—and faith.

PART I: FORCES

CHAPTER II

The Air Forces of Europe

The atmosphere of Europe is becomingly heavily charged. Its tendencies inevitably have a reminder of 1914, yet with differences. People everywhere are talking of 'war'. It is easier for men to see the ways in which war may come than how it can be avoided. The hopes that they express have no firm ring of confidence. On the other hand, there is curiously little accent of fear in the forebodings they express. Fear may be the ultimate source of the forces that are gathering, but it does not emerge on the surface. France has been fearing things so long, and so many things, that the edge of her fears may have become dulled. This may help to explain the strange state of resignation that seems to have overtaken the French just at the time when the dangers they have long anticipated are coming closer to realization. Elsewhere on the Continent it is difficult to gauge the measure of the fear because it is submerged in the intoxication that is so palpable. Men are once again talking and singing, with a martial fervour that sends a chill through a sober listener. It is true that they will make intermittent declarations of their repugnance to the idea of another war—if this be true, they have a peculiar way of expressing their dislike. But different as the angles from which the peoples of Europe are viewing the possibility of war, there is a common slant in the view they take of its nature.

Their thoughts instinctively fly upwards—and their imagination flies faster. Memory, of air attacks in the last war, is as much the propellant as any knowledge of air developments since. To anyone who analyses the comparatively slight material results of air raids in 1914-18, it is remarkable to find what a profound psychological impression they made, and have left. Small as was the force employed in these raids, it caused a greater and wider nerve strain than any other agent of warfare. The effects have not disappeared with the cessation of the cause: they are traceable in the general tendency among the public, whenever they think of war, for the thought to be associated immediately with the idea of being bombed from the air. And from this apprehension springs a natural exaggeration.

During these last years, the armaments race has begun again. It is an ominous reality. But here again imagination travels faster than the facts. In 1934 the British public was startled by the declaration of a great newspaper magnate that Germany had 25,000 military aircraft. In 1935 he informed the House of Lords that Germany possessed 10,000 bombers each capable of carrying about a ton of explosives. If the estimate had not mounted as one might have expected, considering that there had been a year's interval for expansion, the picture was certainly painted on a large canvas. The Russians have a reputation for generous-size estimates of any German military preparations: at the same period the Assistant Commissar for War credited the Germans with a total of 3700 military aircraft, including reserves. Even this figure was considerably in excess of what French experts calculated—and the French, since 1914, are not inclined to minimize any menace that Germany possesses.

If fear be the predisposing cause of war, ignorance is the most potent of the factors that nourish it. The fear of the unknown breaks down armies in wartime; in peace time it drives nations, like the Gadarene swine, down to the abyss. Unhappily, it is again becoming epidemic to-day through a fresh wave of 'secrecy'. Fear and secrecy react on each other. 'Spy-mania' is one of the products. This ugly rash is again breaking out on the face of Europe; and no symptom could be more ominous. Its justification is probably slender, as usual. For the knowledge that matters is rarely gained by the methods that thrill the lover of sensational spy-stories: safer, in every sense, is the knowledge that comes by the application of ordinary deductive methods to a mass of data that is common property, fitting together the insignificant fragments on a foundation of technical understanding until they form a mosaic from which a clear picture emerges.

Air strength is normally reckoned in terms of first line aircraft—which represents the number of machines actually in service with formed units. Subject to certain qualifications that I shall touch upon, it gives a reasonable idea of the number of aircraft which could be engaged on the outbreak of war, and thereby enables one to arrive at some calculation of the scale of air attack that a country might launch.

The creation and expansion of the German air force has been carried out in such a haze of secrecy as to foster exaggerated assumptions. Yet there is reason to doubt whether its first line strength exceeded 1200 machines at the end of 1936. Expansion, however, has been moving rapidly, with vigorous governmental aid at every step, to overcome the disadvantages of a late start. By the spring of 1937 it is expected that the German Air Force will attain what is believed to be its immediate goal—a first line strength of 1500 machines. That it did not reach this earlier was due to the difficulty of training personnel and organizing units as fast as the manufacture of machines, which has been proceeding at a rate that was probably in excess of the capacity to absorb them. The accident rate in training is reported to have been extremely high, although the details have been hidden. Another significant feature of the German Air Force is the high proportion of bombers of various types. Fully half the force appears to be composed of bomber squadrons of various kinds, and more than half of these are equipped with large machines that can carry a bomb-load of upwards of a ton, with a radius (out and back distance) of about four hundred miles—far enough to reach the capitals of any of Germany's neighbours. This may help to account for the reluctance which the German leaders have recently shown to consider any agreed check upon air bombing.

Germany, also, has specialized in the construction of civil aircraft that were easily and quickly convertible into effective military machines, and probably a further 200 could have been reckoned on this account. This asset, however, is now losing much of its old significance with the achievement of the air force expansion. So long as Germany was trying to hide the fact that she was developing a military air force it was convenient to have a reserve of pseudo-civil machines that could be converted into bombers in emergency. Now the need for this device has passed. Nevertheless the pilots and personnel carry out several months regular training each year, and there is little doubt that in war they would be immediately formed into regular squadrons, equipped with military aircraft which are held ready for them in peace. The civil aircraft themselves would more likely be utilized for training purposes. There are also the auxiliary and sports associations, in which well over five thousand pilots are said to be in training; from these might emerge enough squadrons to form an additional force of 300-400 machines, besides providing reserve pilots for the Regular Air Force.

The strength of the British Air Force, before an expansion programme was somewhat hurriedly embarked upon in face of the ominous European situation, amounted to only 880 first line machines. The process of expansion, moreover, has been complicated by Italy's invasion of Abyssinia and the consequent tension in the Mediterranean: the diversion of instructors to emergency duty naturally interfered with the training of new personnel. At the end of 1936 the total regular strength was just over 1100. But the needs of India and the other overseas territories, as well as of the Navy, reduced the total regular strength at home to a little under 900 first line machines. Under the present programme of expansion, whose completion has suffered from delays, it should reach a total of 1500 by the spring or summer of 1937, and 1750 by the autumn.

France long had the highest strength among the Western Powers, her total first line strength, being at one time not far short of 1700 machines; it is now probably about 1500. But of these barely 1100 are available at home, the rest being overseas, in North Africa, the Levant, Indo-China, etc. Moreover, most of the French machines are not of a very modern type, although new types of greatly improved performance are expected to come into service gradually from the early months of this year. The number, too, is being increased fifty per cent. An existing factor which has to be taken into account is that France's proportion of bombers is much less than Germany's. But the new French machines will be of much larger bomb-capacity than at present.

The Russian air force is now the greatest in Europe. Its first line strength is reported to be over 3500 machines, and may be as high as 4000. It includes at least 500 large bombers of long radius—of which, because of her geographical distances, she has made a special point. The strength of the Russian air force, together with its striking range, forms the ground on which Hitler is claiming to go beyond the level of parity with the air forces of his Western neighbours. Another feature which Russia has developed is the employment of swarms of machines designed for the attack upon ground targets, in conjunction with the army. Many of her machines are of an obsolescent type, but she is reported to have made better progress than many people would have expected in the creation of the ground organization necessary for the efficient use of such a large air force.

Italy is another country where the veil of secrecy has been tightly drawn. Since the expansion which followed the coming of the Abyssinian war her actual first line strength is probably about 1500 machines. Out of this nearly 200 are said to be still in Eritrea and Somalia, engaged in clearing up the Abyssinian situation, and about the same number is in Libya and the Dodecanese. But Italy can probably exercise the strategic mobility of her air force better than any other country with overseas possessions. For she can concentrate at home in peace, for training, and yet reinforce Libya and the Dodecanese at short notice whenever required. This strategic mobility is growing with the extending range of aircraft—and Abyssinia as well will soon be reinforcible by air as easily as Libya is to-day. Italy has now a large output of new types of bombers of high performance, with a speed of about 220 m.p.h. and a radius of nearly five hundred miles. These have been turned out by the factories as fast as possible. With such a radius, it would be possible, from Libya, to reach not only Alexandria but Port Said, and also the ports in Southern Greece. Only the extreme ends of the Mediterranean would be beyond their stretch.

Such risks as these have called for reflection by the statesmen whose countries carry the main burden of the League and would have to bear the brunt of any 'mad-dog' attack. It is common knowledge that when the possibility arose in the autumn of 1935, the bulk of the British fleet was withdrawn from its historic base of Malta to the extremities of the Mediterranean—a precaution that was a striking testimony to the strategic influence of air-power on sea-power, and the more striking in view of the way that sailors tended to depreciate the new weapon so long as hard facts had not to be faced. That candid recognition of the risk may prove of practical benefit in promoting the adaptation of their own defence systems to modern conditions. Moreover, it gives no encouragement to Italy, on a sane calculation, to precipitate the risk. For her strategic situation as a whole has weaknesses so marked that, on a long view, they should be a check on rash impulses. Apart from the fact that so large a part of her land forces and resources are engulfed in East Africa, precariously dependent on a tenuous lifeline from the homeland, Italy's own situation has handicaps that are inherent in geography:

her long coastline, the narrowness of the country, and the nearness of her main centres to the sea or to neighbouring frontiers, are factors that cannot be ignored. The factories which produce her new long-range instruments of warfare are themselves within uncomfortably short range of the less obvious points from which the forces of other countries might take off. Compared with France, for example, the strategic situation of Italy is on balance unfavourable for any contest in the air. Her vital centres are far more accessible than are those of France to the Italian air bases. The comparison may be extended from the question of the moment to the European problem as a whole. The more one reflects on the involved problems of modern warfare, the more importance seems to attach to the factor of 'vulnerability'—the relative vulnerability of the different countries—in any comparison of strengths.

This in turn has a bearing upon the research for technical surprise which is now being so actively pursued. Those who contemplate taking the offensive in any future European war are impelled to seek a new master-key both by the certainties and uncertainties of the problem. They are forced to recognize that the methods of the last war will not suffice; that nothing but a protracted struggle and an inconclusive result can be expected from the use of armies equipped with the weapons of 1918 merely improved. They fear that such a prolongation of the issue may produce developments that cannot be foreseen, causing a rapid shifting of the balance. The combination of these thoughts is an urge to the search for quick results. In 1914, the military chiefs hoped to decide the issue within a few weeks, and bent their efforts towards this object. That was short enough—and much shorter than the event, after their plans had miscarried. Now, they are coming to the view

that the first few days, or even hours, may be crucial, and
to see that unless they can obtain a decisive advantage
within this brief time it may be unattainable on any calculable basis. Hence their eagerness to find new weapons
that may overcome defence without past delays.

The scope for such technical surprise is not limited to
the invention of new weapons. It may be obtained by an
unexpected multiplication of strength. In 1914 the Germans surprised the French by incorporating their reserve
formations in their striking force, thus deploying nearly
double the numbers that the French expected to meet in
the opening clash. This device may be repeated to-day
with air forces, and it is the possibility which lends instability to the system of calculating air strength in terms
of first line machines. For each first line machine, most
countries aim to maintain three or four in reserve, to make
up the wastage that is likely to occur during the first few
months of a struggle, before the factories can attain their
expanded war rate of production. But an aggressive-
minded power may consider that the risk of being caught
short at the end of a month or two is less than that of failing to gain the maximum advantage in the first days. Or
at any rate that the prospects of early success are worth the
risk. Hence, it may decide to employ a part of its reserve
aircraft with its first line units, increasing their size or
their number. The extent to which it can do this, and the
extent of the surprise attained, will depend on the efficiency of its arrangements.

But if the gamble fails the last state may be worse than
the first. There are so many incalculables. A quantitative
advantage on one side may offset some unrealized qualitative advantage on the other; either may be upset by
some inadequately appreciated advantage in vulner-

ability, or by the belated discovery that the effect of an attack is not equal to what was necessary to repay the effort and justify the risk. Weather conditions, psychological conditions, economic conditions, political contingencies all play their part in complicating the problem. The uncertainty which exists as to the actual state of the various nations' forces is nothing to the uncertainty which prevails as to their effect. If the former engenders the fear which leads to war, the latter justifies fears that may deter the decision to embark upon war. It is a certainty that the vitals of each country are exposed to its neighbours' action. There is one greater certainty—that there is more uncertainty than ever before about all the other factors with which strategists and statesmen must reckon. Compared with the present state of flux, it was simple to make military calculations in the past. The elements of strength were to a great extent calculable. To embark on war then was no greater hazard than that of betting on the favourite—and yet the favourite has often lost. To-day, it is like backing a horse that has never run, and whose breeding even is unknown. Any professional gambler might think it wise to refrain; statesmen should be as wise.

CHAPTER III

The Armies of Europe—The Totalitarian Powers

Napoleon delivered himself of the saying that 'Providence marches with the big battalions'. He was often careless about self-contradiction and also about the way his sayings might be misinterpreted. This one was not altogether borne out in his practice, although he certainly relied on weight of numbers more than most of the great Captains. Such a tendency was inevitable owing to his disregard of the possibilities of making his forces qualitatively decisive through superior training or superior weapons. It was fostered by his unlimited resources—until the man-power of France was exhausted. Even so, his victories were obtained more by manœuvring power in massing superior numbers at the decisive point than by a mere total superiority.

His words, however, made a deep impression. And they were read in the more obvious sense. A generation later his famous German interpreter, Clausewitz, expressed the conviction that 'superiority in numbers becomes every day more decisive'. He at any rate had more excuse than the military authorities who, in all countries, have repeated his creed for a century. For when he wrote the mechanical age was only dawning, whereas his followers persisted in this delusion while mechanical weapons were continually multiplying in nature and effect. They forgot how Alexander conquered Asia, how Hannibal defeated the Roman armies in their own land, how Belisarius reconquered the Roman Empire, how Genghis Khan swept over Asia and Europe, with forces far smaller than those opposing them. They forgot the still clearer proof of the value of superior armaments which was provided when Strongbow conquered Ireland with a few hundred knights, an astonishing lesson in the power of a technically decisive handful which was repeated in Cortés's conquest of Mexico, Pizarro's conquest of Peru, and Clive's conquests in India.

When the World War came in 1914, the fallacy of the 'big battalions' was exposed by the mechanical progress which enabled one man sitting behind a machine-gun to account for more than a score, or sometimes a hundred, or sometimes even a thousand, who were advancing upon him with rifle and bayonet. The more the number of the attackers, the more the number of the dead—that was all in many cases. The contrast between qualitative and quantitative values was exemplified in another way at Cambrai on November 20th, 1917, where the use of only 378 tanks and some 4000 tankmen to assist a mere six divisions of infantry, produced a greater gain of ground and a greater shock to the enemy at a cost of some 5000 casualties, than the use of several dozen divisions had achieved at Ypres in a three months' effort at a cost of 400,000 casualties. The contrast also illuminated the qualitative difference between different technical means— for at Ypres the British Higher Command rested their hopes of breaking down the enemy's resistance on the use of 3000 guns and 120,000 gunners, who fired some four and a half million shells in the preliminary bombardment alone.

Yet, in spite of all the experience which shows that numbers have little real meaning, the governments and generals of Europe still, as a whole, continue to count their forces in terms of 'numerical men'. And the public is naturally of the same tendency. Such figures are more easy to grasp than the difficult and intricate assessment of qualitative values. If they throw little light on the military problem they at least help to show the taxpayers' burden— the pay and upkeep of the individual soldier forms by far the biggest proportion of any military budget. Since no survey of the armies of Europe would seem factual without these 'false' figures, I will insert a few in this account. They are as accurate as can be determined under the conditions of censorship and mystification which now prevail in many parts of Europe. And if the sum should be a million or so out, it will not much matter militarily from any practical point of view. The real power of the armies of the three great totalitarian states, with which this chapter is concerned in particular, does not lie in their numbers of men under arms. The vast numbers, however, have significance as the symptoms of an impediment compulsorily contracted by the nature of such states.

Germany

Since the advent of the Nazi regime, the German Army has carried out a great expansion and undergone a great transformation, not altogether to its qualitative advantage. By the terms of the Treaty of Versailles it was limited to a strength of 100,000 men voluntarily enlisted on a long-service basis, and was forbidden the use of tanks, aircraft, and heavy artillery. These compulsory limitations encouraged an attempt to surpass them subtly by developing a force of superior quality and mobility. Surprise became its keynote—'every action', declared the post-war German manuals, 'should be based on surprise . . . ruses and wiles of every kind ought always to be used to deceive the enemy'. General von Seeckt, the rebuilder of the German Army after the war, had been the brain of Field-Marshal von Mackensen in the war, devising the plans which led to the Gorlice break-through against the Russians in 1915, and to later successes. He gave the post-war army a doctrine of mobility, and put forward the view that a small, quick-moving, quick-hitting army of picked troops could, under modern conditions, discount the numerical superiority of an old-fashioned mass army. That view was genuinely shared by some of the more original-minded German officers. But the majority merely made a virtue of necessity; brought up in the creed of mass, they hankered after the size which to them still represented strength and, no less important, a reflected prestige. Similarly, despite the experience of the war and their straitened post-war means, they still clung to the old belief in the offensive; officers like the present Field-Marshal von Blomberg, who sought to adapt tactics to modern conditions and advocated such methods as the luring defensive, found it difficult to convince the bulk of their comrades.

The idea of the 'qualitative' professional army had not really taken firm root when the Hitler revolution gave the Army a chance to revert to the old love of mass. The Nazi movement of its very nature made such a reversion almost inevitable. Many of the Regular officers were undoubtedly apprehensive of the effect of diluting their carefully trained units with undisciplined enthusiasts of the Brown Shirt type, and found still more cause for concern in the claim of the Brown Shirt leaders for a share in the officering of the new national army. They were ready to welcome all the support that the new regime gave to the growth of the Army and of martial ideas, but not to accept a partnership in the control. Their policy prevailed, on this point, helped by Hitler's need of the Army to maintain what he had created, or unloosed.

At Geneva, before she left the League, Germany had claimed the right to expand her army of 100,000 men, organized in seven divisions, to an army of 300,000. While the statesmen argued, the process of expansion went on. The aim was to create a force of twenty-one divisions. The manufacture of tanks, artillery, machine-guns, and aircraft was rapidly developed. The way for conscription was paved by the introduction of six months labour service, and the training was so directed that the Labour Corps soon came to have a marked military value—more, indeed, than the Brown Shirts.

Then, in March 1935, conscription for the Army was announced, and, simultaneously, the expansion of the Army to thirty-six divisions, organized in twelve army corps. The news came as a shock in neighbouring countries, increased by the importance customarily accorded to numbers. Yet, curiously, there was a tendency to underestimate the new total through ignoring the proportion of corps and army troops; 450,000 was suggested as the probable figure, whereas it was likely to exceed 550,000. The first contingent of conscripts of the 1914 class (now aged 21) was called up in October. An average year was expected to yield about 300,000 young men. At the same time the men between twenty-one and thirty-five (the classes 1900-13) who represent Germany's lost classes of trained reserves have been called up for short periods of training lasting six weeks to two months.

In August 1936 a fresh step was taken, by extending the period of conscript service from one year to two. This may be partly designed to offset the lean birthrate years represented by the 1915 to 1919 classes, but is likely to increase the total under arms. Moreover, it is known that Germany has formed three armoured divisions which are additional to the thirty-six divisions provided for by the Army Law of March 16th, 1935, while there are reports of the formation of two more. The fact has a reflection on Hitler's declaration in the Reichstag a few days later: 'The German Government have announced the extent of the expansion of the new German defence forces. In no circumstances will they depart therefrom.' It would seem that a further increase is not regarded as a departure.

These new-style formations were not shown to the foreign officers and military publicists who were invited to see the German Army at work in the autumn manœuvres of 1935 and 1936. In the infantry divisions which have been seen, the transport of the battalions and the field artillery was still horse-drawn, but they were well provided with machine-guns, anti-tank guns, and mortars. The division has some 400 machine-guns, light and heavy, and their proportion of anti-tank guns—two and a half pounders drawn by a light car—is higher than in the French or any other army; they form a divisional unit of three companies with a total of about forty-two guns. The most interesting new feature of the division is a mechanized reconnaissance group, which comprises a company of armoured cars or light tanks, one of anti-tank guns, one of four light mortars, one of machine-guns, and two companies of infantry in lorries. They are used to push ahead of the division's advance, seize tactical points, and occupy them with machine-guns, and then press on to a fresh objective. The staple of the division is composed of three infantry regiments, each of which is formed of three battalions, a mortar company, a machine-gun company, and a troop of cavalry. The battalion is organized in three 'rifle' companies, each having nine light machine-guns.

There is an apparent shortage of officers, owing partly to the wise desire to maintain the standard, if also to a reluctance to give commissions except to those who have passed through the orthodox professional channels. But the training of the troops has made a strong impression on those who have watched it; they move more dispersed than the French, and are no less active in movement, while their equipment is far more modern—the Versailles Treaty has here had its compensations. Their new 105 mm. field-howitzers and their anti-aircraft guns are highly efficient weapons. But the general composition of these divisions and their handling shows little advance on the ideas of the last war. With increase of size the German Army seems to have rather lost sight of the need for subtlety and surprise which Seeckt insisted on in the post-war era.

There is more prospect in the new armoured divisions. They are said to consist of three parts, one for probing, one for hitting, and one for holding. The 'punch' is formed by a tank brigade, which is believed to consist of three regiments totalling about 600 tanks. The number of mechanized vehicles in the division as a whole is said to be nearly two thousand. At present the tanks are of a fast but light kind, weighing only about six tons, with two machine-guns in a turret capable of all-round fire. The Germans are seeking a larger, 'medium' tank, but it is doubtful if a satisfactory one has yet been produced. Against a country with an open frontier or an army inadequately equipped with anti-tank guns, their new armoured divisions might prove a formidable factor in the opening phase of a war, but there is cause for doubt whether the Germany Army has yet developed either the equipment or the tactics to solve the problems created by a strong and thoroughly modern defence.

Russia

The Red Army, by contrast, is undoubtedly the most powerful in its tank forces, while also the most original in methods, although new and old ideas are strangely intermingled. The most archaic feature is the prominent role given to horsed cavalry—no less than sixteen cavalry divisions are maintained—and the way they are handled. On manœuvres great masses of horsemen are plunged into tank-infested areas with little regard to the differing degrees of vulnerability. In peace it looks like a colossal circus; in war it would probably mean a huge cemetery. This Russian attempt to repeat Balaclava in face of machine-guns is evidence that the Red Army has not succeeded so far as its progress in other directions suggests in shedding the mental conventions of its predecessor.

The reliance on mass is a general symptom. In numbers of men the Red Army far exceeds any other. A population which has now grown to 170,000,000 provides an annual contingent of recruits which in recent years has always been well over a million and this year is over two million. The peace-time strength of the army has now been raised to 1,300,000. They provide eighty-four infantry divisions apart from other formations. The men taken for the Regular Army do two years continuous service, while those who are not required for this do several months training in the territorial militia. The Regular Army now represents 73 per cent of the total forces, and the Territorial Militia 27 per cent. It is said that the Red Army chiefs could mobilize 6,000,000 men at a fortnight's notice, and that by 1938 the total trained reserves will reach 10,000,000. This apparently does not include the youths below military age who, to the number of several millions, are receiving preliminary training under the auspices of the Osoaviat-khim and the Young Communist League. More significant is the statement that upwards of half a million have qualified as skilled parachute-jumpers and many thousands as aeroplane or glider pilots.

The bulk of the Army is maintained in the West, but the Far Eastern Army is said to number nearly 300,000 men, while the doubling of the track of the Trans-Siberian railway facilitates its reinforcement in emergency. But as Tukhachevski pointed out in his 1935 report: 'If the Germans had to expend some fifteen million kilometre-tons in order to concentrate one infantry division in Liége by means of the railway from Berlin, 200 million kilometre-tons are required of us in order to transfer such a division from Moscow to Vladivostock. Thus we must be very cautious in counting on the rapid transfer of considerable masses of troops over so-called internal operation lines.' The strain on the railway for supply has been much reduced by accumulating supplies on the spot in order to make the Far Eastern Army self-sufficient—it has been wittily said that to the soldiers stationed here the tin-opener is almost as indispensable as the rifle. At the same time agriculture and munition factories are being developed here as a more permanent foundation for military effort. This is part of the general scheme by which the industries of Russia are being organized and distributed on a strategic basis—with a predominant easterly trend in order to safeguard them from hostile air attack. The largest source of munitions is now established in the almost inaccessible area near the Ural Mountains. But this only solves half the problem. If the Red Army attempts to concentrate its immense forces to act in any particular theatre there will be an inevitable congestion of the routes of supply in that area. Here lies a continual danger of breakdown.

The units of this mass are certainly far more impressive in quality than the old Czarist Army. The discipline is unmistakably good, yet free from the old brutality. The men's bearing on the march combines smartness with elasticity. In physique and intelligence they look a very good type. The officers are professionally enthusiastic and much better educated than their predecessors—no army takes a keener interest in foreign ideas and all news of military progress. On manœuvres there is much evidence of skilled organization and staffwork. The elimination of the corruption which was rampant on the administrative side of the Czarist Army should alone go far to reduce the risks of defeat through shortage of equipment and supplies.

The most striking features of the Army are its development of tank and air-borne units. There are said to be about 6000 tanks—over a thousand have been seen on manœuvres in one area alone. The small number of breakdowns is evidence of their mechanical efficiency as well as of the standard of training in the crews. If the designs show no marked originality, and are obviously indebted to various foreign models, it would seem that the

Russians have had the ability to adopt and adapt the best points of each. There are great numbers of two-men light tanks which can 'swim' rivers and are based on the Carden-Loyd amphibian, first produced in Britain by the Vickers firm. They have also quantities of rather larger machines copied from the 6-ton Vickers. But the machine on which they mainly rely for the modern-style cavalry role is one developed from the American Christie tank. It is well-armoured, weighs about twelve tons, and yet has a speed of over 30 m.p.h. on its tracks, while for long strategic moves these can be taken off and the tank then runs on its bogie wheels. Beyond this, to deliver the decisive assault there is a 'medium' tank of no less than twenty-seven tons, carrying a gun of field-artillery calibre as well as machine-guns, yet travelling almost as fast as the Christie-type tank. They have even a small number of 'Heavy' tanks, which look like moving fortresses and must weigh at least fifty tons. But, in face of the growing power and variety of anti-tank defence, the Russians prefer to rely on machines of high speed and good obstacle-crossing capacity combined with a fair thickness of armour, rather than increase weight and size at the expense of pace.

While they are now ahead of all other countries in the development of armoured mobile forces, their ideas on the use of such forces are not so well thought out; here they seem to have assimilated many ideas from abroad without digesting them. That, at any rate, is the impression gained from a study of their published views and from personal discussions. Likewise on their manœuvres the higher tactical handling of these forces is not equal to the actual handling of the machines by their crews. This reflection applies also to the handling of the ordinary infantry forces, and their formations are apt to offer too good a target. The undue disregard of the effects of modern fire is even to be noticed in the methods employed in their low-flying attacks on ground columns which are much favoured; these seemed to invite casualties needlessly. This general tendency may be in accord with the Russian tradition, but the scales of warfare are tilting increasingly against it. If it is inherent in a doctrine of war which contemplates the use of masses, that is no reason for believing that the masses, despite their increased efficiency, will prove capable of overcoming modern defence. The Russians might have a better prospect if they relied simply on their mechanized forces. For this would also minimise the worst risk they run in taking an offensive with such vast numbers—that the military machine will break down under the burden on its own communications when the strain is increased by the pressure of air attack.

In one way the Russians, however, are better equipped than any army to produce the enemy's breakdown, and even earlier. The agent lies in their new parachute forces, which were much in evidence during this autumn's manœuvres. In one area, for example, a force of 1200 men together with 150 machine-guns and 18 light field-guns was carried 100 miles in troop-carrying aircraft and dropped on an aerodrome behind the enemy's front. Within eight minutes of the release of the parachutes the force had assembled on the ground and driven off the defenders. The spectacular nature of such an operation may be as likely to make professional soldiers sceptical of its potentialities as to cause an exaggerated estimate of its menace among the public.

It is easy to perceive the practical difficulties which such an expedition might encounter if carried out under war conditions; the dangers it might run both in its passage through the air, in the descent to the ground, and in maintaining itself when landed. Nevertheless, any instrument of surprise starts with a big advantage in war—audacity pays, especially when allied with mobility. Because of its range and power of variability the 'parachute stroke' has possibilities that it would be foolish to underrate. Its indirect strategic influence may be much greater than its actual results.

All armies, and nearly all commanders, are acutely susceptible to the threat of a blow in the back, and to the interruption of their communications. The knowledge that the enemy has parachute forces that can be dropped near important bridges or other crucial points in their rear is likely to increase this fear. The risk may well cause the higher command to strengthen all detachments and posts on the lines of communication, thus producing a subtraction of force from the main concentration many times larger than the parachute forces which the enemy possesses. Added to this is the psychological strain. Thus, by the mere threat of their existence such forces have a promise of great effect—greater than any damage they may actually do.

Italy

In view of the essential antithesis between mass and mobility it is a curious phenomenon that both are being simultaneously developed all over the Continent, without regard to the consequences. No country carries quite so far as Italy the conception of the 'nation in arms'. The male child is put in uniform when he is scarcely out of the cradle and may stay in it until he is put in the grave—since the

The Armies of Europe—

hard-worked Italian peasant is often not very long-lived, even apart from the risks of war. At six years of age he is enrolled in the 'Balilla del Lupa' (Wolf Cubs), in which besides wearing uniform he is taught to march, to shoot with the rifle and the machine-gun, to wear gas-masks and carry out anti-gas drill, and to inure himself to life under canvas. Boys who are bad at drill are treated as if they had failed to pass their scholastic examinations for promotion to a higher form. At eight he enters the ordinary Balilla corps, and continues there until eighteen, when he undergoes a more intensive system of military training, until at twenty-one he is called up for his conscript service with the Army, which normally lasts eighteen months. After his release he has to carry on his post-military training until the age of fifty-five—and even then he joins the civilian cohorts that are part of the civil mobilization scheme during war-time. The Italian Press was unusually accurate when it applauded this introduction of life-service with the remark that history had no parallel for such nation-wide militarization.

The actual number of the Italian Army is a variable quantity. In the past it has usually been about 400,000 men, but shortly before the Abyssinian War it was raised to 600,000, and during this 1,000,000 were mobilized. In addition the Fascist Militia totals some 400,000 men. The Army, exclusive of the colonies, is organized in thirteen Army Corps, yielding a total of thirty-one infantry divisions. There are also three mobile divisions mainly of motorized troops, with a small proportion of armoured vehicles. Tanks have not been much developed. They have a few hundred Fiat tanks, but these are very small and limited in obstacle-crossing capacity. They are mainly used as armoured machine-guns to assist the infantry attack.

The Totalitarian Powers

The infantry division comprises nine battalions, as is usual on the Continent, but until recently three of these were merely kept in skeleton. It is rather weaker in artillery support and also in automatic fire-power than the French. The Italian Army's progress towards mechanization was for long retarded by lack of money, reluctance to be dependent on outside fuel supplies, and the fact that its probable theatres of war were mountainous, thus seeming to offer small scope for mechanized mobility. On the other hand, this type of country has had an influence on the training of the infantry, which has aimed to develop agility by a most strenuous course of physical exercise. The hillsides near any military centre are dotted with gymnastic apparatus, and it is astonishing to see whole companies of men going through a series of vaulting, jumping and balancing exercises which seem severe enough to test a professional acrobat. Likewise the marching of the Italian infantry, both in pace and distance, seems all the more remarkable when one takes note of the slender scale of rations on which these physical feats are performed. They have also begun to exploit a new kind of mobility by following the Russian lead in forming parachute units. In mountain warfare these may have notable effect, as a pass or narrow valley can be held by a few men against many, so that by dropping these parachute units to seize such points in the enemy's rear his reinforcement may be prevented, his supplies interrupted, or his retreat cut off.

By a curious contrast, the higher training of the Italian Army had until recently a tendency to restrain rather than exploit the use of its natural assets. Tactical methods were even more deliberate than in the French Army. In part, this was inspired by the aim of correcting the haphazard ways of the past by a rigorous mental discipline attuned to

the new national trend. If it served a practical purpose, it
certainly had the less beneficial effect of cramping manœuvre and tactical mobility. Operation orders were so
long and detailed that, after reckoning the time for writing
and reading them, they seemed to leave little time for
executing them—if the enemy were not to be allowed too
much grace.

It was thus, in form and in outlook, an old-style army
which was shipped out from Italy to Eritrea in 1935.
Mechanized vehicles and aircraft were no more than a
trimming to the masses of infantry. Yet the trimmings,
coupled with the primitive enemy's similar obsession with
mass, saved the Italians from the impasse, and even peril,
to which their own old-fashioned ideas had brought them.
In the outcome, the campaign was determined by the
progressive success of the machine in overcoming human
and natural obstacles. As the data of the campaign have
become available, analysis has tended to confirm the
contemporary inference that the machine-gun and the gas-
projector proved the decisive weapons, aircraft the decisive arm, and mechanization in general the foundation of
the Italians' success. It forms a striking vindication of those
who, in the face of doubts and obstruction, have for years
foreshadowed the importance of these new factors. For
Europe this war is a writing on the wall—and the more
significant because it has been engraved on a remote
mountain-wall. For here was a theatre of war so wild and
rugged, and so strategically inaccessible, that aircraft and
landcraft were operating under an exceptional handicap.

The handicap on their action was at first increased by a
handicap on their effect which sprang from the methods
of the Italian command. They began the invasion of Abyssinia after the style of the invading hosts in 1914. By rely-

ing on mass they impeded their own mobility, so that what was gained by the advent of mechanized means of movement was largely offset by using them merely to feed and maintain great masses of infantry. The supply of such large forces as were employed demanded a well-developed system of roads. The building of these roads called for a great number of labourers, together with the troops to protect them. To feed and otherwise maintain them caused a great increase in the transport demands and in the traffic over the new-built roads. That scale of traffic destroyed the roads almost as fast as they were built. So the difficulties were multiplied by the very means taken to overcome them.

Thus the Abyssinian war began by providing a fresh illustration, in a somewhat different form, of the lesson of the last European war—that armies are impeded more than helped by their own growth, so that quantitative superiority of force carries its own antidote. That experience merely confirmed the neglected warning of the famous eighteenth century master of war, Marshal Saxe, that 'multitudes serve only to perplex and embarrass'. He saw, like Sherman a century later, that there is a limit, determined by mobility, to what one may call the *economic size* of an army. It takes unusual art to gauge—mass and mobility are hard to reconcile. Unless the mean, or means, can be found, the use of force is liable to be stultified by its own forces.

It was fortunate for the Italians that there was no air force to oppose them. That missing factor was their salvation from something worse than congestion and internal disorder. At the end of 1935, after three months campaign, the Italian masses were at a standstill with nothing to hit, while the overburdened communications needed to feed them were providing a target for guerrillas—it would have been much worse if these narrow mountain routes had been bombed from the air. In this state of stagnation, discontent was growing in the territory around them and among their native allies. Then the Abyssinian leaders came to their rescue by attempting a series of massed attacks, thus providing a target for machine-guns on the ground and overhead. In exploiting the Abyssinians' recoil, the Italian command turned their infantry masses into road-makers and relied for their own thrust on relatively small motorized spearheads, while mustard gas was sprayed to shield their own communications against the enemy's interference, and also to demoralize the troops and populated areas behind the enemy's front. The advance of these mobile columns was covered by a long-range and flexible barrage of air bombers, while their supplies were in part brought up by air transport.

It is significant that although the Italians were strategically on the offensive almost throughout the campaign, they combined it, almost as consistently, with the tactical defensive. In the four battles which mainly contributed to turn the scales of the war, and settle the fate of Abyssinia, the defeated side attempted most of the attacking. The first three, even Amba Aradam, seem to have been a tale of repeated Ethiopian assaults to forestall or stem the Italians' advance; and in the final battle the Emperor's army shattered itself against the Italians' fire-defence. Thus while the campaign superficially suggested that modern armament gives new power to the attack—at any rate where one side has a definite superiority of arms—its deeper lesson lies in the way the Italians profited from the power of modern defence, applied in a manœuvring advance.

The Abyssinian Campaign should have given the Gen-

eral Staffs of the world other cause for thought. It has shown
the fallacy of their argument that machines are not a substitute for men—by which they mean the weight of the
many, not the quality of the essential few. It has shown,
more clearly even than the World War, that mass has become a dangerous encumbrance when the attempt is
made to concentrate it on the fighting front. Under
modern conditions, and especially the growing menace of
air attack, the larger the army the weaker a country may
prove in war. Technical quality counts, not drilled
quantity.

CHAPTER IV

The French Army

The French Army has for long exemplified the fallacy of the old standards of gauging strength. If its total numbers were counted, it appeared the 'strongest' in Europe, apart from the Russian. That idea was reinforced if trained reserves of men and stored reserves of war material were reckoned. And the impression has thus been spread that the French Army was, at any rate until recently, a serious potential threat to Germany. But the numbers had small offensive meaning under modern conditions; a large proportion were abroad; and most of the war material was old. Although twenty-two tank battalions have been maintained in France most of them were, and still are, equipped with machines of the last war, slightly renovated. They are slow machines, employed to help the infantry forward, yet with a very limited obstacle crossing capacity for that purpose. The Army comprises twenty infantry divisions, five cavalry divisions, and five colonial infantry divisions which serve as a 'mobile force' ready for despatch to deal with trouble overseas.

The total 'strength' of the French Army is some 640,000, but of these nearly 200,000 are serving in North Africa and other colonies. Conscript service is still nominally for one year, but contingents are now being held for an extra year. This is due to the threat of the German military expansion combined with the shrinkage of the annual contingent of young men reaching military age (caused by the fall of the birth-rate during the last war). The shrinkage, together with the need for adequately trained personnel in the mechanized arms, has also led the French to enlist an increased proportion of long-service professional soldiers, who form a corps of specialists. A maximum of 117,000 has been legally sanctioned, although only some 80,000 have been obtained hitherto, as the terms have not been sufficiently attractive. This element is one of several new factors which are contributing to the transformation of the French Army.

Two recent visits to France afforded me the opportunity of renewing, after an interval of some eight years, my acquaintance with that Army. They were also an opportunity of gauging the trend of its military thought. Such actual contact is apt to produce stronger impressions than any perusal of a country's service papers. For even in a country such as France, which has a great tradition of military literature, military ideas are no longer expressed with the freedom of the eighteenth century: that most vital age of military thought, when men like Saxe, Bourcet and Guibert paved the way for the revolution in strategy which the young Napoleon Bonaparte was able to achieve with the leverage of the Revolution. Because of that age of fertilizing ideas, the intellectual homage of every military student is due to France. Since then she has suffered as much as any country from the sterilization of thought which came with the increasing professionalization of armies. It is true that in the years preceding the World

41

The French Army

War, she could still produce a Colin and a Grouard, but such minds did not guide her strategy in 1914—as history too clearly tells. Nor did the shattering experiences of the war, which at least brought appreciation of the sober common sense of a Pétain, seem to succeed in breaking the fetters on thought even to the extent that was seen elsewhere. In France perhaps more than anywhere the subordination that must prevail in the sphere of action was extended into the sphere of conception, with a consequent barrenness. Orthodoxy was exalted to such a pitch that it became the most powerful of contraceptives.

Thus when I last saw the French Army it seemed to me almost the most backward in ideas among the armies of the Great Powers. After eight years for reflection upon the experience of the last war it showed small sign that reflection had borne fruit. Its horizon was bounded by 1918. If war should come again it apparently intended to resume where it had left off. That was better than the cry of 'Back to 1914' which had echoed in some other armies during the years of reconstruction; but they had begun to move forward subsequently, if only in thought, whereas French thought had, in general, remained stationary, despite the bold leap into the future that was made in the immediate post-war utterances of some of the leading soldiers of France. The cause may have been that in France these original ideas were sprinkled from above, by generals who soon disappeared, whereas in Britain they were like springs welling up from below.

In French military doctrine and training all else was subordinated to the production of a great volume of fire, by methods that were as studiously deliberate as the rate of movement they promised. The best thing that could be said of the doctrine was that it recognized the importance

of material factors, especially the effect of fire, and re-
canted the fallacious belief of 1914 that the unshielded will
of the soldier was proof against bullets and shells. But it
seemed to ignore the truth that fire is a means to movement, and that the effect is lost unless it can be followed up
quickly. The division was still the profusely armed but
complex organ of war-time pattern. The French seemed to
have conceived of nothing more than the preservation of a
powerful but rigid fighting machine, a machine which was
likely to break down from its own internal friction if it
should ever be called upon to make a prolonged advance
or retirement. I could not help thinking that the French
had renovated their steam-roller by fitting an extra roller,
but had forgotten to consider its motive-power.

Since this visit, what I had heard from other observers
had tended to confirm the impression. They spoke of the
extreme deliberation of operations, of detail carried so far
that it became an encumbrance. More recently, I had
heard rumours of development, but not sufficient to prepare me for the change which I found.

By contrast with eight years earlier, it struck me as a
remarkable evolution—much greater than our own in the
same period. And the development has been not only in
ideas but in application. If even to-day military thought in
France does not leap forward quite so boldly as among the
most progressive British soldiers, practical steps have been
larger.

Two cavalry divisions have been completely mechanized, mainly with armoured fighting vehicles, although
they have a proportion of 'motor-dragoons' in light cars
and on motor-cycles. A heavy mechanized division is to be
created in 1937, to provide a still more powerful punch,
particularly for a counter-stroke against any hostile mech-

anized forces which might penetrate, by surprise, the fortified frontier. In addition, some ten infantry divisions have
been motorized; their artillery is all tractor-drawn, their
infantry regiments are provided with little armoured
carriers for mortars, machine-guns, and ammunition, and
can themselves be moved by lorry convoy. As regards
supply, it is significant that the French now consider the
possibility of maintaining the divisions at a much greater
distance from railhead than we have yet contemplated.

The creation of these new-type formations, so different
from the rest of the active forces, and from the bulk army
of mobilization, is naturally leading the French towards a
new picture of warfare. It tends to resemble the vision
which General von Seeckt and others cast on the screen of
the future during the years when the German Army was
being rebuilt, although modified to suit the technical, geographical, and political conditions of France.

General mobilization is a process that works slowly in
putting an army into the field: so slow indeed, that if
mobilization and concentration were made as in 1914, the
army would court the risk of never reaching the field. Air
pressure on the congested traffic arteries might cause a
premature collapse. Even at the best, an interval of a week
or two must elapse before these forces can come into
action. But the new-type formations, helped by their special
composition as well as by their rail-free mobility, may be
ready within a time that we commonly count in hours.
To keep them in waiting while the bulk army was assembling would be a precarious discount of the time-
factor, even if the enemy's action allowed the attempt.

Thus, in the new picture, the first phase of a war is
fought out by the mobile forces together with the frontier
garrisons. The second phase, of conflict between the mass

forces, is provided for as a possibility—although some regard it as a doubtful one. Naturally, the picture is clearer in the minds of the younger men who are now rising to positions of influence than it is among those whose minds are filled with memories of how they conducted war in 1914-18. But the fact of this changing outlook is unmistakable, and it has a bearing on British military problems which deserves attention.

I have referred earlier to the modifications in the French picture produced by national conditions. They become most manifest in regard to the employment of the new-type formations. French thought revolves more than ever around the particular problem of safeguarding France against invasion—a problem essentially defensive. And French military thought inclines to share this tendency, certainly more than at times in the past. Thus the new-type formations seem to be visualized, above all, as a means of strengthening defence—by switching fire more quickly to a threatened spot and by developing a counter-offensive more promptly. To many there may be novelty in this 'defensive' view of the value of mechanized forces. But it is justified on technical grounds. Despite the obvious increase of offensive power conferred by mechanized forces, the reinforcement of the defensive may well prove greater still, indirectly. On a long view, it might even be said that this has been the trend of the growing mechanization of war through the centuries.

From the contemporary point of view, it is politically as well as militarily significant that the French should be mainly concerned to fit the new development to their defensive problem—of resisting the invasion which they apprehend. I had the impression that their ideas on this aspect were much clearer than on any wider aspects. That reflection made me cast my mind across the frontier; I thought of those who in Germany have been haunted by fear of invasion—a feeling that is widespread if not so deep-rooted as in France. If they could have shared in my contact with the actual scope of French military ideas, their fears might have been allayed. Statesmanship may suffer as much by failing to grasp what soldiers are thinking as by ignoring public opinion. The former is the more stable of the two.

It was ironically said of the Kellogg Pact that its effect was not to abolish war, but merely the declaration of war. So also, in the world to-day, 'defence' is a conventional euphemism which embraces offence. The embrace, however, may be willing or reluctant. If one follows the trend of military thought in the different countries one may get as shrewd an idea of the predominant attitude as in following the more fluctuating course of policy. To gauge it one must go beneath the surface: for the offensive is so much a part of the military tradition, and so much more appealing than the defensive to the soldierly spirit. On the surface of the training grounds, attack exercises predominate. Indeed, to a casual observer, the armies of the least warlike countries might well seem the most belligerent—since the more shadowy a country's military problem, the more probable that its army will spend its time in practising the type of action it is unlikely to fulfil. Armed forces are most ruled by force of custom when dangers are least concrete. Training tends to become a truer expression of purpose when political conditions produce concrete possibilities.

The fact that the French Army shows a firmer grasp of defensive contingencies than of offensive ones would seem a reasonable clue to the attitude of its leaders. The preponderance of the defensive finds expression in the frontier fortifications to which so much of their money and attention have been devoted in recent years. That newly fortified line, for the most part running just inside the frontier, has been widely discussed.

It consists, as is well known, of a chain of forts and casemates—the proportions varying not only according to the ground but to the money available. The 'forts' (according to details which have appeared) themselves consist of a mushroom-like cluster of concrete casemates linked by underground galleries; these lead to the living quarters, magazines, and power stations which serve each cluster, and are likewise buried deep. The sector first constructed was from Longuyon, opposite Luxembourg, to the Vosges; this covered Metz and the Briey industrial area, although a gap was originally left on either side of the Sarre River between St. Avold and Bitche, where a succession of streams parallel with the frontier helped to form a natural barrier. Subsequently this gap has been filled, in part at least, and the chain of fortifications has been extended along the Rhine to the Swiss frontier, to supplement this river barrier. The defence of the approaches through Belgium and Belgian Luxembourg has also been taken in hand, work being carried out along the line of the frontier towards Maubeuge and Lille. According to plan, the intervals in the chain were to be covered by the interlacing fire of the casemates, but could also be more substantially filled by field entrenchments and the whole covered by wire entanglements. This, I believe, is now being done. And the fortified chain is to be extended to Dunkirk in the north, and to the Jura in the south, along the Swiss frontier.

Such a fortified line, although better designed, naturally

The French Army

lacks the depth of protection afforded by the vast trench systems which developed in the war. Stronger in meeting the first shock, it is intended to gain time rather than to be a final barrier. It is, above all, a shock-absorber, to cover the process of mobilization. Its effectiveness thus depends on the adequacy and readiness of the forces which normally garrison it, and on the promptness with which support can be given. The main danger lies in a surprise attack which might overwhelm a sector before the emergency was realized; a further danger now on the horizon is a penetration of the intervals by mechanized forces, which might disregard the forts or leave them to be 'mopped up' by a second wave of invaders.

It is for this reason that the French are so concerned with the new risks of the *attaque brusquée*. Some of them visualize the possibility of hostile mechanized forces crossing the old demilitarized zone by a swift bound during a single night and delivering their stroke early next morning. All of them now appear to realize, from this point of view at least, the great acceleration of the *tempo* of warfare which modern developments foreshadow.

The technical conditions of warfare have tended more and more to enhance the advantage of the defence, and to discount the numerical superiority which an invader may possess. Thereby they have much diminished the chances of successful invasion. In consequence, however, they have largely concentrated the remaining chances in the possibility of achieving an initial surprise. Unless a decisive advantage is gained in a short time, the paralysis of the offensive is likely to be established more firmly than ever—unless the endurance of the defender should be undermined by pressure from behind, through the internal collapse of the country and the cessation of supplies.

The French Army

In 1914 a fortnight elapsed after mobilization before the advance of the main armies began. An aggressor who nowadays waited so long would have a poor prospect of gaining a decision. If this knowledge, when assimilated, may prove a powerful deterrent to aggression, it inevitably tends to focus the thought of a would-be aggressor on the ways of achieving a short-time penetration by surprise. There are some in France who fear it so much, and become so absorbed in contemplation of their own risks, that they hardly pause to ask whether the possible invaders have the organization or the means to execute it. The General Staff, with their superior sources of information, preserve a firmer grasp of existing possibilities without overlooking the future.

Meantime the problem of immediate concern is to adapt their own organization to the current of changing conditions. One need is to remodel the mobilization scheme so as to produce an effective force in support of the frontier garrisons in the shortest possible time—a time that we must now count in hours rather than in days. That mobilization scheme must also take account of the new risks threatened by hostile air attack during the main process of mobilization and concentration. Concentration must not spell congestion. It should be in the current but not on the surface. Rail and road movements must be more flexible, and the whole must be more distributed.

The other need is to develop mechanization as a means of saving time in arrival and intervention. The fortified region itself is garrisoned by units of varying composition which are 'hand-made' to suit the sector allotted to them; they can be brought up to strength at short notice with reservists drawn from the neighbouring district. But for the prompt support of the region, and for manœuvre

The French Army

based on this pivot, mobile formations are necessary. The need is now being met.

As a start, the 4th Cavalry Division was transformed into a light mechanized division, and the 5th is now being converted. The fighting part of the division consists of what are called *auto-mitrailleuses*—light and medium armoured vehicles on tracks which we should describe as tanks—cavalry tanks. They are all fast machines. The other part is of mixed composition to fit its mixed role of reconnoitring the enemy and seizing 'stepping stones'; it has a regiment of *auto-mitrailleuses*, at present on wheels, and a regiment of *dragons portés*—cavalrymen mounted in light and handy unarmoured vehicles that are capable of moving across country. Each has a strong infusion of motor-cyclists—a type of the troops which the French have developed notably.

In the infantry divisions which have been motorized the artillery is entirely tractor-drawn—light and medium lorries being used for the purpose. Compared with our own mechanized artillery it has a marked advantage for strategic road movements, owing to the fact that the guns are carried on a low trailer, from which they can be dismounted in half a minute on reaching the battlefield. The use of these trailers, lifting the gun-wheels off the ground, enables the artillery to travel long distances at speeds up to 40 m.p.h. without damaging the more delicate mechanism of the gun.

Chenillettes—armoured carriers somewhat similar to the British Carden-Loyds—are being introduced in these divisions for the transport of the infantry mortar, machine-gun, and ammunition. Motorization is at present only partial in the infantry, although they are commonly embussed for long moves. But several regiments have been completely motorized for the trial of a new organization.

Here one may interpolate that the tank units, as distinct from those of *auto-mitrailleuses*, still belong to the infantry arm. This is partly explained by their low speed, but is also due to the fact that the French have never gone back to the belief that attacking infantry, in face of machine-guns, could dispense with armoured support. Realization of the difficulties of supplying the artillery with sufficient ammunition for the creeping barrages of the last war has also tended to emphasize the need for tanks. Where employed, a section to a company is allotted to aid each infantry battalion. Twenty battalions of so-called light tanks are maintained at home, but most of them are still equipped with renovated war-time machines; only a few have been provided with the newer type Renaults which weigh 11 tons (their armour being of 30 millimetre thickness) and have a maximum speed of 11 m.p.h. There is also one independent tank battalion, the embryo of the new heavy mechanized division. The monster 70-ton tanks which were introduced some years back did not give satisfaction, and the French are still looking for an efficient heavy tank of rather less weight; but a large medium tank of some 25 tons is said to be now in production, and a heavy tank of 37 tons under trial.

The development of mechanization in the army is creating fresh problems of personnel. Thanks to the economy of time achieved by the present system of training, and to the admirable simplification of drill, the ordinary infantry attain a remarkably high standard in proportion to the shortness of their service. But it is more difficult to provide adequately trained personnel for the mechanized supporting weapons and the mechanized services in general. For these needs, the French are tending

The French Army

to rely on the increased professional element, which now forms a corps of specialists. Here, however, a fresh problem arises—not only how to recruit sufficient numbers but how to recruit a sufficiently high grade of man. The trend of modern warfare emphasizes the importance of finding a solution. For the unskilled man, in the services as in industry, is losing his utility. Quality outweighs quantity on the modern battlefield.

CHAPTER V

The British Army

The British Army as voted by Parliament consists of some 152,000 officers and men, and of this total 34,000 are serving abroad. But a further 57,000, stationed in India, belong to it, although while serving there they are not paid for by the British public. Thus nearly half the Regular Army is employed on foreign service even in quiet times. The troops at home are organized in five infantry divisions—one less than before the war, owing to the disbandment of the Irish regiments. Behind the Regular Army there is the Territorial Army, composed of civilian soldiers who spend a fortnight annually in camp, besides training in the evenings at their local drill hall. Its establishment is 182,000 but its strength at present is under 140,000; it has been recently rising, however, after years of decline.

The British Army has many points of difference from those of the Continent. While they are large, it is small; while they are raised by conscription, it depends on voluntary enlistment; while they have short-service, it has long-service—seven years is the normal; while they are raised from all classes, it is drawn from the poor.

The British Army

In the past it largely depended for filling its ranks on those who were too uneducated and resourceless to find better-paid employment; and while the officers were drawn from the other social extreme it was a family principle that the Army was the vocation of those sons who were not likely to shine in other professions. If there has been some change in this basis, it persists sufficiently to be a handicap in days when the trend of warfare places an increasing premium on intelligence. Moreover, its social tradition tends to make the British Army highly conservative. On the other hand, it has in a measure escaped the narrow professionalism which marks some of the Continental officer corps through the fact that so many of its officers had independent means, and also through the variety of its service.

This brings us to the greatest difference between the British and the Continental Armies. While their primary purpose is the defence of their own country—a euphemism which embraces the attack on a neighbouring country—that of the British Army is the defence of, and maintenance of order in, the British Empire. These duties have governed its basic organization. In the nineteenth century it became so predominantly a colonial service army as to become quite unfit, both quantitatively and qualitatively, to face the contingency of a European war. Thus in 1868 Mr. Cardwell, then Secretary of State for War, established the principle that there should be a battalion at home for each one maintained abroad. Under the 'Cardwell System' the units at home provide drafts for those on foreign service, and the regiment, instead of being a fighting organization as in other armies, consists of linked home and foreign battalions, which never serve together but merely interchange officers and men.

The British Army

Besides finding drafts for the overseas garrisons, the home army has also to provide a potential expeditionary force, either to act as an Imperial fire-brigade in guarding a serious outbreak in the overseas territories, or as a contribution to the collective forces ranged against an aggressive European power. This last role, if deeply rooted in British history, was only revived a few years before 1914, when an expeditionary force of six divisions was erected as part of the Haldane Reforms. If its size was puny compared with the armies that the continental powers could mobilize, and its equipment barely as good as theirs, it had a definite qualitative advantage through longer training; from its hard experience in the Boer War it had learnt the value of marksmanship, and thus in 1914 its volume of aimed rifle-fire took the Germans by surprise and created the impression that it possessed quantities of machine-guns. This fire capacity gave it a weight beyond its numbers, and, combined with the natural 'sticking-power' of the British soldier, enabled it to renew its traditional record in repelling attacks. But it showed less aptitude for the offensive, and as its numbers grew through expansion on a national scale, it tended to expand them prodigally but unprofitably. In the tank, however, it produced the most important new offensive weapon of the war; and in the last phase this weapon, together with the improved technique which developed with experience, helped it to gain distinction in forcing entrenched positions.

After the war Britain gave up conscription, and went back from her war-time army of millions to one even smaller than in 1914. Yet in one respect this post-war army took the lead among the European powers. Instead of being content to copy continental ideas and practice, a

E   55

new school of military thought arose which went back to an older tradition and thence went forward, via its war-time experience with tanks, to a fresh conception of mobile mechanized warfare. These ideas, although at first regarded as heresy or fantasy, gradually made headway and eventually won acceptance. They also focused the attention of the military world on the experiments carried out by the British Army, and have now borne fruit in the general mechanization of armies.

But in this translation of theory into actual equipment Britain herself has fallen behind. The political desire to postpone measures of rearmament, the inherent conservatism of the senior military chiefs, the inelastic requirements of the Cardwell System and the retarding power of India—these are some of the factors that have put a brake on material progress. Another is the characteristic British tendency to seek technical perfection instead of going into production as soon as it has found something that will be fairly effective. The result is that the chief foreign armies have already a far larger quantity of modern mechanized troops when Britain, despite her much smaller army, is only beginning its general re-equipment.

It was not until the end of 1935 that the War Office reached the point of embarking on a big scheme of reorganization and modernization. The cavalry were to be mechanized, part being equipped with light tanks and part, provisionally, with a new kind of light motor vehicle, with large wheels and oversize tyres, that can travel across country—it looks like an adaption of the Irish jaunting car, the seating being so designed that each man on board can jump out easily, and go instantly into action on foot. It is intended to create a Mobile Division—to take the place of the old Cavalry Division—which will consist of two mechanized Cavalry Brigades, mainly composed of light tanks, with a Tank Brigade (the British Army has only one) attached and detachable. At the same time twenty-six battalions of infantry out of a hundred and thirty-six are being converted into mechanized machine-gun units. It was originally intended to have one of these battalions in each infantry brigade, but it has now been decided to employ them as divisional and corps troops, while the infantry brigade will be reduced to three 'rifle' battalions. These, being relieved of their heavier and more complex weapons, will be easier to handle and to train, while their manœuvring power is being improved by the motorization of their transport. Although called 'rifle' battalions, each of them will have fifty-two light machine-guns—one in each little section of half a dozen men—thus increasing their fire-power.

But, owing to the decision having been left so late, and even then delayed by fresh changes of mind, the manufacture of all the new equipment required is likely to take some years. Meantime the successive emergencies in Egypt and Palestine during 1935 and 1936 have stripped the home army of equipment and men, leaving the expeditionary force a skeleton. This state has strengthened the case of those who argue that the home army should be designed for use as a mobile Imperial Reserve, not as a potential field army for the Continent. Some who hold this view would concede the possible value of employing a small but highly mechanized force in suitable circumstances, where its quality might turn the scales, while doubting the wisdom of any large-scale participation in a continental land struggle. Others would prefer that we definitely eschewed the idea of playing a part in Continental warfare, leaving to the Air Force any such intervention if it should be called for by Britain's obligations.

The ruling view of the Army's role in another war has for years been shrouded in a traditional haze. So far as can be judged, by anything that Government spokesmen have said, it does not seem to differ materially from that which prevailed before 1914. It would almost seem that they are building on a memory instead of on a modern foundation. Yet even if the conditions had undergone no serious change the value of a repetition should come in question. Despite the traditional purpose of British interventions on the Continent, and the immediate cause of our entry into the last war, it was not to the direct aid of threatened Belgium that we sent our Expeditionary Force. Instead, it was designed to serve as the wing-tip of a French offensive. Owing to the perilous miscalculation of the French plan the force soon found itself fulfilling a defensive purpose, and in that role rendered aid of undoubted value to our French Allies, if it thereby slipped further away from the Belgians. In the light of history there is reason to think that if it had gone direct to Belgium it might not only have been an aid to the Belgians but a more effective aid to the French. For by threatening the flank and communications of the German move into France, it might have thrown the invasion out of gear long before it reached the Marne—the more we learn of the inelasticity of the German plan and the nerves of opposing command the more likely this seems.

The 'Belgian' course was favoured by some of our best soldiers; it was abandoned for the French plan, not on a weighing of their respective merits, but because of prearranged steps in the latter direction. It is a warning of the dangers involved by the intricate arrangements necessary for the transport of a field force. Even if we recognize the political hypothesis of a fresh attack in the West, as feared by our neighbours, we should be chary of basing our military steps on a false assumption. Before we contemplate sending a field force as in 1914, we ought to visualize what it would do if an invasion did not go the same way. Suppose the invaders avoided Belgian territory, which stretches some two hundred and fifty miles east of the Channel, are we to contemplate our field force being sent right across to the eastern frontier of France? On military as well as on political grounds such an avoidance of Belgium must be regarded as quite possible; this is even the view of a considerable section of French military opinion. Estimating, from an enemy's point of view, the loss of time and increase of risks involved in the detour, they are more concerned with the dangers of an *attaque brusquée* on their own frontier. The same thought may have had an influence on the recent Belgian tendency towards a re-establishment of their old position of neutrality. And this neutrality might prove a reality. If we take the case of a German attack on France in which Britain went to the latter's aid, it is quite conceivable that all parties might find predominant advantages in the exclusion of Belgian territory from the theatre of conflict. Even apart from this possibility, the tendency of Belgian policy should make us ponder the new problems which would arise in employing a field force on the Continent in a war where Belgian territory was denied to our forces yet at any moment liable to be crossed by the enemy, while lying on the flank of our communications.

We ought, also, to consider the new risks to such a force that are threatened by modern military conditions. The risks that were incurred in 1914, in landing a field force of 100,000 men in a foreign land, were much less than those we should run to-day—when it may have greater distances to cover, and when both railways and roads will lie under the menace of air attack. Broken communications are bad enough when an army is in its own territory, or one where it has complete control. In face of air attack, we cannot ignore the risk of our field force being stranded in the depth of France with no prospect of reaching the front, or of maintaining itself in the interior. In such a plight it would be more nuisance than help to any ally. And the farther it has to travel the more does this risk grow. Beyond it is the doubt whether it could achieve an adequate effect in face of present tactical obstacles, if it came into action. There is reason to ask whether the complexity of the problem is fully recognized either here or in France. Before we accept the argument that the despatch of a field force is necessary on political grounds we ought to be sure that the instability of the military foundations has been recognized. Also, that the Government has made two points clear to the French—first, that they might get more value from increased air assistance, which would naturally become effective sooner, in place of a field force; second, that the despatch of a field force does not imply a willingness to reinforce it without limit, and to expend the massed man-power of this nation in another four years' process of exploring by trial and error a problem which can be, and could have been, examined scientifically. Those who demand the means should be careful to reassure the nation that they have taken the measure of the problem, and have a clear view of the aim.

Secondary to this question of purpose, and consequent organization, is that of recruiting—which, in characteristic British style, has hitherto been made the primary issue in discussion of Army issues. During the past year it has become the dominant theme in speeches delivered by ministers and generals. While there is cause to regret that it should have obscured issues which ought to take precedence, it none the less remains a problem that must be solved.

If we are to find a remedy for the existing difficulty of recruiting men for the Army, it is important to establish its true proportions, and probe the causes. The present deficiency in the Regular Army is some 10,000 men. The deficiency, therefore, is just over five per cent. This may not seem very serious, especially to those who realize that, in modern war, weapon and motor power count for more than man-power. It may even be thought that a shortage in the infantry might have an indirect compensation, in stimulating necessary changes towards a more modern type of army of less adipose tissue. Quality certainly weighs more than quantity in the scales of modern war. On the other hand, it must be remembered that a shortage of men coming forward to join the army is apt to be symptomatic of a deficiency of quality. The more difficulty there is in attracting recruits the less likely it is that those who are accepted will be of the quality that is desirable. Only a large field of selection will enable the standard of intelligence to be raised, as it ought to be. A similar reflection applies to the Territorial Army which on present establishment has a deficiency of about twenty-five per cent. On the existing basis of organization that is, clearly, a serious deficiency. The establishment of a Territorial infantry battalion has been reduced to barely six hundred, a number which would not be regarded as excessive even by those who believe that the conditions of to-day require smaller and handier units than in the past. Many of the battalions in the South are at present unable to take more than half that number to annual camps: this is too weak for effective training, or to give officers and N.C.O.s the necessary practice in command.

The general deficiency cannot, of course, be considered without reference to the basis of organization. Any deficiency is relative to some standard—a fact often overlooked—and in the Territorial Army that standard was fixed many years ago by its staple organization in fourteen infantry divisions of twelve battalions apiece. Two of these infantry divisions have now been converted into anti-aircraft divisions, but it is certainly debatable whether such reorganization goes far enough: whether so high a proportion of infantry and the comparative scarcity of more modern arms fits the conditions of modern warfare and our prospective military problems. The question deserves more attention than it has received. On the other hand, there is no question that the infantry as well as the more technical arms and services need a much higher quality of personnel than in the past. Thus here again we are brought back to the principle that in order to raise the level of quality it is important that a greater quantity should be ready to serve. Units which are full can afford to pick and choose; units which are half-empty may be driven to take what they can get. How can the situation be improved?

Recent speeches by those who are officially concerned with defence have sounded a common note—that if conscription is to be avoided the voluntary system must somehow produce a better flow of recruits. It is questionable whether such a note is wise. Its reiteration has excited remark in many quarters, creating the impression in

The British Army

some that the 'if' had a veiled meaning, and that the defence authorities were already contemplating steps towards conscription, despite the Prime Minister's reiterated pledge that it should never be introduced in his time. To raise suspicion is to raise opposition, so that the directness of such an approach to the problem tends to frustrate its own end. At the least it may impair the prospects of rallying the different sections of public opinion for a common effort to surmount a real problem. It is likely that the conscription note had no deeper meaning than to prompt a better response to recruiting appeals and a more energetic support to our traditional system; even so, it might be better eschewed because of its liability to be misread as a threat. Englishmen do not take kindly to such an approach. Their inclination is to react against it.

At present there is a lack of harmony in the arguments for defence. Until the right call is sounded we cannot expect the response to be strong. On other grounds, too, it is premature to doubt the possibilities of the voluntary system. Before entertaining such thoughts we ought to satisfy ourselves that everything possible has been done to make the Army attractive to the best type of youth. The appeal of mechanization is as clear as the distaste for footslogging, but mechanization is only just becoming general and we cannot expect to see its fruits at once. Again, there is much scope for increasing the interest of the soldier's training, and its value in developing qualities and faculties that will be an asset in civil as well as military life. The Regular soldier's lot has been improved in many positive ways, but the necessity of removing negative restrictions has not received equal attention. There has been too great a time-lag in the adaptation of discipline and barrack life to the civil conditions of the day, and to the growth of education. The Army to-day, both its officers and its men, is one of the most abstemious sections of the nation; yet it still preserves restrictions, on the individual's freedom when off duty, that were a necessary safeguard in a past age when drunkenness was habitual. Custom preserves too many petty constraints, and off parade the soldier is still treated too much like a child, instead of as a man engaged on a military job. It is certainly significant that those who have visited the new German Army remark the comparative freedom of its discipline, its increased appeal to the spirit, and decrease of the punitive element, contrasting it favourably with our own. Even apart from recruiting, the military arguments for modernizing the forms of discipline are strong. Modern warfare demands an ever-rising degree of intelligence and initiative. An automaton is out of date. These reflections at least deserve consideration. For the reluctance of the young citizen to join the Army is unmistakable, and can no longer be explained away by any popular belief that the danger of war is a remote possibility. The Army must be made fit for the future, psychologically as well as materially.

Some of these conditions apply with no less force to the problem of recruiting for the Territorial Army. It is too easy a line of treatment to blame pacifism for the deficiency. We must first be sure that nothing has been neglected that lies within the power of the Government and the military authorities to put right. There has been a marked improvement both of attitude and of conditions recently, and more is in prospect. But the Territorial Army has suffered years of ill-nourishment; to anyone who has known it during those years there is more cause for wonder that it is not dead than that it is still weak. We can hardly expect an instant change to be produced by better treatment—a changed impression inevitably takes time to spread. And there is still much to be done in the way of providing modern equipment, developing the interest of training, and removing the things that chafe. How much these factors mean was shown by the bounding vitality of some units in the years of general discouragement. The Northamptonshire Territorials who became famous as 'John Brown's men' afforded an object-lesson in what was attainable by a leadership which moved with the times, and knew how to combine 'live' training, common-sense discipline, and an inspiring appeal, to generate a current of enthusiasm which ran through a whole district. It should be possible to renew such an achievement to-day, and to extend it. The conditions are more favourable in many practical respects. The Government as well as the War Office are manifesting through their spokesmen that the importance of the Territorial Army is appreciated more fully than ever before—and that the means to nourish it will be forthcoming. That atmosphere is bound to have a bracing effect, as well as the nourishment.

But the 'body' itself must be adapted to the conditions of the present time, both in organization and in methods. If the Army, Regular, or Territorial, is to attract men of intelligence it must be able to convince them that their effort will not be wasted. They want a clear idea of the purpose of the Army under modern conditions, and a reasonable assurance that its organization and training are fitted to that purpose. There is a warning that it would be well to heed in the experience of a much esteemed commander of Territorials who not long ago made wide-spread enquiries, especially among the N.C.O.s in his division, in an endeavour to ascertain why recruiting was poor. The answer he received was epitomized in the remark: 'What can you expect? The men now growing up are the sons of the infantrymen of the last war,' the men of the Somme and Passchendaele.

The Secretary of State for War showed his recognition of such doubts when, in a recruiting speech towards the end of 1936, he declared:

'If there is to be another war we need not be afraid of having to go through Passchendaele again, of sitting in the mud of Flanders in the way many of us did from 1914 to 1918.'

But something more than words of assurance is required to remove from men's minds the impression of an experience so deeply embedded. It will not even suffice to tell them that more guns, machine-guns, and tanks have been added to the Army—for they will say to themselves that as many more of these weapons have been added to the armies of possible opponents, so that the additions probably cancel out to make the sum still a strategic zero, and the prospect another stick-in-the-mud stalemate. There is not likely to be much chance of persuading men that the next war will be different unless and until we can show them an army essentially different in composition, equipment, proportions and tactics.

CHAPTER VI

The Rearmament of Britain

The appearance and atmosphere of England show but a slight reflection of the armament race now in progress throughout Europe. There is none of the bustle of military preparations which is so manifest on the Continent. The landscape is not coloured by uniforms. But unobtrusively there is a considerable measure of activity. The most noticeable sign, perhaps, is the number of new military aerodromes—there are forty more than at the end of 1934. Some of the great motor factories, too, show large extensions for the building of aircraft. The British Air Force is fast, if not furiously, expanding to a formidable scale, while the other forces are more gradually acquiring a new complexion. These developments, however, will take time —and Britain has much leeway to make up. Meantime her defence problems have developed faster.

The conquest of the air has laid low her old sea-wall of seclusion, and brought her into uncomfortably close neighbourhood with the Continent. The rebirth of Germany in arms has affected her situation indirectly even more than directly, because of its impetus to the general expansion of forces, which works to the widespread dis-

67

advantage of a scattered empire which has so many points of contact with the domains of other nations. And her situation, from a military point of view, is more complicated than it was before 1914. She was committed by post-war engagements to a generalized effort to resist any aggression against other countries, and to a more specific guarantee in Western Europe: although recent events have loosened the former tie it remains a potential source of entanglement.

Meantime old friends have become estranged, while becoming more formidable as military powers: with this development goes an appetite for new territory which, accentuated by their martial tastes, threatens a clash of interests. Italy lies athwart Britain's main trade-route to the East, through the Mediterranean and the Red Sea. Japan is encroaching on its eastern extremity, thus imposing a two-way stretch on British resources which is all the more of a strain owing to the increased length of her communications and their intermediate susceptibility to pressure. And there is the still more uncomfortable possibility of a new combination of pressure at the point where Britain's Mediterranean and Cape routes converge. Even when goodwill prevails it is not easy for countries in which an essentially different form of government and basis of society exists to reconcile their respective aims. Britain's coasts and causeways are now lapped by totalitarian tides.

After the World War the British forces were rapidly reduced, and the country returned to the traditional system of voluntary enlistment which it had temporarily abandoned when the war was in its second year. The Army was brought back to less than its pre-war size, which had naturally been much smaller than the conscript armies of the Continent. The Air Force, which had been built up to the highest level of any by the end of the war, was reduced to a skeleton—from 185 squadrons to 28, of which only three were available for the defence of the home country. With the Washington Treaty Britain gave up her long-standing claim to predominance on the seas, and agreed to a condition of parity with the next strongest naval power.

In 1922 the Geddes Committee, appointed to consider economies in national expenditure, went so far as to suggest reducing the Air Force to a mere eight squadrons. The older services—conservative in a double sense—were more than content to see their young sister's allowance cut down if it saved a little more for themselves. But a check was imposed after strong Press criticism initiated in *The Times* by General Groves, a former member of the Air Staff. And just afterwards a state of tension developed with Britain's former allies, when the French marched into the Ruhr to impose their will on conquered Germany. The British, making plain their dislike of this invasion, felt a strong sense of personal discomfort when they awoke to the fact that a considerable part of France's 126 air squadrons were assembled within reach of their own coast.

The outcome was the announcement by Mr. Baldwin in 1923 that, apart from overseas requirements, 'British air power must include a home-defence force of sufficient strength adequately to protect us against air attack by the strongest air force within striking distance of this country'. He stated that the force was to consist of 52 squadrons, to be created as quickly as possible. The expansion started promptly, but was checked in 1926 when still a long way from completion. Three years later the official spokesman of the Air Ministry disclosed to Parliament that Britain had sunk to fifth place among the world's air powers. Yet the incomplete programme was again suspended, first to meet the economic crisis, and then to meet the hopes of a general limitation raised by the Disarmament Conference which assembled in 1932. During these years all service expenditure had been steadily pared down. If the Navy suffered least, as the favourite child of British tradition, the modernization of its capital ships was put off longer than in either the United States or Japan, while its own youngest and least cherished child, the Fleet Air Arm, had to be content with crumbs. The Army, faced with a shrinking purse, conservatively preferred to save on new equipment rather than at the expense of historic units. Although younger brains had given the British Army a technical lead in the means and methods of mechanized warfare, to the older heads modernization seemed less important than the maintenance of infantry numbers. In this endeavour they even allowed the reserves of ammunition to sink below what would be needed if the Army had to take the field. Nevertheless the Army and Navy together were taking six times as much money as the Air Force from the total allotted for defence—a little over a hundred million pounds a year. The disproportion gave a curious reflection to the Government's admission that: 'The advent of the air weapon has lost us our age-long security as an island nation, and has left the greatest city in the world more open to the dangers of air attacks than any of the other capitals in Europe.'

This prolonged curtailment of expenditure on the forces, while fostered by the urge for economy, was justified by the Government's formal assurance to the heads of the services that no major war need be anticipated within a period of ten years ahead. The ruling was renewed annually—until it lapsed, and the country suddenly found itself confronted with the possibility of a war within much less than ten years.

The strengthening and re-equipment of the British defences continued to be postponed so long as some hope, if a diminishing hope, hung on the Disarmament Conference —although well before this the Continental powers and Japan had obviously begun rearmament. The pace of this quickened with the advent of the Nazi government in Germany, and its unconcealed measures. Eventually the British Government took account of the danger and made a detailed examination of the state of their own forces. The result awakened them to many deficiencies—and the impression would have been worse if they had studied the technical trend of modern warfare enough to gauge the more serious qualitative defects. Even as it was, their confession of national deficiencies contrasted vividly with the complacent assurance that they had dished out to Parliament year after year in answer to a few critical voices.

The immediate result of this enquiry was that in July 1934 the Government adopted a five-year programme for increasing the Air Force, and raising the home defence part of it to seventy-five squadrons. They were soon led to quicken their step, and shorten the time of their programme, owing to evidence of Germany's rapid development in the air and the expansion of other air forces. Early in 1935, France had 1650 first line machines, Italy 1050, and Russia over 2000, while Britain had 1020, of which 688 were at home. By the end of the year she now aimed to have 1180 altogether, and in 1936 to have 1310. Ground defences against air attacks were also increased. Until then London alone had any such defences, and they were provided by merely two skeleton brigades of Territorial anti-aircraft artillery and searchlight units—com-

posed of citizen volunteers, who go to camp for a fortnight
a year and do occasional evenings' training during the rest
of the year. It was decided to break up two Territorial
infantry divisions and convert them into anti-aircraft
troops, to man a long belt of defence running from the
south coast up the east coast, so that it would cover the
north country industrial areas as well as London. This
conversion is not yet completed, nor the provision of the
necessary guns and searchlights. A research committee of
scientists has also been formed to study new means of
countering attacks.

At the same time that this immediate defence of Great
Britain was thus taken in hand, extra money was provided
for beginning the modernization of the Army and Navy,
although their actual size was not to be appreciably increased. Indeed the Army found difficulty in recruiting up
to the existing strength of approximately 200,000, and by
the end of the year was 10,000 short. Although £4,000,000
was added to the Army vote—a 10 per cent increase—a
large part of this was absorbed by the need to make up
depleted reserves of ammunition, and barely half a million
was allotted for modern mechanized equipment. With the
Navy an increase was restricted by Treaty conditions, and
the construction of new ships was limited to normal replacement: it included three new cruisers. But during
recent years the already difficult problem of guarding the
immense length of the trade-routes with naval forces
smaller than before the war, has been complicated by the
development of submarines and of torpedo-carrying speedboats in several of the Continental navies, notably those of
Italy and France. On top of this looms the menace both to
merchant shipping and their naval guardians, as well as to
the ports on which they depend, that comes from shore-

based aircraft—anywhere those trade-routes are within
the ever-growing range of the air-weapon.

The new programme had barely been decided when a
new series of shocks caused its upward revision. In March
1935 Germany startled the world with the announcement
of her reintroduction of conscription and the formation of
an army of thirty-six divisions, or some 600,000 men—
fifty per cent larger than the French. It was followed by
Hitler's intimation, to the British ministers who had gone
over to Berlin for friendly negotiations, that Germany
already possessed parity in the air with Britain and was
aiming at parity with France—which meant a superiority
to the prospective British air force. If there was some
doubt about his first assertion, his second was plain. And a
fortnight later the German Government disclosed that it
was again building submarines.

The sequel was that in May 1935 the British Government decided to raise its own intended air strength by
fifty squadrons, and to have a home defence force of 1500
first line machines within the next two years. This involved the construction of an additional thirty air stations
beyond the eighteen new ones already planned, and also
the training of 2500 new pilots as well as of 20,000 other
personnel. Although still hoping for any agreed limitation,
the British Government was no longer content to let preparedness wait on hope.

But the process of expanding the Air Force and renovat-
ing the Army was to suffer an unforeseen complication; it
came from Italy's invasion of Abyssinia and the tension
this act of aggression caused with Britain. As the chief
upholder of the League Covenant, she was naturally the
target if sanctions should culminate in war. If she was
better placed than any of the other powers to hinder the

despatch of Italian forces to Abyssinia, should the League's intervention go so far, her own communications were also exposed to possible interruption by Italy. A sudden realization of this awkward position (which is discussed at more length in Chapter 9) led the British fleet to leave its Mediterranean base at Malta, which lay close to the Italian air bases, and move to the far end of the Mediterranean. At the same time the military garrison needed strengthening. But the position in Egypt, also, became precarious in view of Italy's increase of force in Libya; the assembly there of mechanized divisions and powerful bombing squadrons was an obvious threat to the security of Egypt and the new harbours of the British fleet. It led to a hasty despatch of air and army units thither, which imposed a severe strain on existing British resources. It temporarily upset the expansion of the Air Force by taking away the experienced officers and N.C.O.'s who were needed as instructors for the newly recruited pilots and mechanics. Although the Army sent barely the equivalent of one division, out of the nominal five maintained at home, the rest of the army had to be scraped of equipment in order to make that detachment an effective fighting force. All the modern type tanks, a mere hundred or so, were sent out, leaving the home forces to carry on with long obsolete machines, supplemented by ordinary light trucks masquerading as tanks, until the manufacture of war material could catch up with the needs that had too long been neglected. The available stocks of mechanized transport, wireless sets, and many other kinds of modern equipment, were almost as badly drained. The whole army at home was left bare of what it needed for war until manufacture could overtake deficiency.

The emergency revealed not only the shortage of men

and material but a failure to make adequate arrangements beforehand. Hasty improvisation had to make good the absence of plans. The impression produced by these deficiencies, coupled with the uncertain state of service opinion on various technical issues, such as the effect of aircraft against warships, raised doubts whether the Government, in deciding upon measures of rearmament, had any clear picture of their aim. There was widespread anxiety lest the increasing outlay of money should fail of its purpose through faulty distribution; lest it was being governed merely by the endeavour to satisfy the demands of the three services, and based on a compromise between their separate interests, instead of being laid out on a fore-thoughtful plan. That anxiety found voice in *The Times*, which urged the need of viewing defence as a whole, and co-ordinating the activities of the three services as well as their supplies. This lead was supported by a growing volume of authoritative opinion, which included the testimony of several former service chiefs to the limitations of the existing system and its tendency to work by mere compromise. The proposal to develop a more powerful organ of co-ordination was strongly resisted in some quarters, but the Government eventually yielded to the weight of public opinion (see Chapter 15) and in March 1936 appointed a Minister for the Co-ordination of Defence, as well as three permanent, if junior, members to the Joint Planning Committee, at which the representatives of the three services meet. The Minister was not to be in charge of a department, but would act as the Prime Minister's deputy on the Committee of Imperial Defence, preside when necessary at the meetings of the Chiefs of Staff of the three services, and would also be in supreme charge of the supply organization and industrial planning. This was a step forward, if it did not go as far as was desirable: there was a danger that the new Minister might become too absorbed with the problems of providing the fighting services with equipment to have time for adjusting and combining their respective plans.

Sub-committees by the dozen have been set up to deal with the different items of munition supply, with the provision of raw material and its manufacture, with man-power, food-supply, grain storage, as well as with such questions as the protection of merchant shipping, the development of anti-aircraft defence, and precautions for the protection of the civilian population in air raids. A detailed survey has been made of the industrial field, to examine and clarify the material, operative and technical resources of the country. Hundreds of engineering firms have been inspected to see whether their plant is adaptable to munition production in war-time. Production for present needs, however, has been delayed by lack of the necessary machine-tools and gauges. The maintenance of the population itself is an even more complex problem. Two-thirds of the food required is at present imported from overseas— a total of some 50,000 tons a day. Agricultural production has been increased about 14 per cent in the last few years, and the country could be self-supporting in potatoes, eggs, vegetables and milk. But this is not possible with meat and cereals. In Britain there are, at any particular moment, only about six to twelve weeks' stocks of some of the main kinds of foodstuffs required. The renewed portents of war have reawakened the British people to the risks they run through their dependence on imported food, and consequently on the sea-routes by which those essential supplies are brought. It is this realization which, more than any threat from a specific quarter, has impelled the British

The Rearmament of Britain

Government to hasten the repair and expansion of its forces. It has also governed the direction of their main effort.

With the Air Force the interruption caused by the Mediterranean emergency was soon overcome, if not overtaken. The production of new types of machines, of much higher performance and greater range, has been speeded up so much that they are being delivered long before the date originally contemplated. The intended strength of the force at home has also been raised to 1750 first line aircraft, exclusive of the Fleet Air Arm, which is to be increased to at least 450 machines. The creation of the new squadrons, however, has been slower. Of the 72 which were to be raised by the end of March 1937—to make a home defence total of 124—only about 26 will now be complete, with a further 22 formed on a one-flight basis. The remainder should be formed, it not at full strength, by the late summer. With the Navy, which had a relatively lesser problem, the rate of construction has been quickened to the extent that some of the new ships are expected to be ready nearly half a year earlier than the scheduled time. Five of the new class of 9000 ton cruisers are expected to be ready within the next year: they have a speed of 32 knots and an armament of twelve 6-inch guns, as well as eight 4-inch anti-aircraft guns. Similar progress is being made with the building of destroyers, while two new 35,000 ton battleships were laid down in January 1937, with three more to follow shortly. And the completion of the Singapore Base is being hastened. Last winter the Government decided to raise the cruiser strength from 50 to 70—the number which has for years been claimed as a necessary minimum by those directly concerned with the defence of the sea-communications: in 1914 there were 125 cruisers, new and old, available.

The Rearmament of Britain

The situation is less comforting in regard to the deficiencies of the Army. The belated official acceptance of modernization and mechanization has caught its munition plants in a state of inadequacy for large-scale production, and a shortage of skilled labour has aggravated the difficulty. Even to-day it lacks any anti-tank guns, any modern light machine-guns, any assault tanks, any fast medium tanks that are fit for war. The motorization of its transport will take some time to complete. A new light machine-gun, the Bren, has been adopted to replace the wartime weapons that are still in use, and deliveries are expected to begin late in 1937. Some of the new anti-tank guns and anti-tank rifles may be available earlier. But the Territorial Army is even worse off and will have to wait longer.

A realization of the defective state of the Army has helped to give a new emphasis to an old theory—that Britain, even if she cannot avoid entanglement in Continental issues, should at least eschew the idea of landing an army on the Continent. A small field force from Britain, inevitably late in arrival, would seem to have little chance of influencing the issue or retrieving any advantage which an invader might gain by surprise in the first days of a new war; and the necessary peace-time preparations for its despatch to foreign ports are difficult to make without causing offence. By contrast, the air force could act from its own shores and could intervene in the first hours. The promise of such help would be more comfort to a threatened neighbour, and more deterrent to a would-be aggressor, than any force of the 1914 pattern—a mere drop in the bucket of a Continental struggle between mass armies.

This view made headway in Government circles last winter, but in the end the force of past custom prevailed, and the idea of sending a field force was again adopted.

The Rearmament of Britain

Since then, however, there have been fresh developments, both in the international and in the technical sphere, to strengthen doubts of its wisdom. And the fresh strain caused by the Palestine emergency has shown how limited are the resources of the Army for dealing with Continental in addition to colonial problems. That experience has given renewed force to the argument that Britain should limit her Continental commitments to possible action by air and sea. On this question largely turns the trend of her strategic policy, and of still broader issues.

PART II: PROBLEMS

CHAPTER VII

The Tactical Problem—and a New Solution

It is setting expectations high to count on any programme of rearmament and mechanization to bridge the gulf that now separates armies from their desire—for successful attack. My own view is that these potential developments in offensive power are far exceeded by the actual growth, largely unrecognized, of defensive power: and that the progress of mechanization hitherto has already reinforced the capacity for resistance more than it has any good prospect of strengthening the capacity for attack. Not only fire, but the means of obstruction and of demolition, may now be moved more swiftly to any threatened spot, to thwart a hostile concentration of force.

The question which armies must face is whether they have any chance of overcoming resistance on present lines, even when developed. An alternative way of approaching the problem is to seek a tactical solution, not merely a material one. If we are doubtful of overcoming the defence by an increase of offensive strength, as we have cause to be, is there any prospect in a different solution by an improvement of *art?* So heavy are the present odds against effective action on land, however, that something more than the art of the individual general is needed. Even if an army could breed Napoleons, which no army can be expected to do under its peace-time professional conditions, they would make no headway without an antidote to the paralysing machine-gun. Armies need to develop a new technique, and, then, to develop their tools to suit this new type of art.

Four years ago a committee composed of the younger generals was appointed to investigate the lessons of the war, and to see whether they were adequately applied in our training. The experience then sifted and collated should have shaken our satisfaction with customary methods. It is common knowledge that this re-examination of war experience led to the conclusion that surprise was of paramount importance, both in attack and in defence, and that the greatest lesson of the last war was that no attack on an enemy in action was likely to succeed unless his resistance was already paralysed by surprise in some form. It is known too, that this committee expressed the emphatic opinion that our methods, both during and since the war, were too stereotyped; also that the vital importance of surprise and of the indirect approach ought to receive greater attention in the training of the Army.

There has been some evidence of efforts to apply this admonition—but they have not gone wide enough. Exercises have too often become a competition in obviousness. Instead of developing ingenuity, the main effort has too often been towards simplifying the enemy's problem in defending himself. This tendency was the sequel, paradoxically, to the fresh concentration of attention on training the Army for European warfare—the very type of warfare in which investigation had shown the paramount importance of surprise. Under the influence of this

The Tactical Problem—and a New Solution

'European' keynote methods became more stereotyped rather than more subtle. Instead of going forward to the trial of new ideas, they went back to the repetition of old practices. If this is the best we can hope for, there should be no hesitation in bowing to the present paramountcy of the defensive, and resigning ourselves to the conclusion that it would be better to relegate the Army to a merely protective role—as a lesser evil than its futile sacrifice.

There were, however, some features in the work of the troops, as contrasted with the ruling ideas, which held out some promise of greater effect. One was the increased skill and subtlety which many of the troops showed in concealing themselves from air observation. Another was the cultivation of night sense and increased use of attacks in the dark —by some commanders at least.

These developments point a path by which further progress is possible. By the skilful use of *obscurity*, in its various forms, the attack might recover some of its lost power. Whereas to-day a mass attack merely spells massacre, a 'masked attack', under cover of darkness or fog, natural or artificial, has potentialities that have scarcely been tapped. Obscurity is a strong antidote to the defensive machine-gun and may prove a better protection than armour. Its risks are mainly those of confusion; they are certainly less than those of annihilation, by machine-guns with a clear field of fire; and they can be greatly reduced by training. The superiority of well-trained troops over normal troops is much more pronounced in the dark than in daylight.

The use of obscurity, however, requires judicious adaptation to the type of troops, and a recognition of its limits. Darkness is a better cloak than artificial fog to attacking infantry because, if skilled, they can see through

85

it; when moving in fog the man on foot has difficulty in keeping his direction, while he becomes a target the moment he emerges. Thus artificial fog would seem to have greater promise as a cloak for armoured fighting vehicles, equipped with direction finders. But night, despite its advantages for infantry who are trained in night fighting, has the disadvantage of limiting the effective depth of their attack. They may storm a position under cover of it, but if they press on, the risks of confusion are likely to increase disproportionately to the distance travelled. For control can hardly be kept once advancing troops are engaged in actual night combat. The actual assault may go well; the difficulty comes in re-forming and pushing on afterwards. Perhaps the problem of exploiting the night attack, and extending its reach, may eventually be solved by some form of flood-lighting the battlefield when the enemy's position has been stormed.

In places that afford plentiful cover—woods, villages and rough ground—infantry may be able to overcome hostile machine-guns and make headway by the use of what one may call the 'stalking attack'. It is a method which puts a premium on individual skill, and it offers considerable scope for development. But enthusiasm for it should not blind us to its limitations. It is a method which only fits special conditions; it is bound to be slow if it is to be efficiently executed; and it cannot be counted on to produce large-scale results. It is of its nature a preparatory or supplementary part of the attack rather than a separate form of attack.

We are thus left with the 'masked attack' or the 'armoured attack' as the two main forms of the offensive that seem to have any promise of breaking into an enemy's position, and ejecting him. But there are more

86

ways of overcoming the enemy's army than by storming its positions, just as there are more ways of winning wars than by winning battles. It is for the art of war to find them, and the need is the greater now that the strength of the defensive has made the storming of positions such a dubious proposition. The enemy may be forestalled on positions; he may be levered out of them by manœuvre; he may be left in them while his general situation is weakened by developing pressure elsewhere, in directions that his position does not cover. As a sequel or otherwise, he may be caught in motion, without having time to take up a defensive disposition.

There may be more scope for such alternative forms of action than is realized by those who still think of another war in terms of the last. The present trend of conditions is by no means favourable to the formation of continuous fronts, at any rate in the early stages of a war. Mass armies do not lend themselves to mechanization, and since the mechanized fractions will be available earlier than the rest, there is a likelihood that the crucial first phase of a war will be fought out between these opposing fractions; thus we should see relatively small forces on large fronts. Furthermore, the assembly of the masses on the frontiers will be hindered by the danger of air attack on the marching columns, and by the jeopardy of supply when their communications are exposed to interruption over so large an area in rear.

A factor common to all these alternative courses is the time factor. If the advantage is to be gained there must be an acceleration of action. The scales of war are inclining not to the side which has the 'big battalions' but to the side which 'gets there' first. I would suggest that it is an axiom of modern war that 'a hundred men with

G   87

machine-guns who arrive at a spot first are stronger, at least in daylight, than five hundred and sometimes a thousand who arrive second'.

This, in turn suggests the value of using any fragment of one's force that is mechanized, or can be motor-moved, to jump ahead and secure key-points. Nothing has been more disappointing in recent years' exercises than the way that mechanization has been wasted by moving units and formations at the pace of their slowest portion, owing to the desire to move complete. It shows a too general disregard of another modern axiom, arising from the advantage of defence over attack, which we may express in the phrase that 'possession is nine-tenths of the war'.

Soldiers to-day are predominantly concerned with the problem of attack, so dubious of solution. They might wisely spare a little time to study the possibilities of a form of action which would throw the burden of that problem on the enemy. I refer to what I would term the 'baited offensive', the combination of offensive strategy with defensive tactics. Throughout history it has proved one of the most effective of moves, and its advantages have increased as modern weapons have handicapped other types of move. By rapidity of advance and mobility of manœuvre, you may be able to seize points which the enemy, sensitive to the threat, will be constrained to attack. Thus you will invite him to a repulse which in turn may be exploited by a riposte. Such a counterstroke, against an exhausted attacker, is much less difficult than the attack on a defended position. The opportunity for it may also be created by a calculated withdrawal—what one may call the 'luring defensive'. Here is another gambit of future warfare.

Whatever form of action be adopted, its effectiveness

The Tactical Problem—and a New Solution

will depend on concealment of intention. The mystification of the opponent acts upon him like a paralyzing drug. The surest method of producing it, as centuries of experience have shown, is that of *wide extension*. It is a method unsuited for use by military mediocrity. But in skilled hands its risks are far outweighed by its advantages. By operating on a wide front, one thickens the fog of war for one's opponent yet minimizes it for oneself. It is a psychological smoke-screen which disturbs the mind and may shake the nerve of the stoutest adversary. Under cover of it, one has the best chance of seizing points of leverage. The introduction of mechanized mobility has added to its potency while increasing its safety. But of itself it aids rapidity—by reducing the congestion inherent in the practice of operating on narrow fronts.

There have been some instances in recent exercises of a tendency towards movement on wider fronts, but it has not gone nearly far enough for its promise to mature. The greatest hindrance is the dogma of 'concentration', imperfectly understood. It is not easy for the simple mind to grasp that concentration is in essence a matter of effect and not of form. The adaptation of methods to changing conditions is retarded by the soldier's customary reluctance to change his traditional terminology. By putting new ideas in old potted terms we cramp the growth of this understanding. I learnt this lesson when compiling the post-war infantry manual. To eradicate the practice of a rigid linear advance and of direct reinforcement—a 'building up of the firing line' which merely piled up the casualties—it was necessary to replace the terms 'firing line' and 'supports' which many, from habit or sentiment, desired to retain. The benefit of their disappearance was unmistakable. But to-day, in a higher sphere, we still suffer such needless handicaps. We still call the preliminary distribution of forces, however widely disposed, the 'strategic concentration'. We ought to drop this terminological absurdity. Again the idea of advancing on a wide front is cramped by the term 'advanced guard', which is associated with the practice of moving on a narrow front— with the whole division on a single road. We are likely to be fettered to this obsolete method until we strike out the term.

The greatest need to-day is to recognize the evolution that is in process. Until the end of the 18th century, a physically concentrated approach, both strategic (*to* the battlefield) and tactical (*on* the battlefield) was the rule. Then Napoleon, exploiting Bourcet's ideas and the new divisional system, introduced a *distributed* strategic approach—the army moving in independent fractions. But the tactical approach was still, in general, a concentrated one. Towards the end of the nineteenth century, with the development of fire weapons, the tactical approach became *dispersed*, i.e. in particles, to diminish the effect of fire. But the strategic approach had again become concentrated—this was due partly to the growth of masses, and partly to the misunderstanding of the Napoleonic method. To-day we must recognize the need of reviving the distributed strategic approach, if there is to be any chance of reviving the art and effect of strategy. But two new conditions—air power and motor power—seem to point to its further development into a *dispersed strategic approach*. The danger of air attack, the aim of mystification, and the need of drawing full value from mechanized mobility, suggest that advancing forces should not only be distributed as widely as is compatible with combined action, but be dispersed as much as is compatible with cohesion. And the development of wireless is a timely aid towards reconciling dispersion with control.

If there is to be any hope of reviving an army's effectiveness, except in mere protectiveness, it lies in the development of such new methods: methods which aim at permeating and dominating areas rather than capturing lines; at the practicable object of paralyzing the enemy's action rather than the theoretical object of crushing his forces. Fluidity of force may succeed where concentration of force merely entails a helpless rigidity. The sea is stronger than a steam-roller, and should replace it as our military ideal. The main difficulty is the doubtful ability of soldiers trained on present lines to rise to the level of this new technique. Unless they can do so, it would be wiser to abandon any dreams of attack, and resign ourselves to the present fact that the defensive is the only role an army can effectively play in a modern war where both sides are fairly equal in equipment.

CHAPTER VIII

The Capital Ship

The capital cost of the last capital ships we built before the Washington Treaty was some £7,000,000 apiece. Since then constructional costs have risen; whereas that of H.M.S. *Nelson* was £177 for each standard ton, compared with a pre-war battleship cost of £78, the constructional cost of the recent cruisers has been £204 to the ton compared with £71 in 1914. The cost of new battleships will be at least £8,000,000 each. Beyond that must be reckoned fully half a million pounds a year for its direct maintenance, apart from the cost of graving docks and repair plant. Since the building of battleships will absorb so large a proportion of the money that can be found for defence as a whole, it is essential to enquire whether the result promises to repay the cost.

Because of the high valuation which Englishmen have come to place upon sea-power, from centuries of experience, there is a tendency to shirk this question—especially in Whitehall. It would be a happy thing for us as a people if the conditions of sea-power had not been affected by new developments. For that reason we should be specially on our guard lest the wish should father any unjustified assumption—as it certainly did before the Mediterranean emergency produced an awakening. Is it a full awakening? Have we taken the measure of our present sea problems? The question whether aircraft can sink battleships is but a small part of the greater issue whether the battle-fleet can fulfil its strategic role. Under the conditions now developing, has a rebuilt battle-fleet the promise of contributing in a way commensurate with its cost to the security of our sea communications and the flow of supplies upon which the nation's life depends? Is it still the necessary foundation of the operations of the lighter craft which actually execute this task?

In considering these questions we have to take into account the fact that twenty years ago the submarine attack on our shipping routes nearly brought us to disaster despite the unassailable supremacy of our battle-fleet. If we are disposed to forget this, other powers do not. And it would be folly to shut our eyes to the fact that they are counting on aircraft and high-speed surface craft to multiply greatly the past potentialities of the submarine for direct attack on sea traffic. We should take account also of the fact that before a new battle-fleet less susceptible to air attack can be built several years must elapse: during that time the means of attack may be improved proportionately. Moreover, a battle-fleet is dependent on bases. The bases that we might develop to-day as safely out of reach may be within easy range of air attack three years hence. The problem is a bundle of complexities. In default of a better answer, the comment is frequently heard that so long as other countries proclaim their intention to build large battleships we must follow suit. This merely shirks the real question. It may also play into others' hands, by enabling them at some cost to cause us to divert a much larger proportion of our expenditure into a channel which they inwardly regard as irrelevant to the vital issue.

Let us hope that they are mistaken; and that doubts of the continued efficiency of our traditional shield are misplaced. But a heavy responsibility lies on the Government for the thorough investigation of these problems. If a combined defence organ had been established years ago the task would have been easier.

In deciding upon its defence programme in 1935, which included the laying down of two new battleships, the Government was naturally guided by the case presented by the Chiefs of Staff Committee, as then constituted. Of its members, it could hardly be expected that the Chief of the Air Staff should have opposed the claims of the others. And it would be strange if the representatives of the older services, after a lifetime spent in dealing with familiar material, should not hold the shoemaker's belief that 'there is nothing like leather'. Men rarely reach such a position, especially in peace-time, unless they conform to the accepted ideas. Even in the slow changing past, accepted ideas have commonly proved out of date when tested by war's reality. The likelihood is greater to-day. Since the Services are separate there is no such thing as a professional 'Combined Serviceman'—trained in studying war as a whole. The nearest approach to it is in those who have been through the Imperial Defence College during the past eight years. And it is significant that its first Commandant, Admiral Richmond, has strongly questioned the value of the big battleship under modern conditions. In a letter to *The Times* on December 21st, 1935, he pointed out that the real question is not whether the battle-fleet may be sunk by air-bombers but whether it can fulfil its functions—whether, as effective bombing range extends, it will 'be able to take up and maintain a position close enough to its opponent, either at sea or in harbour, to ensure that that enemy cannot move without the risk of being brought to action'. For if that cannot be done 'the fleet becomes incapable of exercising control'. Here is a question that deserves enquiry. It bears on a point made by the then First Lord of the Admiralty, Lord Monsell, that 'in the last war our Battle-Fleet in the North Sea was able to prevent the German Fleet from getting out into the Atlantic' and 'destroying our trade'. It is by no means certain that such a danger was prevented only by the battle-fleet, but even if it be accepted we have to remember that we were greatly favoured by our geographical situation. Would it apply to-day when spaces are greater, bombing ranges ever increasing, and bases more distant from an enemy's naval ports?

To meet the doubts which were widely felt and expressed, the Government in the spring of 1936 belatedly appointed a sub-committee of the Committee of Imperial Defence to investigate the question of the vulnerability of capital ships to air attack—a question which was but a fraction of the issue. The Sub-Committee consisted of four ministers; with the First Sea Lord (the Chief of the Naval Staff) and the Chief of the Air Staff as expert advisers. Their report was published in November 1936. It may help to clarify public opinion on a number of points which are constantly in discussion, and naturally came up in the course of the investigation. It brings out factors that partisans are apt to ignore. The conclusion is of a cautiously negative kind, as was to be expected in view of the limited state of knowledge at the present time on many of the points at issue, and the natural reluctance to make grave decisions on a basis which is largely speculative. The dominant feeling of the sub-committee is obviously expressed when they dwell on the risks of a false decision, ask whether we ought to take the lead in doing away with capital ships, and answer: 'Surely not, unless the question is settled beyond all possible doubt.' A question which remains, however, is whether it would have been possible to have gained more light on the problem without waiting for the actual experience of war.

In regard to determining the effect of bombs on ships, the sub-committee declare that they are satisfied that the Admiralty 'have taken all proper steps to that end', but go on to recommend further experiments, emphasizing that the provision of funds and material should not be allowed to stand in the way. In view of the immense sum of money that is to be sunk in the building of new battleships, surely it should not have been impracticable to have carried out adequate bombing tests on those which have been sent to the scrapheap? Again, on the question of the accuracy of bombing, the sub-committee remarks that some of the factors are 'at present a matter of opinion, but we do not think it need so remain. We recommend that experiments, jointly agreed and jointly analysed, should be carried out to determine the facts.' It is clear there was cause here for dissatisfaction. On the effects of anti-aircraft fire, the report refers to 'the unreal conditions' under which tests have 'hitherto taken place'; it suggests that the difference between the Admiralty's and the Air Ministry's point of view might be 'considerably narrowed down by making, as we recommend, peace-time practice assimilate more closely to war conditions'. It urges that the two staffs should work in closer touch 'for their joint benefits'. The impression is left that the eighteen years since the war have not been adequately utilized for ob-

The Capital Ship

jective research. The neglect may be to the joint detriment of the country and the taxpayer.

The many elements of doubt on these technical and tactical issues must have increased the sub-committee's difficulties in studying the broader issues. For they found it necessary to go beyond their terms of reference, since a strict interpretation would have made the field of enquiry artificially narrow. It would, as they justly point out, 'be unsatisfactory to deal with the vulnerability of capital ships to air attack without taking account of the extent to which they may become liable to this form of attack'. At the same time the sub-committee 'tried to confine within necessary limits' their survey of the wider aspects. To determine what are necessary limits, however, must have been difficult. There is no true dividing line between technical, tactical, and strategic values. In historical experience, nothing is more upsetting to calculations than the tendency, natural though it be, to consider the problems of war in bits. At every step the bit needs to be related to the whole. The report bears evidence of the difficulty which this investigation found in endeavouring to keep within limits. It wanders into the field of strategy and out again; the excursion was necessary, but its extent is too short. In concluding it the sub-committee remark: 'It is possible to state the matter in its simplest terms. The advocates of the extreme air view would wish this country to build no capital ships (other Powers still continuing to build them). If their theories turn out well-founded, we have wasted money; if ill-founded, we would, in putting them to the test, have lost the Empire.'

While there is much truth in this contrast, it is too simple strategically. We were in peril of losing the war in 1917, although we had a far larger battle-fleet than to-day, because of the havoc that a comparatively small number of submarines played on our trade routes, and because the destroyers which were wanted to combat that threat were being kept to safeguard the battle-fleet. If Germany had invested in submarine building earlier, some of the money which she devoted to battleships, that menace might well have proved fatal. That is an example of the strategic factors which should be borne in mind when weighing the capital ship question. The sub-committee, while recognizing the risks which the battle-fleet may run in the narrow seas, rightly emphasizes the importance to us of free passage for our trade on the oceans, which 'cannot at present be covered by our own land-based air forces'. It then remarks that 'it would not be impossible for the capital ships of a hypothetical enemy, in the absence of a powerful British fleet, to place themselves, without interference, across our trade routes'. Here certainly, is the strongest argument for the maintenance of capital ships.

Yet it is well to consider the degree of possibility, and to remember the difficulty of 'placing' a battle-fleet at a great distance from its bases. For a practical estimate, too, it is desirable to avoid too vague an hypothesis, and to ask what Powers there are which possess battleships that could be used to interrupt any vital section of our trade routes. Two of them lie at distances which seem to minimize the possibility of interrupting any vital route. The others lie in land-locked areas from which emergence would be very hazardous to them in face of strong flotilla and air forces. If there was an outstanding feature of the last war at sea it was the general reluctance to hazard irreplaceable battleships in waters where submarines might be lurking, thereby imposing a marked strategic limitation on the use of battleships. Those hazards are, at the least, multiplied

The Capital Ship

to-day by the development of aircraft and high-speed motor torpedo boats, which might be carried on the defender's ships, and perhaps also of his ocean-going submarines. Nevertheless, if there is a serious chance of such a venture being attempted and succeeding, we may be justified in building battleships to meet it. Even so, there are further considerations worth attention.

The navies of to-day are seeking to increase the speed of their battleships. What if we were to find, too late, that the enemy's battleships, which had reached the oceans, outpaced ours, and were able to sweep the trade routes without being brought to battle? Might we not regret that the money spent on battleships had not been invested in more aircraft-carriers and flotilla craft? The whole question of future war is shrouded in uncertainties, deeper than ever before in history. Because of the risk of enemy battleships placing themselves on the ocean trade routes, it may be the safe course to build battleships ourselves—although the insurance premium would seem high compared with the risk. But it is well to realize that in covering this risk we are necessarily taking a risk in other aspects of the strategic issue, since the total money that can be devoted to defence is not unlimited.

CHAPTER IX

The Future of the Mediterranean

It is characteristic of British policy not to look far ahead. This habit is carried to a pitch that can only be appreciated by anyone who has enjoyed an inside view of the workings of the machinery of government. It seems to be beyond the understanding of foreigners, especially of the Latin or Teutonic kinds. They find it not only disconcerting but incredible. Hence the undiminished, because perpetually reinforced, currency of the phrase *'perfide Albion'*. If you try to give them a realistic picture of the way that British policy works, they treat the explanation with a politeness that barely conceals their suspicion. To them it is but one more manifestation of the subtlety with which the British pursue their long-range designs. I have often quoted Harold Nicholson's novel *Public Faces*, as a perfect picture of how the machine works and great issues are apt to be decided. But to a Continental reader, its humorous treatment of the subject seems to convey the idea that it is mere fantasy, instead of, as it really is, proof of the power to see the facts with a true sense of proportion.

The inability of foreign statesmen and diplomats to comprehend the 'immediacy' of British policy leads them

into many pitfalls. They misjudge its course by crediting
it with a long-term plan; and then stumble again because
they fail to realize that underneath its opportunistic
surface is not a plan but a principle—or, rather, an
instinctive pattern formed by tradition. Sometimes these
Continental misjudgments turn out to the benefit of
Britain; sometimes otherwise; but they are usually detri-
mental to Continental plans. And Britain herself has
undoubtedly benefited by the elasticity and adaptability
which have been preserved by her reluctance to plan
ahead. But this tendency, although often an advantage
in the sphere of foreign policy, increases the strain on
defence policy. Few emergencies have found Britain
adequately prepared to meet them. Here is the clue to the
familiar saying that in a war she 'only wins one battle—the
last one.'

The military disadvantages of this dislike of looking
ahead were forcibly brought home to the British by the
situation produced in the Mediterranean in the early
autumn of 1935 when Italy launched her Abyssinian
campaign in defiance of the League of Nations. As a leading member of the League, Britain was committed to an
endeavour to arrest Italy's course. It placed her in a
predicament which few had foreseen. The post-war
friction between France and Italy, followed by the growth
of Fascist Italy's armed power, had focused attention on
the conflict of interests between the two Latin powers. In
this, Britain saw the need of her services as mediator, and
likewise recognized the divergent possibilities of a clash
between Italian and German interests in Austria. She took
little account of possible trouble between herself and Italy;
Italian propaganda in Malta was an irritation, but seemed
a local symptom that could hardly develop in view of the

The Future of the Mediterranean

long-standing tradition of friendship between the two countries and Italy's dependence on imported raw materials, together with her obvious susceptibility to the pressure of sea-power. These old-established assumptions helped to obscure the newly roughened edges of Britain's own position in the Mediterranean. Her repose was abruptly disturbed in 1935. When the reality of the Italian threat to Abyssinia was at last appreciated it produced a rise of popular indignation almost comparable to that caused by the violation of 'little Belgium'; and the effect, in pushing the Government forward, was accentuated by the backsliding of the Laval Government in France. Forced to give a lead at Geneva in upholding the Covenant, the British found themselves thrust still more into the foreground by their strategic position astride Italy's sea route to East Africa. This made them the natural target if sanctions were to culminate in war. Italy emphasized the point by despatching mechanized divisions and powerful bombing squadrons to her Libyan colony, close to the borders of Egypt. Britain hastily strengthened her forces there, though it meant a temporary interruption of her Air Force expansion at home and stripping the Army of most of its still meagre supply of modern equipment. More precarious still was the position of her main fleet base at Malta which lay within easy range of the Italian air bases; to keep the fleet there, liable to a surprise onslaught by bombers or to lurking submarines was a risk that made the Admiralty hurriedly swallow the vocal disdain of these oversea and undersea weapons in which they had been but recently indulging; the fleet was withdrawn from Malta to the far end of the Mediterranean. Here, certainly, it might block the passage of Italian transports, if the League issue was pressed thus far, but how far it could keep a free passage for Britain's own sea traffic was a question that left the British public wondering.

Some twelve years ago, in a little book on *The Future of War*, I suggested that the controversies over the bomb versus the battleship, or the torpedo versus the gun, tended to overlook the end in their ardour over the means —and that, instead of becoming entangled in an interminable dispute over technical values we ought to 'direct our course by the compass of grand strategy'. While the power of the fleet might still be paramount on the oceans, it was clear that it had been strategically affected in the narrow seas by the newer weapons. 'The vital question of the future is how this transfer of power over the narrow seas affects the international situation—particularly that of Great Britain, which is concerned with both spheres of sea-power.' After studying its bearing on the seas around the British Isles I passed on to 'the Mediterranean, another long and narrow sea channel through which runs our artery with the East, and where our main naval force is now concentrated. Note that our ships, naval or mercantile, must traverse the *length* of this channel, and worse still, have to filter through a tiny hole at each end—the straits of Gibraltar and the Suez Canal—while midway there is a narrow "waist" between Sicily and Tunis barely ninety miles across'. After pointing out how the potential *radii* of submarine attack from the ports on the European and African coasts intersected this long single line of British sea communications, the question was posed: 'Is it not obvious that if in a future war any Mediterranean power was numbered among Britain's enemies, her fleet would find it difficult enough to protect itself against submarines, let alone protect merchant convoys and troop transports? When to the proved menace of submarine

The Future of the Mediterranean

power is added the potential effect of aircraft attack against shipping in the narrow seas, it is time the British people awoke to the fact that, in case of such a war, the Mediterranean would be impassable, and that this important artery would have to be abandoned. Thus, as a strategical asset, the Suez Canal has lost a large part of its value in face of modern naval and air development—for in such a war we should be driven to close the Mediterranean route, and divert our imperial communications round the Cape of Good Hope.'

It is worth quoting this, not to prove that the writer was wise before the event, but because of its continued bearing on a problem that is not yet solved and on events that may be still to come. I was by no means the only critic who drew attention to the new dangers in the years that have intervened. Yet when the Italian crisis arose, not only was the main British fleet still stationed at Malta, but practically nothing had been done to prepare a 'switch' route round the Cape for our sea-traffic. Under pressure of the emergency, part of the traffic from the East which normally passes through the Suez Canal was actually diverted round the Cape, and hurried steps were taken to send out reserves to the bases along that route. But it became clear that bunkering and port facilities would have to be considerably enlarged if the whole of the traffic was to be sent that way. Also that the naval bases would have to be renovated and developed.

The mentality which had been responsible for the neglect of such obvious precautionary needs can perhaps be best epitomized by an extract from a letter which I received in August 1935 from one of the highest officers of the Empire: 'You have evidently been crammed up, as I fear that both the Government and the public at home have, by the Air propaganda. . . . There is only one way in which the Air can win a war and that is by bombing women and children; and that will never bring a great nation to its knees, but only inferior people. You know perfectly well that the Navy laughs at the Air now. They have got protected decks, and with their "blisters" and multiple machine-guns and multiple anti-aircraft guns, they don't fear them in the slightest.'

Close on the heels of this letter the Fleet abandoned Malta—for fear of what it hadn't feared. The letter is significant not merely as an example of the obscurantism induced by the military prejudices against novelties; it shows how the very men who are concerned with the bigger problems of defence are apt, through their training, to focus their attention on mere tactical details, so that they can overlook the fact that the security of a fleet depends on the security of its bases, not merely on its guns and armour. Also, the bigger fact still, that the purpose of a fleet is not merely its self-preservation, but to preserve the security of the sea-routes.

It is questionable whether these facts have been fully impressed even by the alarm of that autumn. Since then, Britain has exerted herself to remodel as well as strengthen her naval dispositions in the Mediterranean. Thereby she will be in a better position to deal with any recurrence of an Italian threat to her fleet. But it is not easy to see how any reliance can be placed on the use of the Mediterranean route for her own sea-traffic, if such a conflict should arise.

Britain's Mediterranean problem has two main aspects. First, that of ensuring the safe flow of the traffic from the East which uses this short cut. Second, that of maintaining her sphere of influence in the Eastern Mediterranean, and the forces which safeguard her position there. There is a tendency to regard the second as a corollary of the first, but historically the order of development was the reverse. This fact should be borne in mind when considering the treatment of the problem under the new conditions of to-day. Britain's concern with the Eastern Mediterranean was forcibly demonstrated throughout the first half of the nineteenth century, not only in the struggle against Napoleon; but it was not until late in the second half of the century that it became of paramount importance to her sea-communications with India and the East. The Suez Canal was the child of a Frenchman's imagination; and Ferdinand de Lesseps's scheme was stoutly resisted by Lord Palmerston who, seeing it merely as a French attempt to repeat Napoleon's design of conquering Egypt, instructed his diplomatic agents throughout Europe to do all they could to prevent the construction of the canal. In the end the British Government remained the solitary opponent—and failed.

Few failures have been more richly compensated. For this shortening of the route to the East resulted in a ten-fold increase of Britain's trade with the East. It also went a long way towards securing her military position there —by accelerating her power of reinforcing her garrisons. The Canal, begun in 1859, was opened ten years later. And within five years, Britain became the chief share-holder through the foresight of her un-British Prime Minister, Disraeli, in purchasing from the Khedive seven-sixteenths of the total share issue, at a price of £4,000,000. This stroke of Imperial policy was extended in 1882 by the occupation of Egypt, following the intervention of Britain to suppress Arabi's anti-foreign rising. The occupation, intended to be temporary, became permanent in the process of reforming the administration. It brought great

The Future of the Mediterranean

compensations, but also a chain of complications. It assured the security of the Canal, that hundred-mile pipe through which now passed Britain's main line of communication with the East, but it imposed a great and growing burden in protecting both the Canal itself and the rest of the homeward route, since, unlike the Cape route, this passed through a sea bordered by other naval powers. Henceforth the British had to maintain a considerable proportion of their naval strength permanently in the Mediterranean as custodians of the route.

The strain became severe under the indirect pressure of Germany's naval expansion in the decade before 1914. The growth of their fleet in the North Sea faced the British with a difficult choice between weakness in one quarter and vast expenditure to maintain predominance in both. They found a compromise in an understanding with France whereby they concentrated their strength in home waters and France concentrated hers in the Mediterranean. This proved a tie greater than they had realized in the crisis of 1914, since, with the first threat of war between Germany and France, they found themselves morally committed to the duty of safeguarding the northern coast of France against the German Navy. And in the war the dangers of the Mediterranean route were demonstrated by the high percentage of commerce destruction that was achieved there in proportion to the small force employed by the attacker—there were rarely more than half a dozen submarines operating at any one time. One U-boat alone attained a total 'bag' of half a million tons of shipping. A German naval historian records that 'U-boat commanders going into the Mediterranean were much envied by their comrades in home waters owing to the extraordinary possibilities offered by operations in the

The Future of the Mediterranean

Mediterranean'. Yet this campaign was carried on at an immense distance from their home bases and under the great difficulties caused by the hazardous passage past the British Isles and the lack of convenient bases in the Mediterranean.

After the war, with the collapse of Germany's naval power, the British Navy returned in strength to the Mediterranean, and its main fleet was based at Malta. On the surface it seemed to re-establish the old security of the route to India, and although the continued attention given by the French and Italians to submarine construction caused some uneasiness, the ultimate conquest of the U-boats in 1918 tended to make British naval opinion forget the extreme handicaps under which the U-boat campaign had worked, so that the confidence bred of success in the final issue caused an undue discount of the future prospects of the submarine when employed under more favourable conditions. Such conditions are certainly offered to a guerilla campaign in the Mediterranean waged by a naval power which is there in home waters.

It is the advent of air power, however, which has most affected the Mediterranean situation. Its influence did not develop early after the war, although its shadow began to stretch across the inland sea. Italy had no serious air force until Mussolini rebuilt it. Spain has never had one. France herself was too remote from the traffic-route, and although her African colonies bordered it, they were separated by a wide expanse of sea from their sources of aircraft supply. Even if a war between Britain and France had been politically conceivable, the British fleet and its aircraft carriers might have had a powerful effect on the strategic situation of the French by interrupting the passage of trade and reinforcements between France and French North

Africa. Moreover, the scope of shore-based air attack was limited by the comparatively short radius of the machines possessed by the post-war air forces.

The situation has radically changed with the rise of Italian air power, the development of bombers that have a radius of 400 to 500 miles, and the promised attainment within a year or two of double this radius. Thereby the 100-mile canal from Suez to Port Said has been extended into a 2000-mile 'canal' from Port Said to Gibraltar. Port Said itself lies less than 400 miles from the Italian air bases in the Dodecanese, off the south-west corner of Asia Minor. While limited at present, they are being developed. On emerging from the Port Said bottle-neck, shipping might have a short run of sea-space with only the lesser fear of being caught in the open. But the route then passes through the mere 200-mile channel between Crete and Libya, dominated by the Italian air-base at Tobruk. An alternative route is round the north coast of Crete, but this passes within a bare 100 miles of the Dodecanese islands. Beyond Crete the routes inevitably converge on Malta, a mere 70 miles from the coast of Sicily and less than 200 from Tripoli. Thereafter the channel narrows until it is less than 90 miles across between Sicily and the African coast at Cape Bon. Before any shipping could emerge from this danger zone it would be in a fresh one, created by the Italian air bases in Sardinia, which lies within 100 miles of the African coast. Thus for more than half the length of the Mediterranean shipping passes within easy bombing range of Italian air bases, and for fully three quarters might run the risk of attack. The danger will soon grow as the new types of bomber recently designed, and in process of accelerated production, come into general use.

The Future of the Mediterranean

But a new danger has loomed up, even earlier, to menace the one free stretch of the route—and the bottleneck at the far end. This is the possibility of a militaristic Spain, filled with the desire to renew its Imperial role which is already reflected in some of the interviews given by General Franco, and linked with Fascist Italy by a common ambition as well as by the sense of help received in the course of the present rising. In that quarter, too, Nazi Germany might find scope for developing an indirect leverage on her own neighbours in favour of her ambitions. A powerful Spanish Air Force, supplied or constructed by foreign aid, could be a serious menace to the last lap of the Mediterranean route. And Gibraltar in turn might become as untenable as a base for the British fleet as Malta proved in the last emergency. Strategically, the danger is so obvious that it is difficult to understand the eagerness with which some of the most avowedly patriotic sections of the British public have desired the rebels' success. Class-sentiment and property-sense would seem to have blinded their strategic sight. The danger would be extended by the establishment of air and submarine bases in the Balearic Isles; and extended still further, by the similar use of the Canary Isles—since this would threaten Britain's use of the Cape route. There have been reports, formally denied, of a secret promise of these two strategic points to Italy and Germany respectively in return for help rendered. Though the denial may be accepted, this does not remove the potential danger. The availability of bases in these islands for the possible use of a strong sea and air power would be scarcely less ominous than the actual cession of the territory.

The prospect deepens the dark hue of the Mediterranean's new complexion. It jeopardizes the outlook for

The Future of the Mediterranean

France as well as for Britain. France hitherto had, on the whole, more scope for exerting pressure on Italy than the other way round. Her dependence on imported raw materials, and thus on sea communications, was less than Italy's; unlike Italy, she had ports outside the Mediterranean; her sea-traffic from Africa could diminish the chance of interference by hugging the Spanish shore; it might even be possible to avoid the sea passage by using the Spanish railways. Moreover, Italy's industrial centres, lying close to the northern frontier, would be more endangered by air attack than those of France. A Spain in league with Italy, and developed into a formidable military power, would change the balance heavily to the disadvantage of France —who may find increasing cause to regret the tacit encouragement she gave to Italy's successful defiance of the League over Abyssinia and the consequent enhancement of Italy's military prestige.

But the potential effect on Britain's position strategically stretches further. The Spanish development can hardly fail to have an influence on the steps that have been taken to reorganize the British dispositions in the Mediterranean. When the tension arose over Abyssinia last autumn, the main part of the British fleet was withdrawn from Malta to Alexandria. But this has defects as a permanent base, apart from being in Egyptian territory. Also it lies within bombing range of the Italian air-bases in Libya and the Dodecanese—some 350 miles from the former and 400 from the latter. These considerations have prompted a study of other possible bases. Cyprus is one. Disraeli secured possession of it at the Berlin Congress of 1878 and presented it to Queen Victoria with the remark: 'Cyprus is the key of Western Asia.' But four years later its value was eclipsed by the occupation of Egypt, and ever since

The Future of the Mediterranean

Cyprus has lain in strategic neglect. After the war, however, the harbour of Famagusta, on the south coast, was improved and enlarged, while in 1931 Imperial Airways temporarily made Limassol a stopping place on their Middle East service. The salt lake near here is suitable for flying boats while the great central plain forms a natural air-base. Another possibility is Haifa, the Palestinian terminus of the oil pipe-line from Iraq. Haifa is at present the most secure from air attack, lying some 660 miles from the nearest air-base in Libya, and 450 from the Dodecanese. But with the rapidly increasing range of aircraft even the most remote base would be brought within bombing range before its development and fortification could be completed, while the farther away that the fleet and its own aircraft carriers are posted the more its own power of action against an enemy is handicapped.

Confronted with this dilemma, the present inclination of the British Admiralty would seem to be 'to damn the risks' and trust in the superiority of its own offensive power. Preparations along these lines are foreshadowed by the recent statement of the First Lord of the Admiralty on returning from a tour of inspection in the Mediterranean. He declared that there was no intention of 'abdicating our position in that sea, or of scuttling from Malta', and added: 'It is simply a question of adapting ourselves to the new conditions, and of making the fullest use of our own air power.' The question may not be so simple to answer, satisfactorily, when all the conditions are appreciated, but the determination is clear. Malta is to remain the primary base of the British fleet, and its defences are being strengthened, while the potentialities of Cyprus as an air and naval base are being developed. Cyprus lies 270 miles distant from the new bases which Italy has made in

The Future of the Mediterranean

the Dodecanese, and since it offers accommodation for a larger force, while the British also have a superiority in sea-borne aircraft, there is a prospect of converting any threat from the Dodecanese into a boomerang. With superior naval and air force, too, the islands of the Dodecanese might be effectively isolated from support and supply from Italy. So might Libya, while the Italian colonies, old and new, in East Africa are largely dependent on the goodwill of the power which holds the gateway from the Mediterranean into the Red Sea. These aspects of the situation are worth recognition.

Likewise in the western half of the Mediterranean, the new danger to which the French communications with North Africa are exposed does not lessen the inherent weaknesses of Italy, due to her immense length of coastline, the accessibility and vulnerability of her focal points, and her greater need of sea-borne supplies. If she strikes she can hurt, but she runs even more risk of getting hurt. Besides the formidable naval and air power of France, there is the pressure which the British naval forces might be able to exert if they are used with good judgment, and avoid being trapped in harbour. With so great a length of coastline, the protective screen afforded by submarines and shore-based aircraft might not prove impenetrable, while the strain on Italy's armed resources is increased by the number of her detached territories. The British Mediterranean Fleet has already been strengthened and a large proportion of the new ships now under construction at home are likely to be sent to reinforce it further.

It is a bold bid which Britain is thus making to maintain her threatened position in the Mediterranean by establishing a more formidable deterrent to interference. Inevitably it has some element of a gamble, because of the uncer-

tainty which veils so many of the technical issues of
modern warfare. But its chances will certainly be increased
or decreased according to the 'load' that her forces carry.
If they are called on to maintain the use of the Mediterranean as a mercantile traffic-route from the East the odds
will be heavily against the attempt succeeding, while the
effort will dissipate and endanger their own strength. If the
British Admiralty is prepared to abandon this route and
divert all normal traffic by the Cape route, its forces in the
Mediterranean may play an important strategic part. The
diversion increases the distance from Bombay to England
by nearly eighty per cent—from 5900 miles to 10,400
miles; from Singapore by over forty per cent—from 7900
miles to 11,400 miles; but from Melbourne, only ten per
cent—from 10,700 miles to 11,800 miles. The increased
distance would cause delay, and a consequent check in
the flow of supplies unless and until more shipping was
employed on the route. But even a delay would not have
very serious effects on Britain's supply situation. For only
twenty per cent of her imports at present come through the
Mediterranean. And of these eleven per cent come from
countries within that sea, so that a readjustment in the
scheme of supply regarding these commodities would in
any case be inevitable to meet the conditions of war. But
the use of the Cape route for the remainder of the Eastern
trade would simplify the strategic problem of the British
in a war with any Mediterranean power. By the virtual
closing of that sea as a traffic-route it might be more
effectively utilized as an area of offensive operations
against an opponent who could not disencumber himself
similarly.

A people who are anxious for peace and a quiet life are
naturally inclined to look at a strategic problem from the

The Future of the Mediterranean

point of view of their own security, and thus to overlook the disabilities of a potential opponent. The way that Italy has enlarged her forces and extended her bases of offensive action has undoubtedly complicated Britain's problem in assuring the security of her trade-routes and overseas territories. But in the process of extending, Italy has entangled her bases with those of Britain to an extent that is awkward for herself. This strategic entanglement may prove a check on aggression, and thereby become an unforeseen 'bond' of peace.

A new disturbing factor has been foreshadowed by the possibility of Spain's development into a military power with warlike tastes and Fascist ties. This would be a potential threat not only to the French communications with her African colonies, but to Britain's power to control the western outlet from the Mediterranean. A naval force could hardly be maintained at Gibraltar in face of a hostile air force on the mainland.

These possibilities inevitably increase the insecurity of the British position in the Mediterranean, while they also introduce a new insecurity into the Cape route. Even so, the fresh complications might not prove wholly adverse. When so many heavily armed powers are confined in so narrow a space, each with their bases interwoven, and that space is being continuously narrowed by the growth of modern weapons, to start a war there would be like shutting up a bunch of mad cats in a cage. The picture, and the uncertainty of any calculations, might deter even the most warlike statesman.

CHAPTER X

The Role of the British Army

I

There is cause for appreciation of the steps now being taken to repair and modernize our defences. There is, also, a tendency to make them cause for congratulation on the security we shall have attained when the present programme is completed. If expressed more moderately the notion is travelling in the same direction as the recent assertion of Herr Rudolf Hess: 'Every new gun, every new tank, every aeroplane, gives an additional security to the German mother that her children will not be slaughtered in an accursed war.' A more realistic view would tell us that our situation is, and is likely to be, far less secure than it was before the new armament race abroad compelled us to strengthen our own forces. Nor can we have much hope that the completion of the programme will be more than a stage in an extending programme. Nevertheless, there is no security in remaining weak when surrounded by those who believe that virtue rests with the violent. Arming becomes unavoidable for those who are unwilling to be victims. The question is, then, how to arm to the best effect proportionately to the expense. It requires not only a clear idea of the aim but a sure gauge of the resources and their relative values.

In such a trial of strength a nation's capacity to stand the strain depends not merely on the extent of its resources but on their economic distribution. That lesson is engraved in our history. Where Spain, Holland, and France broke down in turn under the double strain of spreading their military effort in the attempt to bestride both the land and the sea, we conserved our strength, helped by geography, by concentrating on superiority in one element. To-day the two elements have become three by the addition of the air, which brings the consequent risk of a triple strain. It lies with our defence policy to minimize this, by maintaining a sense of proportion. Security in the air is as necessary to us as security on the seas; we cannot safely concentrate on one at the expense of the other, although by wise distribution and combination we may be able to diminish the total burden thus created. Moreover, in each case there are standards by which we can gauge our needs; it is true that if we stand alone these represent an appalling effort and expense, but they can be scaled down on the basis of collective security, in proportion as such a basis can be established.

In the sphere of the land forces we are, fortunately, free of any standards imposed by the strength of the Continental armies. The only essential requirement is to maintain forces sufficient to defend, and maintain order in, our overseas territories. For those forces a mobile Imperial reserve is needed. Anything beyond this is not a strategic obligation, although it may be prompted by political considerations. The use of a field force to prevent hostile air and submarine bases being established close to our coast may be desirable strategically, but is not strictly essential. Its value should be weighed against its cost—lest it be at the expense of the necessities—and against its risks both political and military. Its practicability should also receive due attention—can it be provided without detriment to the essential function of the army? Can it be sufficiently effective under the modern conditions of war, and the limitations imposed by geography? To answer such questions we must try to estimate those conditions and the fitness of the Army to meet them.

The experience of the last war left the defensive still superior to the offensive in land warfare. For it would be rash to draw different conclusions from the last phase when morale was crumbling and resources were becoming exhausted. Thus anticipations of a change are merely built on hope—the hope that the subsequent development of certain of the new weapons of the last war may suffice to overcome the power of defence, even though this has also been developed. Military history is such a tale of misplaced hopes that we need to examine such assumptions with care before building any wing of our defence policy upon them.

The one factor which is clear is that our field force, should we use one, will need the power of attack in order to fulfil its purpose under the conditions that can be foreseen. For, if it is to be sent complete with all its arms and transport, it cannot be transhipped to the Continent and brought into action until some time has elapsed—in 1914 this was three weeks, and although accelerated mobilization arrangements may reduce it to some extent there is the question whether the modern risk of air attack will allow it to be moved by as direct a route as in 1914. By the time it arrives, the war, owing to the accelerated tempo of modern plans, is likely to have taken a definite turn. The aggressor may have been stopped on the frontier; in this case our field force might have no purpose except to be used in an offensive against his frontier. The aggressor may have penetrated some distance and then have been stopped; in this case our field force would be called on to help in ejecting him by an offensive. The aggressor may be still pressing on—even in this case, the counter-offensive is the most likely form of action we should be called on to undertake. All these prospects imply that a field force, if it is to be sent, should possess the power of attack. Is there any adequate prospect of it possessing this power?

The past year's training did not go far enough to provide much light. The 1st Division was rushed off to Palestine when it had only carried out the first of its divisional exercises. Its precipitate departure upset the crowning stage of the Guard's training and spoilt the prospects of the 4th Division troops who had been brought to the Sussex Manœuvre Area: when they carried on with a curtailed programme this was abruptly terminated by an outbreak of foot and mouth disease. The bulk of the 5th Division was missing from the training areas of the Northern Command, being still detained in Egypt. The 3rd Division was not assembled for collective training last year, although the separate brigades had some useful exercises; but when one of them was brought by sea from Plymouth to be pitted against another which was training in the New Forest, the promise of this amphibious exercise was partly marred by the weather. The 2nd Division alone had a full run; its transport was last year completely motorized, although the number of substitute vehicles—which did duty under a label for the real article—inevitably detracted from the effect and lent a doubt to the deductions that might be drawn. The most suggestive feature was the effective use of bus columns to quicken manœuvre. Each division is now to have a troop-carrying company R.A.S.C. capable of moving four battalions at a time. The utility of such embussed moves is greatly increased now that the infantry transport itself, being mechanized, can accompany the troops. Such moves can thus be employed far more often in the strategic sphere, while they can now play a part even in the tactical sphere. Their value for accelerating the advance, for enabling wider outflanking efforts, for changing the axis of attack, and for giving infantry an entirely new power of pursuit, was shown in several of the exercises. At the same time the limitations of the large road-bound coaches or lorries which compose such bus columns were made manifest, which suggested the need for lighter and handier vehicles to carry a portion of the infantry, who would precede the bus column and clear the way. Up to a point this new motor-power has good promise of improving the army's power in the offensive, so far as resistance can be overcome by manœuvre, and so far as the country allows scope for it. But it does not solve the problem of overpowering the defence, a problem which seems to be becoming harder and harder.

Of the non-divisional formations, the training of the 1st Cavalry Brigade, still horse-mounted, was broken off by the threat of foot and mouth disease; the 2nd Cavalry Brigade, now in the process of mechanization, suffered a handicap in developing its new technique because the process was still incomplete, from lack of machines—or the proper machines: its light tank regiment had to work with inferior substitutes. On several occasions during the Army training horsed units put up a good performance. There is a tendency among soldiers, however, to lay more stress on such minor manœuvres' achievements than they can safely bear, overlooking the short duration of exercises, the narrow limits of the areas, and the absence of bullets. To draw any reasonable deductions it is necessary to relate these mimic actions to the realities of the battlefield, and to think how the bit of war represented in an exercise would be likely to fit into the general pattern—enthusiastic members of any branch or activity of the Service are too apt to view war in bits instead of as a whole. The effect is, too often, that the greater is subordinated to the lesser.

The enthusiasts of the Tank Brigade have in the past been accused of this tendency, but here the charge can hardly be sustained, since the present scale of our tank forces is insignificant compared with the importance of the role, and the variety of functions, which military opinion throughout the world now allots to the armoured fighting vehicle in future warfare. The nominal 200 tanks of our solitary tank brigade are a puny total compared with the thousands of tanks in the chief Continental Armies—the Russian alone is said to have about 6000, and the bulk of them are more up to date than our own. The only modern machines we have are light tanks so small and limited in obstacle-crossing capacity that they would be rated as featherweights by the Russians' standards; they have great numbers of similar machines, but their 'light tanks' are equivalent to our 11-ton medium tanks, if intrinsically superior, while their medium tanks are machines of about 27 tons. Moreover, our medium tanks are still of a fourteen-year-old type, now quite unfit to be sent into the field and still less fit to go into action against modern anti-tank weapons. Yet in the past year's training the Tank Brigade was reduced to nothing more than these obsolete machines, apart from 'make-believe', as it had been stripped of its light tanks, and also of its wireless sets to meet last autumn's emergency in Egypt. It was fortunate that the Tank Brigade contains such a band of enthusiasts—they certainly had to call on their enthusiasm to the full in order to vivify training under such handicaps. Its deficiencies become greater in comparison with the growth of its role. During the war the infantry depended on tanks to help them on to their objectives. Some years later, with the advent of the fast tank, it came to be seen that in these armoured vehicles lay the best chance of reviving the moribund role of the Cavalry—as mounted fighters. Yet we have only one tank brigade. The light tanks are comparatively modern machines, but they lack the speed and obstacle-crossing capacity needed for their role, to serve as the probing fingers of the brigade. The clenched fist is formed of medium tanks, and those we have are little better than dummies. Apart from their mechanical obsolescence, they are so thinly armoured that they could not be risked in a punch except against tribesmen who do not possess any armour-piercing weapons. If, as appearances sometimes suggest, responsible members of the Government as well as the public imagine that this tank force could be used in a European war, it is well to sound a warning: to send our present tank force into a modern battle would scarcely be better than manslaughter.

While we have not got the machines for this revived cavalry role, we have now added a fresh role, itself a revival from the last war. This is the use of tanks as a direct help to the infantry advance. A clearer recognition of the power of machine-guns to stop infantry, of the growing number of machine-guns in the Continental armies, and of the hopelessness of relying on the artillery to subdue their fire, has driven us back to seek a solution on the lines we followed in 1916-18, lines that the Continental armies

The Role of the British Army

have never abandoned. In consequence, our authorities have decided to form battalions of 'infantry tanks' on the scale of one to a division. By breaking up the tank brigade temporarily and using its machines for a role for which they are not designed, the army had some practice during 1935 in the methods of tank and infantry co-operation. But it was largely hypothetical. These new machines-in-aid-of-the-infantry have still to be produced, and we may have long to wait. Moreover, there is a widespread doubt whether the kind of machines that are contemplated are likely to prove suitable.

This state of mechanical obsoleteness and inadequacy is depressing in face of the fact that we took the lead in tank development among the post-war armies, besides being the pioneers in the realm of ideas on mechanized warfare. The seed has borne fruit—in all other countries. Owing to the years of thought that have been given to the subject here, we are still ahead of others in methods, and the standard, of tactical training. But we can hardly hope to maintain even these assets without adequate machines on which to form experience. In the years that have passed, the demand for progress was continually met with the argument that nothing could be done beyond experiments because money was lacking. To this, the advocates of progress replied that it was better to reduce quantity, especially of what was obsolete, in order to ensure that the forces which were maintained were efficient; that if money for modern equipment could only be obtained by cutting down the number of men, this was sounder economy, and a lesser risk, than allowing the army to become technically unfit to cope with modern conditions, since with armies, as with species, the power of survival depends on adaptability to environment. But to the conservative school the idea of disbanding units was abhorrent, while the maintenance of the overseas garrisons without an equivalent number of units at home required a reorganization more drastic than they cared to face. The Cardwell system, having been established over half a century, had become sacrosanct. As those who by seniority were in the seats of authority tended to be conservative, in habit if not in instinct, the quantitative view prevailed. The modernization of the Army was postponed year after year. There would have been more justification for this attitude if the prospective role of the army had been reduced to that of Imperial policing, although even for that function quality combined with mobility can diminish the need for mere quantity of men. Moreover, it is folly to fight tribesmen, even, on their own terms, since the terrain gives them superiority when weapons are equal. But the Army authorities did not reduce their conception of the role of the Army. There had been an expeditionary force organized and trained for European warfare before the last war; there must continue to be such a force; the picture was too firmly fixed to be changed. The revival of international tension and renewed growth of armaments abroad, despite its accentuation of our own military weakness, merely hardened that Continental conception. But it hardly accords with the reality of the army's situation. The unfit state of our potential expeditionary force is the result of the past policy of sacrificing equipment in order to keep mere numbers: numbers that, even as kept, are but a drop in the Continental bucket.

II

If we contemplate providing a field force for use on the

The Role of the British Army

Continent it should, as the problem is at present visualized, possess the power of attack. For by the time it can arrive, even at the earliest reckoning, there is not likely to be much scope for a purely strategic offensive, while the time will have passed when the capacity for mere defence might be enough. It should be capable of undertaking the tactical offensive, with a fair prospect of success, if it is to justify the cost of its provision and the risks of its despatch—risks that are increased to an incalculable extent in face of hostile air power. We have only to take account of the present state of the Army and its deficiencies of equipment to realize that at the moment we have not got a field force adequate to the purpose. The question remains whether it would be adequate when the present programme of re-equipment is complete. Before attempting an answer, it is worth while examining the basic elements of the tactical problem that the force would have to solve if it gets to grips with the enemy without its strategic advance being interrupted by air attack.

The predominant condition of the last war, on land, was the superiority of the defensive. During four years this superiority amounted to supremacy. The main cause was the machine-gun. In the spring of 1918 the Germans were able temporarily to overcome the Allied defence, partly through the aid of a new technique, but even more through the unforeseen help of fog, which blanketed the opposing machine-guns at the outset of their first three offensives. Later, when there was no fog, their offensives failed. And even their successful offensives petered out in face of slender opposition when this was reinforced by their own difficulties in maintaining momentum. In the late summer and autumn of 1918 the German defence in turn was overcome by the combination of tanks with natural and arti-

125

ficial fog. Even so, the Allies never succeeded in solving the problem of exploiting initial success, not even as far as the Germans had done. The cause of their greater, and conclusive, success lay in the moral and physical bankruptcy of the foe, whose military ruin could be traced to the expense of his own spectacular offensives earlier, and was completed by the sickness, physical and mental, of his troops which was produced by economic pressure. The coming of the Germans' collapse found the Allied armies baffled, at least for the time, by the problem of keeping up armed pressure.

Analysis of these conditions provides no warrant for the belief that the offensive, save locally, had succeeded in reducing the superiority of the defensive. They rule out the idea that infantry who have to attack over the open can, even locally, be expected to overcome infantry whose machine-guns are ensconced behind cover, so long as the defending side is morally unshaken. The new light machine-guns are certainly an improvement on the Lewis gun, for use by advancing troops, but there is no ground for supposing that they are going to make a decisive difference against an enemy who is below ground, and nowadays has more machine-guns, light and heavy, than the defence ever had in 1914-18. High-angle fire, since it drops the projectiles over the cover, is more promising; but we cannot expect a decisive difference to be made by a battalion's handful of four mortars, against fifty or sixty machine-guns on an opposing battalion front. There were mortars in the war.

We have increased the artillery support slightly by converting light artillery—the former 'pack' artillery—into field, thus providing a scale of twenty field batteries to a division instead of sixteen; we have increased it still more indirectly because eight of these batteries are in 'army' brigades and can be concentrated on any divisional front where they are most needed. There are also the equivalent of four medium batteries to a division. Even so, the possible scale of artillery support is a trifle compared with what it was in the offensives of the last war, and we know how little it achieved then. By contrast, any defending force in Western Europe to-day will have far more machine-guns to check the attack than it had then. Moreover, if motorization has quickened the application of fire-power in the attack, it promises to help the defence even more by enabling him to rush machine-guns to any threatened spot and counteract any surprise that the attacker achieves. The defending machine-guns will be able to fire from behind cover, whereas the attackers, at any rate in the immediate future, will have to be brought forward in unshielded vehicles. They might make more difference if they were mounted in armoured vehicles and could bring their fire forward to close ranges.

What further possibilities are there of overcoming the established superiority of the defence? Leaving gas out of the reckoning, we have to pin our hopes of a solution to *obscurity*, *armour*, and *art*. Attacking infantry have at present a good chance of overcoming the machine-gun in the dark, although art and high training are required to profit by the opportunity and avoid the risks of confusion. Even so, they cannot safely press the attack more than a short distance; to exploit the effect there must be enough armoured vehicles available, or some form of floodlighting the battlefield must be invented. Also, it would be unwise to bank too heavily on the attack in darkness, for the defence may find means of keeping their front continuously lighted.

The Role of the British Army

The attack in fog has perhaps greater possibilities, on the basis of experience; but we cannot count on enjoying a natural fog when we need it. Smoke-screens are a useful substitute, but those of the past were too local. More hope lies in the development of artificial fog, capable of being projected in larger volume than is possible with artillery smoke-shell. Even so, the defence may not be long in finding means of dispersing it.

Armour is another well-proved aid. The armour may be carried, as in the war, by relatively slow tanks accompanying the infantry. It may be carried by fast tanks acting like cavalry in earlier wars and relying on the speed of the charge or on rapidity of manœuvre. It may be carried, also, by little low-built machines manned by infantry, relying partly on their slight visibility, and giving the infantryman more protection at least than he would have when advancing on foot—the possibilities of such true 'mechanized infantry' have not yet been fully explored. The value of armour can also be increased by combining it with the use of obscurity. Armoured troops, if equipped with direction-finders, may be more suited to profit by natural or artificial fog than are men on their feet. In darkness, too, they are more formidable, if adequately trained for such tactics. And the progress that may be made in dispersing obscurity on behalf of the defence should affect tanks less because of their speed, so long as some obscurity remains.

Nevertheless, the post-war development of anti-tank weapons is a serious and increasing threat to the tank, especially when coupled with the new technique of obstruction. How serious, it is not easy to gauge. We can at least be clear that the chances of the tanks increase with their quantity—and decrease disproportionately when they are few.

The Role of the British Army

At present we seem to contemplate no more than our one existing tank brigade re-equipped with modern machines —which may form part of a mobile division otherwise possessing small power of attack—and four battalions of infantry tanks which have still to be built. With such a small quantity of tanks, the chances of successful attack might well be zero. Against the multiplying anti-tank weapons of to-day, it is certain that hope lies only in swarms—to swamp the defence.

For the rest of the army, the ordinary infantry divisions, there is just a possibility that the development of a new technique in combination with the new equipment might give them some prospect of successful attack, up to a point. This possibility depends on progress in the art of war rather than on its material side. Here, unfortunately, we have to face the fact that the Army's present lack of modern equipment is not the sum of its qualitative deficiencies. Because of their small size our forces need to excel in technical and tactical skill. At present they do not. Hampered by the poor type of recruits it has attracted, by the depressingly slow promotion among the officers, by the peace-time tendency to give staff work preference over leadership, by the lack of men and new means with which to develop the art of command, and by years of an atmosphere in which boldness of thought and freedom of expression were discouraged, the Army as a whole is not up to the standard of skill demanded by the more exacting conditions of modern warfare. It may be no worse than other armies, but it does not stand out like the army of 1914, while the true standard required is relative to the conditions of warfare, not merely to the level of others. Its weaknesses are apparent not merely to the onlooker, who is said proverbially to see most of the game; they are realized by many of the officers concerned with its training. It will be easier to make good the material deficiencies than to remedy these failings. The energy now being exerted may complete the re-equipment of the Army within two or three years. Even under the best guidance, and a better sense of how to promote activity of intelligence, it would take many years to outgrow the legacy of the postwar period and raise the general level of tactical aptitude. There are a fair number of officers who are real tacticians, whose natural aptitude has survived an unfavourable climate, but the proportion to the total is too small. They are like currants in a pudding.

There has been an unpalatable abundance of suet in the exercises seen in recent years. 'Safety first,' seems to have largely superseded Danton's, and Napoleon's, motto '*l'audace, l'audace, toujours l'audace*'. Conformity to the manuals, the confusion due to constant changes of detail, and the excessive emphasis on meticulous order-writing, have produced a slow-motion habit which is inimical to the exploitation of opportunities. Instead of building tactical art on a basis of battle-drill, thus quickening its application, we have turned tactics into a drill in slow time. The effect is seen in an attitude of what can only be described as 'reckless caution'. It is the opposite of real security, while it stultifies the possibility of achieving surprise. To-day we are slaves of the obvious instead of being masters of surprise. Without a far more highly developed battle-craft there can be but a dim prospect of shaking the sovereignty of the defence.

When all the conditions are carefully weighed, the balance seems to be heavily against the hope that a British field force on the Continent might have a military effect commensurate with the expense and the risk. I cannot see

The Role of the British Army

an adequate prospect, even when the present programme is complete, of it possessing the power of attack necessary to wrest from an invader any ground he may have gained before it could arrive. To fit the picture into the actual frame, formed by the zone between the Meuse and the Channel, serves to deepen this impression. And I do not see that a larger force would have a better effect, nor that subsequent reinforcement might make a great difference, for the limiting conditions have little to do with numbers of men. They are essentially qualitative and technical. Moreover, beyond all the difficulties which face the attacker on land lies the danger of his approach being dislocated by hostile attack from the air. And the larger the force the greater the danger.

It may still be considered that the force is worth while on political grounds. That may be a just opinion. But we ought to be sure that those who decide do so with their eyes opened to the fundamental military limitations. Moreover, the latest turn of Belgian policy may well give pause to those who are inclined to assume the need of a field force for the Continent without being clear as to the way it will act and the end it will serve. It has been argued that the action of our field force should be directed to prevent an enemy establishing air bases close to our coast, and to cover the bases which our own Air Force might establish abroad in order to lengthen its range. But the increasing range of aircraft promises to diminish the value of such cover. Apart from this doubt of its need, the type of force required for the particular duty is different to that of 1914, when the plans of the General Staff were dominated by the idea of contributing a general-purpose force of three army corps to join the French field armies in their main offensive campaign. Even if a general offensive of this kind were

practicable to-day, the distant and disconnected cover it
would give might not suffice to protect the air bases under
modern strategic conditions. For that function a specially
designed force might be more effective, and less precarious.
Its design is indicated by the prevailing conditions and
limitations of land warfare—a force small in numbers of
men but amply equipped with fire-weapons of the light and
handy kind, and coupling this power of resistance with high
strategic mobility. Its action, too, should be adjusted to
these conditions, making the most of the inherent advantages of modern fire-defence, and applying tactics of
elastic resistance and riposte.

If, now, there is a doubt as to Belgians' attitude, the difficulties of using a field army effectively may be augmented,
and its risks also. If, on the other hand, we should decide
to give up the idea of intervention with an army, our
military problems would be greatly simplified. We could
concentrate on making the Army at home an adequate
Imperial Reserve, for the reinforcement of the overseas
garrisons, the mobile defence of the overseas territories,
and for such expeditions, truly so-called, as may be needed
to fulfil our historic strategy under future conditions. We
could adjust its scale, organization, and training to this
role—thus avoiding the wide, and increasing, divergence
between what is required for offensive warfare on the
Continent and what is best suited to mobile defence, to
Colonial warfare, and Imperial policing. The forces we
have would need far less development. The very qualities
in the average officer which raise doubts of his 'offensive'
ability under modern conditions are admirably suited for
the performance of these duties. This applies to the men
also. Since Marlborough the British Army has rarely shone
in the offensive, not through want of courage, but from

lack of aptitude. It has been superb in defence, and un-rivalled as an agent in maintaining order. Those qualities will have enhanced value in proportion as strategic mobility is added.

At the same time, the training needs to be recast. Wherever the Army is used, and whatever decision may be taken as to sending a force across the Channel, its mission and action ought to be adjusted to tactical realities. It should not be allowed to waste its strength by becoming engaged in an allied offensive carried out on past and present Continental lines. This does not mean that its action would, or could, always be confined to pure defence. But where a strategic advance was necessary to fulfil its mission, it should normally combine this with tactics of elastic resistance, varied by a lightning riposte to exploit a disordered recoil on the enemy's part, and by dislocating counter-moves. It is folly, nowadays, to attempt direct attack on a properly equipped foe, except at points where the opposition is particularly weak. Even in the past ages of warfare, it has been rare for a strategic offensive to be crowned by a successful attack; modern conditions have emphasized still more the superior promise of the luring defensive or the combination of offensive strategy with defensive tactics. Yet at present, as in the past, the training of armies is predominantly devoted to practising tactics which are essentially unreal, under the spell of a soldierly dream of attack which can only end in nightmare assaults.

III

By comparison with anything achieved in the whole post-war period there has been so much progress in the past two years, notably towards modernizing the means of transport, that one would hesitate to dwell on deficiencies but for the fact that the storm-clouds are moving so much faster. That foreboding fact compels us to face the contingent facts of our own military situation. The best service that anyone can render to those who have the responsibility of making up for past neglect is to recognize, and emphasize, the immensity of the problem that confronts them and the inadequacy, by comparison, of what has yet been done towards meeting it.

Moreover, those who are immersed in so great a labour find in it more than enough to occupy their attention: the detached onlooker may be of service in watching the point of aim, and raising the question whether that effort, on present lines, has an adequate chance of effect. The man in the observation post can see much that is hidden from those who are serving the guns.

When deficiency coincides with emergency it is an awkward, and may even be a dangerous moment, to dwell on the former state. Unfortunately, it is rarely possible to arouse either governmental or public concern with the deficiencies of defence until a possible emergency is more than perceptible: this is a lesson of the centuries. It is a service habit of equal antiquity to denounce the 'politicians' for their failure to anticipate the danger and be fully prepared before it arises. But, even apart from the difficulty of determining what constitutes such full preparedness, the habit is an emotional outlet rather than a practical attitude. The soldier or sailor who adopts it, though he may be a good fighting man, reveals his own disqualification for a part in the higher conduct of war, where strategy and policy are interdependent and interwoven. For another deduction from historical experience, and human nature, is that no government of a democratic type can demand public money for repairing deficiencies until there is a widespread public recognition of the need for repair. One may certainly discriminate between this and the kind of internal renovation which requires no increased budgetary outlay: but it should be the soldier's or sailor's own business to fulfil such tenant's duties without calling upon the landlord. Before having recourse to the latter, the need must be manifest.

There is no such thing as an absolutely right time for arousing public concern. It is a matter of relativity, of choosing a time when danger is sufficiently obvious to procure a response, yet not so close as to make discussion and preparation futile. Inertia will always find an excuse for postponing the issue; sentiments and interests, for covering it up. But to-day there is such a gap between the rate at which danger is growing and the rate at which the Army is repairing its deficiencies that the risk of a frank exposure seems less than that of maintaining the present rate and course. If so, this is a time for plain speaking: for pointing out not merely that deficiencies exist, but of what they consist. For they are qualitative as well as quantitative; mental as well as material. And if the conclusion be that we cannot safely count on the time to repair them, or that the repair may not meet the conditions, we must face the question of modifying the Army's purpose to fit the state of the means.

The adequacy of the Army depends on the question of its functions. Two years ago, the minister who introduced the Estimates enumerated four—the defence of this country, the defence of our naval bases, the maintenance of order in the territories of the Empire and the defence of our interests abroad—the last being the function of what we used to call an 'expeditionary force' and now call a 'field force'. He went on to say that these four purposes were 'all equally important', a statement which might obscure the problem of proportion. For any defence policy in peace, like strategy in war, must necessarily be a reconciliation between conflicting claims. To be equally strong everywhere, against an opponent with equal resources or a superior sense of proportion, entails being too weak everywhere. The impossibility of covering everything is the rock upon which many national policies have foundered. We need to classify our purposes in order of importance, and then to see how far the organization that best serves the major purpose can also serve the others.

Changing conditions affect all four purposes. Although the fear of invasion held a considerable proportion of our troops in England during the last war, the fear had no justification in anything that we knew of the enemy's intentions, nor in the actual conditions: and now, with the development of air power, these conditions have made such an attempt still more improbable. The approach of a fleet of transports to, and the disembarkation of troops on, a hostile coast have become far more hazardous in face of a shore-based air force. Conditions, therefore, would seem to have diminished the importance of the defence of this country as a function of the Army, although the Army may well be called on to maintain order and restore internal communications in the dislocation caused by a hostile air attack. Actual defence from the ground against an air attack is a new duty, but one of a specialized kind.

The defence of naval bases is a duty for which only a small fraction of the army is needed. In fulfilling it, troops have always been subsidiary to the naval forces themselves, and may now be considered subsidiary to the defence by air also; if these are worsted, the situation of the military

The Role of the British Army

garrison would be more precarious than ever in the past.

More important, certainly, is the Army's duty of policing our overseas territories. In keeping quiet uncivilized or thinly populated territories, and also in checking invasion of frontiers, especially the more remote, air power may play a primary part. But for maintaining order in thickly populated lands nothing is likely, so far as we can foresee, to replace the need for troops on the ground. If the Empire is to be maintained, and unless special policing forces are to be created, this duty must take precedence in our Army's functions, even though it is not so definitely an army's function as that of waging war. But the question remains how this duty can be reconciled with that of providing an expeditionary force.

Now there is a fundamental difference between the qualities required for the first three functions and those required for the last. The development of automatic small arms and of mechanized mobility has increased the power of defence, and also the power of trained troops to quell insurrection. But an army in the field is still presumed to need the power of attack, in order to overcome the resistance of hostile troops with similar armament.

The additional armament, and the new types of it, which have been symbolically represented in recent exercises indicate the steps that are now being taken to resuscitate this moribund power. There are other means that may be tried, some of a less material nature. But will such developments suffice to overcome the existing superiority of the defensive, and its probable developments? Unless we have stronger reason than at present to think so, it might be wiser to modify our ideas on the employment of the Army in a modern war. And to spend our money on equipment that will fit this modified role.

The Role of the British Army

What does this reflection imply? At present, one clear factor in the problem is that the offensive is as much at an advantage in the air as it is at a disadvantage on land. This comparison, in conjunction with our present deficiencies, has suggested that the offensive role, of an expeditionary force, might be entrusted to the Air Force. Apart from its greater promise of effect, it could be conducted from our own shores or from bases more easy to secure and more remote from the enemy than the zone an army requires. And it would avoid many of the complications involved, and evolving, when we land an army on the Continent. The Army could then be left to fulfil its Imperial reserve and police duties.

The possibility of simplifying our military problems by such a redistribution of duties certainly deserves serious consideration. An essential preliminary is a thorough investigation, so far as is practicable, of the prospects of reviving the power of the offensive on land. One deduction we can draw from the experience of the last war is that any attempt to restore it which is not radically different from the methods tried then is foredoomed to failure. For the scale of artillery then employed is far beyond our resources, or possible resources at the outset of another war, while the scale of machine-guns that the armies have now, to oppose attack, is much larger than in 1918. If the Army exercises of 1935 and 1936 left one outstanding impression it was the futility of seeking a solution on the old lines. The attacks which had the least effect, and looked the least deserving of it, were those in which the resemblance to 1918 was the most marked.

If it might be unwise at this stage to decide that the offensive activity of armies is beyond resurrection, that cannot be said of an interim arrangement in accord with the existing situation. One strong argument is that such a resurrection cannot yet be predicted with any assurance. A still stronger is that our Army has not yet got the means to which its hopes are pinned. In the interval, it would seem more reasonable to entrust the old expeditionary role to the Air Force than to dream of sending an army into the field with new means that only exist in imagination.

The release of the Army at home from the precariously illimitable duty of providing a field force for the Continent would ensure that it was better able to fulfil its necessary duty as an Imperial Reserve. That purpose requires not only adequate numbers but a force which is thoroughly up to date, if not so heavily armed as would be required for the dubious attempt to force entrenched positions on the Continent.

This would seem the course best fitted to the existing realities of warfare on land. It will not suit those who desire the totalitarian training of the nation for war, as well as the preparation of a potentially unlimited army for intervention on the Continent. Since such ideas are growing in many circles, it is well to consider them at a time when cool reflection is possible, instead of under the stress of emergency. The haphazard way in which our part in the Continental land struggle, with its exhausting demands, was determined in August 1914, should be a warning to this generation.

To-day, owing to technical and tactical conditions, the dispatch of a field army to the Continent does not seem to offer any promise of effect adequate to the risks involved. Since the blankness of the prospect is due to the inherent superiority of modern defence once this has had time to consolidate itself, it is hard to see that in preparing larger forces, to send still later, there is any greater prospect—except of greater waste of lives and resources. On the other hand, with a larger army the risk of it being hamstrung by air attack on its communications would be much increased. The advocates of a field force themselves recognize that the difficulties of transporting it and maintaining it overseas to-day would be much greater than in the past. And there is a further aspect to the problem. The more troops we send oversea the more shipping we have to divert from the essential task of maintaining the supplies of this country, and the more targets we shall offer on the narrow sea passages—which are the most exposed to air and submarine attack. The problem of feeding this country in war is difficult enough without adding to the burden by superfluous and unpromising land campaigns on the Continent.

CHAPTER XI

The Limitation of Arms

Study of the problem of security, under modern conditions and in present circumstances, tends to the conclusion that it is technically unattainable along customary lines. Augmentation of national armaments can no longer promise an adequate insurance even where superiority is possible. Any such superiority is apt to be far more fleeting than it was under past conditions: more easily forfeited by some technical development. Nor is that all that we have to consider. The incalculable factors in warfare have multiplied immensely. To evaluate forces and national degrees of security, in terms of numbers, is an obsolete convention. The instruments of warfare have become so intricate and their effects so hypothetical that the most profound calculation may prove no better than a guess in the dark. In the past, uncertainty turned mainly on the human factors; to-day the material factors magnify the uncertainty, and the men who handle them may become their sport. If the tendency of the time is towards turning men into robots, the machines themselves promise, or threaten, to produce a fresh variability.

While this may eventually frustrate any scheme of

security, it has definitely upturned the old foundations. It is not in the nature of mankind to remain shelterless with content. Rebuilding must be attempted, so new ground must be sought. There are two courses, both converging to the same end. One is on the lines of collective security; the other on the lines of technical limitation—to limit the dangers from instruments that have already outstripped our powers of comprehension. It is easy to point out the uncertainty of either means, but difficult to suggest any alternative that is more than a mere acquiescence in, indeed a hastening of common devastation.

If, in experience, agreements have often been broken, that bare fact does not nullify their value. The more deeply one probes into historical records the more one comes to appreciate the restraining influence which agreements exercise. They operate both psychologically and technically. We are justified in deducing that assurances of help, prohibition of certain forms of action, and limitation of weapons, may be an effective check, if not a complete one. Their effect may even persist after they have been broken. Moreover, although each tie separately may seem a fragile strand, when interwoven they may form a powerful check.

It is important that each should be as definite as possible. The cause of peace has suffered much from idealists who, in their enthusiasm, put forward airy solutions that can be easily pricked by technical objections. And it would be a mistake for Governments to accept any prohibitions or limitations so wide that the unscrupulous can evade them—at the expense of those who keep the letter as well as the spirit of agreements. There is often more restraining power in the cumulative effect of a number of small but practicable checks than in a single sweeping measure formulated in vague terms.

From this point of view the proposals made by the German Government in May 1935 appeared to have promise. They avoided the mistake of being too general, and the opposite mistake of defining each point too rigidly for adaptation in discussion. While the economic situation of Germany, together with the difficulties of quick-time production, may have had an influence on her willingness to accept limitation of the more expensive types of armament, the prospect of a race in such weapons is not to be welcomed elsewhere. Apart from the financial strain, the military advantage of a superiority is doubtful. It is too much like a race of indefinite extent for an unknown stake.

This reflection is emphasized if we consider the proposals in their bearing upon the military problems in Western Europe. A superiority in the size of warships and the calibre of naval guns is of very dubious advantage in the narrow seas. If theoretically possible on the assumption of a limitless purse, in reality its maintenance would be at the expense of the lighter craft needed for defence in these waters.

On land the technical arguments are no less strong for 'abolition of the heaviest arms, especially suited for aggression'; these being the heavier artillery and heavier tanks. It has often been said that one cannot distinguish between offensive and defensive weapons. This is true—if so loose a definition be used. All weapons are offensive, obviously, in the sense that they inflict injury, and all can be useful to the defence as well as to the attack. But not all can be as useful. Here is the crux: not that certain weapons are more offensive in themselves, but that they give a better chance, under modern conditions, of enabling

The Limitation of Arms

attack to overcome defence. And so their abolition or limitation would at least promise a check on aggression by reducing the chances in favour of a would-be aggressor. In general it would increase the security offered by a fortified frontier. Though the risk might still remain of this being breached by some form of surprise, it would be a diminished risk. To circumscribe the chances is worth attempting, and the more so because the defensive is already superior to the offensive on land.

In the air it is otherwise, at the present time. The strongest check is the fear of prompt retaliation in superior force. Hence the importance of measures to ensure this by collective action. But it is also worth exploring subsidiary checks. Arguments for outlawing certain methods of war, such as the bombing of the civil population, have more support in experience than they may have in pure logic. The laws that were broken in the last war had, on the whole, more restraining force than the public appreciated. It may prove difficult to fulfil, or even to frame, an effective prohibition of 'the dropping of gas, incendiary, and explosive bombs outside the real battle zone', but before dismissing the conception its practicable adaptation may well be considered. The unlimited horrors of the Thirty Years War produced an effective limitation of methods by common consent in the century and a half that followed. That example might be repeated. The experience of the last war and the omens of the next unite in a warning of what otherwise awaits us. Practical wisdom may restrain what strict logic unleashes.

CHAPTER XII

Military Training

Military training, whether under historical or under psychological analysis, is found to be divided into two spheres, a higher and a lower—the training of the commander and the training of those who act under command. In the actual practice of training the division has often been ignored or confused, especially in the early preparation of future leaders. The consequence has too often been their ultimate stultification as leaders. This is shown in the rarity of inspired and creative leadership in the organized armies of history. Generals have been legion; artists of war few. Many more, and infinitely more military genius can be traced in the scantier records of irregular and guerilla forces. The obvious explanation is that the natural gifts of these leaders who have emerged straight from the womb of conflict, instead of a professional incubation chamber, have not been cramped or warped by convention. To acknowledge the genius of many of these irregular leaders does not imply that they would have been equally successful if placed in command of a more highly organized type of force, at any rate until they had gained experience of its organization and different application. But it does cast a reflection upon the customary method of training leaders in organized armies. It is significant that in the American Civil War, which was the most fruitful field of generalship in modern times, most of the outstanding leaders were men who after an apprenticeship in the Regular Army had gone into some field of civil activity, which in varying degree freed their minds from the fetters of military convention and routine, while they retained a useful experience of the functioning of the military machine.

The adage that it is necessary to learn to obey before one can command, although it contains an element of truth, has been greatly abused in its actual application to the education of leaders. There has been too little differentiation in it between the spirit of obedience to a common purpose and the mechanical form of obedience. Many of the greatest military leaders have shown themselves exceptionally restive in their early career under the restraints of conventional discipline. One may cite the candid confessions of Grant and Sherman as to their behaviour when cadets at West Point, and their critical reflections in old age on the system of training to which they had been subjected in youth. In British history, such men as Wolfe, Wellington, and Nelson showed themselves even less amenable to the outward forms of discipline. It is only too evident that these and many others became great leaders not because of but rather in spite of their early training—because, instead, their personalities were too strong to be forced into the conventional groove. Thus there is unconscious humour in the fact that such men have been held up as exemplars to the young officers of later generations who were undergoing the same kind of training. Only ignorance of history, or excess of varnish, can explain such unwitting irony. If there are signs of change in the military educational system, a much greater change is needed, and a much clearer distinction, before schools for officers can truly be regarded as an aid towards preparing officers for leadership. That change must be towards the university ideal of education, of training young men to think for themselves, instead of moulding their minds to a sealed pattern.

The obvious difficulty, of course, in the solution of this problem of military education is that officers, although in all grades called upon to exercise command, have also to act under command except in the highest grades. But the problem is not so difficult as it may seem so long as the system of education is based on a true understanding of the spirit of discipline, and the system of discipline is elastic rather than rigid.

The Training of the Soldier

The training of those who simply act under command, and merely handle the inanimate tools of war, is a simpler problem. Not so simple as it used to be before weapons became complex mechanisms and before their long-range effect compelled the dispersion of the combatants on the battlefield, but still simple in comparison with the training of a leader.

The object of the soldier's training is threefold. To make him skilled in handling his weapons under battle conditions. To make him an interlocking and frictionless cog in the military machine, which implies the development of automatic obedience, of instinctive combination according to some practised system of action, and of physical stamina. Thirdly, and above all, to make him conquer his own sense of fear.

Military Training

Military exercises and military discipline have been the two main agencies used to produce the trained soldier. But they have had a purely moral accompaniment in the cultivation of a distinctive military spirit—springing from comradeship and bound up by the strands of *esprit de corps*.

The form of military exercises has naturally varied with the changing nature of weapons and the consequent changes in the fighting formation of military bodies. These exercises may be classified as individual and collective. In their application to the training of the soldier both classes have in the past been predominantly and still are to a large extent, based upon drill—that is, the repetition of certain movements until their performance becomes instinctive. If such drill has the primary purpose of developing working efficiency, it has also been of use, especially in the past, as a supplement to discipline and the military spirit. By a discipline of the muscles the reflexes of obedience were developed so that the soldier could continue to act effectively even when his mind was numbed by fear.

Military discipline, in the strait sense of the term, is the enforcement of instant obedience to orders through the threat of punishment, supplemented by the control of the reflexes established through drill. In the wider sense it is bound up with the soldierly spirit. So far as this is susceptible to analysis, its components appear to be the pride of manhood, the pride of arms (of being an initiate in the martial cult), the confidence that comes from skill at arms, the sense of comradeship, the sense of duty, and the sense of loyalty—to comrades, commander, corps and country.

The proportions of these components have certainly varied. Thus in the citizen-military armies of the Greek city-states and the Roman Republic, patriotism would seem to have been the dominant element—at any rate in

148

the willing soldier's spirit. The same has been true of the armies of the French Revolution and of the 'national' armies subsequently. In the army of ancient Sparta, the influence of its martial cult would seem to have risen to at least equal proportions with patriotism. In the Roman legions from the time of Marius onwards patriotism counted for little, and personal loyalty to a commander took its place. It was in the early part of the first century B.C. that the old oath of allegiance sworn annually was replaced by a personal and permanent oath of loyalty to the commander. As for the mystical sense of membership of a cult we can see its power in Cæsar's ability to quell a mutiny by addressing his men as *quirites* or civilians.

These two elements continued to be predominant throughout the Middle Ages, first in the feudal forces, then in the 'free companies' who hired themselves out collectively, and later in the swelling volume of mercenaries who enlisted in the army of any sovereign willing to pay them.

When standing armies became general, from the seventeenth century onward, the element of personal loyalty to the general declined in importance, to be succeeded by loyalty to the corps—the regimental spirit. Patriotism naturally revived as a motive factor when armies were raised from natives of the country. Yet in all professional armies the martial cult and *esprit de corps* have remained as powerful influences on the soldier's spirit.

No student of war is likely to underrate the strength of the military spirit as a cement to armies, especially those whose ranks are filled with men of some intelligence. Yet, equally, no scientific historian will fail to perceive how much of their fighting power and fortitude, especially in the past, was due to a severely punitive discipline, which inspired a fear that overcame fear of the enemy.

Military Training

Spartan discipline is proverbial, yet it had a larger moral element in its application than that of most armies until recent times. Those who ran away were punished by shame —they could hold no office, could receive no wife, were exposed to insult or blows without the right of reply, were compelled to wear patched and parti-coloured dress, and were only allowed to shave one side of their faces.

Roman discipline, in comparison, was far more physical in its deterrents, the death penalty being frequently inflicted. When a body of troops failed in the hour of battle, a customary punishment was decimation—the putting to death of every tenth man. But it is interesting to note that the Romans subtly appealed to the military spirit in some of their disciplinary measures, by giving them the semblance of punishment for a crime against comradeship and the corps rather than merely against the state. Thus the delinquents were punished by a form of running the gauntlet in which the other soldiers of the legion, armed with sticks and stones, normally battered them to death. On the other hand, the Romans, as an offset to these merciless penalties, created a regular system of rewards for distinguished service, apart from the ordinary incentive of loot.

We find the Roman practice of decimation revived by Wallenstein in 1642 to punish a regiment which had led the flight from the battlefield. If the enforcement of discipline varied greatly in the armies of the seventeenth century, the scale of punishments were very severe. In that of Gustavus, however, they were employed as much to ensure good behaviour in quarters as bravery in battle. And the Swedish Army was certainly a shining contrast to the marauding armies of the day in its conduct towards the people of the territory it passed through. In Marlborough's army discipline was tightened, running the gauntlet and, for lesser crimes, whipping being the chief forms of punishment. The rod, however, was now used to punish many offences for which death or mutilation had formerly been inflicted. In 1712 there was a case of a soldier being sentenced to 12,600 stripes in seven applications.

It was left to Frederick the Great to produce the most severely drilled and disciplined army that the world has perhaps yet known, with the calculated purpose of turning men into automatic machines that could fire five volleys a minute—with a flint lock musket!—while advancing and manoeuvring at a slow march under the enemy's fire, and that could be relied on to keep up these rolling volleys while their rigidly dressed ranks were being torn by bullets and cannon balls. It was a triumph of merciless discipline and drill over human nature. Blind obedience was the keynote of a system in which the death penalty was introduced for the soldier who even dared to grumble at his sergeant's exacting orders.

It was only by comparison that other armies seemed less severely disciplined. Thus in the British Army and Navy the cat-o'-nine-tails, superseding the rod, reigned throughout the eighteenth and far into the nineteenth century, as the regular penalty for offences great and small—a hundred lashes being regarded as quite natural for the latter, and anything up to fifteen hundred for the former. We learn that in the 28th Foot in 1806 any man who failed to pass the inspecting officer's scrutiny of his turn-out was flogged on the spot, and that from ten to twenty men used to be punished at a single parade. If some commanding officers were reluctant to flog, the power was grossly abused by many. Not until the Royal

Commission of 1835 was a systematic limitation imposed, and not until 1881 was flogging finally abolished. Every effort towards reform had been fiercely opposed by senior officers who declared that any limitation would ruin the discipline of the Army.

We should recognize that the men in the ranks were largely composed of the scourings of the slums, so that some excuse may be found in their vicious tendencies for the drastic measures taken to ensure good behaviour. We must recognize that so long as men fought in close formations—from the Spartan phalanx of spears down to the serried lines of Frederick's grenadiers—wherein each man must move in dovetailed uniformity with his neighbours to ensure cohesion, there was a military value in a discipline and drill that turned men into machines.

It was as much due to the growing effect of firearms, which compelled looser formations, as to a growing humanity that in the nineteenth century the methods of discipline became gradually less severe. Even so, old habits die hard and even in the armies of the early twentieth century discipline remained predominantly punitive as a means of subduing the independent will of the soldier and as a means, perhaps overrated, of enabling him to face danger through the conscious or subconscious fear of the more certain penalties that awaited him if he failed. Even to-day there are military students who maintain that instinctive courage is so weak and self-respect so unsafe a support that it is wiser to impose courage through the impress of a martinet discipline.

Yet a different way was introduced, and vindicated, more than a century ago in what is known as Sir John Moore's system of training. Its origin was partly tactical, partly humane. The more intelligent British officers who fought in America were impressed by the impracticability of pitting stiff-ranked formations against the forest craft of the Red Indians, and the need of combatting them with a new type of resourceful light infantry. On Christmas Day, 1755 took place the birth of a corps, the 60th Royal Americans (now the King's Royal Rifle Corps), which became a light to the whole military world. It developed not only a new style of infantry tactics, but under Colonel Bouquet, a new form of discipline, in which the self-respect and self-confidence of the men was fostered by an atmosphere of trust and brutality replaced by sympathy. In preference to imposed discipline there was a cultivation of all the elements of the soldierly spirit to the end that men should acquire self-control. The experience of the American Revolution and the hard lessons taught by the colonists acted as a spur to this new tendency, and eventually led, first, to the formation of the Experimental Rifle Corps in 1800, and then to the training of the Light Brigade at Shorncliffe under Sir John Moore. It gave a new spiritual meaning to discipline and added a moral to a merely physical cohesion with results that were proved in the Peninsular War, where the Light Division was the salt of the Army.

Its triumphs were the more remarkable because the salt was damped, the light dimmed, by many conservative soldiers who lacked the insight and the courage to place their trust in the new system. This adulteration continued in the generations that followed, although partially offset by the rising level of humanity in the people at large. At the present day, one can say that the methods of discipline, if not its spirit, are virtually equivalent to those of Sir John Moore's system. But they should have made a century's progress. By comparison with the immense change in the customs of civil life, we can see that there is far too much stress on physical deterrents even in the most enlightened codes of military discipline. And too little emphasis on intelligence. To-day the revolutionary changes in warfare point the urgent need of a fresh change in discipline. The increasingly mechanical nature of weapons demands the intellectual development of the men who handle them—at any rate of those who act individually or in little groups. When battle was waged essentially between physical bodies there was a value in turning men into machines. Now that battle is being waged more and more between machines the object of military training should be to produce men who will be masters of the machine—by developing their mental powers.

The Training of the Commander

If executive intelligence is becoming more and more needed in the soldier, creative intelligence is and always has been the supreme requirement in the commander—coupled with moral courage. War is a two-party affair, and thus conventionality of thought inevitably tends to confirm this equality of kind, conducing to stalemate. The best hope of tilting the scales and of overcoming the resistance inherent in conflict lies in originality—to produce something unexpected that will paralyse the opponent's freedom of action.

But, in historical fact, such creative intelligence has been rare in the operations of war. And rarer still in preparation for war. Military history is filled with the record of military improvements that have been resisted by those who would have profited richly from them. Between the development of new weapons or new tactics and their adoption there has always been a time-lag, often of generations. And that time-lag has often decided the fate of nations.

The explanation lies not only in the system of training but in a psychological attitude underlying it. The officer has never been taught to approach his problems, and the investigation of experience, in a spirit of scientific enquiry. His early training is directed, above all, to the cultivation of unquestioning loyalty—multiple loyalties—to sovereign, country, service, corps and his superiors. To strengthen him for his fighting function, and for the tremendous trials of fortitude this entails, the development of an intense spirit of loyalty has great value. But, obviously, it becomes an obstacle when the man so brought up turns to investigate the facts of warfare. His compound loyalties create prejudices which inevitably colour his vision and bias his judgment. They may be essential to the soldier in action, but they are a hindrance in reflection—where facts should be analysed in a scientific spirit, with complete detachment from all loyalties save that to truth. To understand this fundamental difficulty of the military mind not only helps to explain its historical records of myopia but may help many who feel bitter at the consequences to judge the case more charitably.

But charity does not imply contentment. It may be that only a philosopher could reconcile the opposing loyalties harmoniously, but something could be done to help the normal soldier in adapting himself to the conflicting roles of loyal executant in war and truth-loyal student of war. The first need is a change of attitude towards criticism and independence of thought. It would be helped if there was a recognition of the psychological commonplace that men of personality and originality—in other words, the men naturally fitted to be leaders—are inherently critical. And in fact the great leaders of the past who are taken as examples were critically minded. A second need is for a new attitude to knowledge, and the encouragement of a spirit of enquiry. Satisfaction with present knowledge is the chief bar to the pursuit of knowledge. It has been so in all branches and professions. If the military profession is no worse than others, that is no just cause for contentment. Nor does the history of armies yield any cause for self-satisfaction to any soldier who digs down into it. In these conditions lack of criticism is a proof of virgin ignorances. Those who have studied war the most cannot avoid becoming acutely conscious that the exploration of war as a scientific subject has scarcely been begun.

Social Effects of Military Training

These can be summarized briefly, or otherwise require a comprehensive historical survey, not possible here. The effects have naturally been far-reaching wherever compulsory military service has been the custom. They have been correspondingly insignificant save indirectly among those peoples who have depended upon mercenaries or upon permanent professional forces, as separation from the normal life of the people naturally tends to give the soldier a sense of isolation that in time accentuates the natural caste spirit arising from pride of arms and the mystical bond of comradeship between men who have faced danger together.

The physical benefit of military training is very marked, so long as it is accompanied by good feeding and housing conditions. Its value, however, lies in the open air life and exercise rather than in the specific forms of military drill, which are certainly inferior to gymnastic exercises. This can be seen in the present Italian army where open-air gymnastics and physical training are carried out extensively. The physical development and activity of the men who have done their military service is remarkable.

The moral benefit of military training varies with the system of discipline in vogue. It is highest when the predominant emphasis is placed on an appeal to the soldierly spirit, and lowest when unthinking obedience is imposed through fear of the consequences. The purely punitive form has little more than a negative value and then only as applied to the lowest form of manhood. In contrast the elements which make up the soldierly spirit are in proportion to their development a foundation of good citizenship.

The mental benefit is more doubtful, save in so far as it provides opportunity for practising leadership or for developing specialized knowledge. Military training certainly tends to stimulate quickness of thought. On the other hand, it inevitably tends to uniformity of thought, if this may be relieved by the diverse tests and intense experiences of active service.

These influences together with the educational facilities that now commonly exist in an army may contribute to a definite increase of mental capacity in a backward community or when applied to backward types of men. In Russia, for example, the idea of using the army as a lever through which to raise the intellectual level of the masses lies at the base of a noteworthy educational experiment.

The wider effects of military training upon society, and the political effects, can be gauged in past history. Thus in the city-states of Greece, whose armies were citizen militias, it seems reasonably clear that the duty of military service did not harm the intellectual development of their finest minds, while it undoubtedly strengthened the sense of citizenship. Moreover, the restriction of military service to free citizens tended to enhance its moral significance. Decay began when, under the strain of the long-drawn Peloponnesian war, slaves and mercenaries were enlisted. On the other hand, it is clear that the drawbacks of military training outweighed the advantages in the case of Sparta, where the nation was turned into the equivalent of a military corps, and the unmarried men lived entirely in barracks. The civilization of Sparta was stunted and the poorness of its contribution to the intellectual and artistic achievements of ancient Greece is only to be explained by its military 'life' as a nation.

If early Rome was almost barren in the arts, its highly developed civic virtues and its contribution to political science cannot, in analysis, be separated from its system of military service. Under the Tullian organization the army comprised all citizens from seventeen to sixty years of age, those under forty-seven being used for service in the field. They were enrolled for a year at a time which, in normal practice, meant a summer's campaign only. But the expansion of 'empire' which followed the Punic wars broke down the old citizen levy system. Marius abolished the restriction of service to men of some property, and from that time onward the army became professional and long-service, with an increasing dependence on the men of subject races and eventually on alien 'barbarians'. If the change assisted the growth of civilization in Rome, it unquestionably contributed to the decline and fall of Roman civilization.

In modern times also, notably in the eighteenth century,

the discontinuance of the duty of military service, and the consequent dependence of states upon an isolated military caste, can be seen to have paved the way to disaster. Sometimes it has been internal, through the overthrow of a government by a minority who alone possessed and knew how to use the lever of force. More often, it has been external, as when the professionally-dependent states of Europe were overthrown by the national armies of Revolutionary France.

The latter danger is reduced with the scientific development of weapons that makes mere numbers of small account. The former danger remains, as may be seen in the state of Germany to-day. This danger is reduced where there is a militia system, voluntary or otherwise, as well as a professional army.

But beyond these deductions, it is too early to make any prediction as to the social effects of abandoning or continuing compulsory military training in states of advanced civilization.

CHAPTER XIII

The Higher Direction of Forces

The re-equipment of our forces is progressing. But it is no less important to ensure that mental re-equipment keeps pace—that there will be minds capable of directing these new-armed forces under the more exacting and intricate conditions of to-day. Everyone is familiar with Napoleon's saying that: 'In war it is the *Man*, who counts, not the men.' Not everyone realizes that this saying has an increased application to modern war. Yet it stands out among the lessons of the last war.

In exploring the history of 1914-18, the impression grows that the personal performance of commanders was often far better than its actual effect. Many of the attacks that have been levied against them miss the real point by overlooking this difference. It was to a large extent the natural consequence of the conditions which bounded the exercise of high command in a war of masses. The remoteness of the higher commanders from the battlefield made it even more difficult for them to gauge the real situation there than it was for them to influence that situation. Whereas in Napoleon's time it had been true to say that the best general was the one who made the fewest mistakes, it was nearer the truth now that the best general was the one who caused the least mistakes. Actual command was split into a myriad fragments, resting in the hands of the company and platoon leaders: the higher commanders had changed into company directors. Deprived of personal experience of battlefield reality, they were handicapped in correcting the inevitable discrepancies of pre-war theory: in checking the theory with the facts, and in adjusting it to the new developments.

It is not easy to determine the effect of recent developments on this 1914-18 condition, but the present probability is that this psychological remoteness may be increased in more ways than it is decreased, at any rate in the sphere of the higher command. And it may be further complicated by the freshness of the problems which confront the local commanders of the new-pattern forces. Mechanization is inevitable; the European country that places its faith in old means and methods might find its faith even more misplaced than was that of the Abyssinians, who had the asset of a remote mountain fastness. Yet mechanization carries with it risks that it would be foolish to ignore. Chief among them is not food-supply but mind-supply.

There is serious cause to doubt whether we shall find sufficient officers capable of directing and handling these high-mobility forces until a new generation, born in the motor age, has grown up. And without the necessary mental adjustment to the new conditions, chaos may result when these forces are launched against those of a similar type. The Italians suffered serious congestion and disorganization in the early months of their campaign, yet they had no modern opponent equipped with aircraft and landcraft to make that confusion worse confounded. The dangers of inadequate mental adjustment have been increased by the years of delay in beginning the process of mechanization and in providing the means of training. For unless there has been time to develop a mechanically mobile sense in peace-time, we are inviting breakdown if we have to attempt a hurried transformation under the stress of war.

But the problems that call for attention go far beyond the sphere of mechanization. This has been recognized by the latest edition of *Field Service Regulations*, which is in many respects a landmark in the chain of military manuals. It is here emphasized that high command in war requires:

'The broadest possible outlook and knowledge, of social as well as of military questions. War is now more than ever a social problem: a major war affects the whole of the national life and every class of citizen, and there is a corresponding civil influence on the conduct of military operations.'

The new *Field Service Regulations* also pays significant attention to another condition which has been slow to gain recognition—the essential similarity between the principles or common-sense precepts which lead to success in war and those which govern any affairs where active opposition or competition has to be overcome. Both the military commander and 'the ordinary citizen who is planning a business transaction' have 'to take into their calculations the possible schemes of rivals'. Too many military plans have broken down through the failure to realize that war is essentially a two-party affair. The very principle of concentration, that was so continually on the lips of the dominant soldiers in 1914-18, becomes meaningless unless the enemy's concentration is prevented by well-devised distractions, which require detachments from

The Higher Direction of Forces

your own. Applied without comprehension, this 'principle' too often proved in practice no better than an unpractical catchword. Its dangers emphasize the importance of imagination—to put oneself in the enemy's shoes and to see things from other points of view. Normal service training in peace-time has hitherto done little to develop such qualities, or the habit of applying them.

While the new *Field Service Regulations* emphasizes the fundamental similarity between the qualities required for military and civil leadership it suggests, more questionably, that a difference arises owing to the fact that 'the conditions of war are utterly unfamiliar to the ordinary civilized man'. It may well be asked what opportunity the professional soldier has in peace-time to become familiar with the stresses of battle. Past experience he may have, but so now have millions of civilians. But even this may be of little service as acclimatization for the conditions of a new war. A better ground for arguing the regular soldier's advantage over the ordinary citizen is that he becomes so habituated to military processes that he can perform them instinctively in the heat of action, so that his functional efficiency is apt to be less affected by the 'friction' of war. Here, undoubtedly, is a real asset.

It applies, however, in far less degree to the higher sphere of war, where it may be outweighed by handicaps that are inevitable in peace-time soldiering. The politician is always 'at war', and the business man commonly in competition with others. They have constant practice in conflict, and unceasing experience of its psychological conditions. Soldiering, in comparison, is a sheltered occupation save in war. The ease with which the will of the superior prevails inside an army becomes a handicap in preparation for dealing with a hostile army. Always revolving between

163

the poles of authority and obedience, the soldier gains little or no psychological experience as a fighter. Exercises in mimic war, regulated by umpires, cannot compare with the exacting tests of the political or the business field.

An appreciation of these conditions may arouse sympathy for the generals of the last war who, from the isolation of a headquarter office, had to direct armies of millions composed of the people in arms, and were pitted against an active foe in a warfare which embraced a diversity of factors that were military only by adoption. There is no cause for surprise that they failed so often to gauge their steps, or the enemy's; rather is it remarkable, when all is weighed, that they adapted themselves even as well as they did to conditions for which they were, by training and environment, so little prepared.

Yet this reflection leads to another, on the way that square pegs were placed in round holes. Although it was a war of nations, and many of the best brains of the nation were drawn into the forces, they were excluded from those military spheres in which 'the broadest possible outlook and knowledge' were needed. The custom of all the forces erected the principle that no one was fit to have a voice in matters of strategy unless he had nearly forty years experience of the military machine. It was certainly a novel principle, since it would have excluded nearly all the great commanders of history, from Alexander, Hannibal and Cæsar, down to Cromwell, Marlborough and Napoleon. And it was the more strange since the twentieth century strategist had to deal with many more non-military factors. But although the principle flew in the face of historical experience and modern knowledge, the records show that it was rigidly maintained—except in the Dominion forces —throughout the four years of war.

The Higher Direction of Forces

By a practical paradox, the civilian was invited to take over the most strictly professional functions of soldiering while he was viewed as an intruder in the higher and hence less technical posts. Any intelligent citizen with administrative experience found it easy to master the details of staff-work—as soon as he had 'learnt the language' his past experience here became a strong asset. In comparison, it was far more difficult for him to become an efficient regimental officer. Proficiency in the operative technique of an infantry or artillery unit, in a regular army, is the product of habit as well as of specialized training.

The higher the plane of war, the more the solution of its problems depends on wide knowledge, broad outlook, and depth of thought: and the less, comparatively, on technical experience. This does not mean that knowledge of military technique is unnecessary: without it, the ablest man would be handicapped, especially in dealing with forces which have a long-established system of operation. The principles of fighting are based on common-sense, but something more is needed to apply them effectively in the handling of armies. The better a man's mental equipment, however, the less time he will take to acquire an adequate knowledge of such technique. And in acquiring it quickly he will have an advantage over the man who has taken thirty or forty years in climbing the military ladder. Instruments and methods will have changed, and often be entirely new, since the other man served his apprenticeship to arms. It is difficult for the older soldier to have a sure grasp of weapons he has never handled, and of methods he has never carried out. Moreover, if his technical experience lies several steps back, it becomes more difficult for him to gauge the next step forward. What he gains by having prolonged experience of command may be offset by lacking first-hand knowledge of the present tools of command.

Nevertheless it was only in the Dominion Forces that the F.S.R. definition had a chance of test. Its results are significant. Since technical proficiency and executive habit count for more in the lower grades, it is to be inferred that a non-professional soldier who proved himself barely the equal of many regulars as a battalion or brigade commander might prove outstanding when, and if, he reached a higher command. That inference was confirmed by actual experience in the Dominion Forces, notably in the case of General Monash.

When the conditions of the war are analysed, it becomes clear that in the qualifications for high command, and still more for strategic direction, there was little in pre-war professional experience that helped a man, while there was much that might handicap the development of his personal qualities. One important qualification remained which could not be quickly acquired; the man who had spent a lifetime in the military profession might here have had a special advantage. An objective study of the past would have been a guide to the conditions that were in development. But for such study professional soldiers had no training and limited opportunity. The discovery of uncomfortable facts had never been encouraged in armies, who treated their history as a sentimental treasure rather than a field of scientific research. Thus the potential asset was left a 'buried talent'.

All were amateurs in that war from the moment when the opening moves broke down, and the real nature of the war emerged from the artificial mould of convention in which the pre-war plans and forces had been cast. The question which remained was how quickly they could learn, and whether their minds could expand to the scale of the problems. The chances of this adaptation, as well as the opportunity for fresh minds, were diminished by a delusion—that they were professionals in the larger sphere.

In retrospect, it can hardly be considered that the results were satisfactory, or that the power of adaptation equalled the need. The question remains whether it will be adequate if another emergency comes, under conditions that are still more complex, even less 'military' and far more difficult to gauge. At present there is small reason to expect a different result to that of 1914-18. It would seem essential both to give professional minds greater opportunity for development and to make more use of other minds. Here is a problem that is inseparable from all calculation of what is 'an adequate standard' of defence.

CHAPTER XIV

The Higher Education of Officers

Is there any solution for the problem outlined in the previous chapter? An obvious one is to raise the standard of intelligence and education required of the prospective officer, but its achievement is not easy. In 1924 the question of the education and training of officers was examined by a committee under Lord Haldane's chairmanship, which included two of the ablest soldiers then in the War Office as well as a leading member, and future Vice-Chancellor, of Cambridge University, Mr. Will Spens. That Committee pointed out that the problem had two aspects: 'It is much to be desired that first-rate brains should be attracted into the Army. It is not necessary, nor is it wholly desirable, that all, or even the majority, of regimental officers should be intellectuals. . . . In consequence, a very difficult problem has to be solved in part by attracting a certain number of boys of high intellectual ability and in securing the proper opportunities of further education for these, and for the rest by attracting and educating a large number of boys in regard to whom stress is laid on character rather than on high intellectual qualifications.' The Committee also declared that 'any adequate improvement in the quality and quantity of candidates must depend upon a larger number of parents being induced to regard the Army as an attractive career for their sons. This implies the necessity of convincing parents that the Army provides openings for brains and character comparable with those provided in the Civil Service or in the other professions. The task of convincing parents may in the end become a matter of propaganda; but propaganda will be valueless unless the system can fairly be said to have been so adjusted as to make it true that such openings exist in fact. Nor is this all. Conviction is only likely to be secured on a sufficient scale by changes in the present system, which will not only provide such openings, but which will also make them sufficiently striking to attract attention.

'It has been represented to us by the many authorities that we have consulted that if it is desired to make the Army attractive as a profession to men of good intellectual attainments, certain conditions are essential: (1) Work must be provided of sufficient intellectual interest. (2) There must be real opportunities for advancement by merit. (3) The remuneration must be adequate.'

Besides emphasizing that a genuine system of promotion by merit was 'essential' if the officer corps was 'to be prevented from stagnating', the report suggested that university candidates should be given special facilities for entering the Staff College early in their service and that the system of proficiency pay should be extended much beyond its existing limits, to encourage the acquirement of special knowledge of some particular military or scientific subject.

The Committee, in conclusion, stated: 'We attach the greatest importance to the whole question of providing at every stage adequate rewards for exceptional capacity. We believe liberal provision in this direction to be essential with a view to encouraging able boys to become officers, and we are unanimous in our opinion that a great opportunity exists at the present time to initiate the suggested reforms. It is not too late to convince the public that the lessons of the war are being taken seriously to heart by the military authorities, and that it is their firm intention to make the Army an attractive career for men of talent. If we wait much longer the public will feel that the Army is such a hopelessly conservative institution that no vital change is possible in the principles on which the post-war army is organised.'

More than a dozen years have passed since the Haldane Committee made its report. Its concrete recommendations have been fulfilled only in small degree, and its intentions still less. For adequate effect, in attracting 'first-rate brains' to the Army, it would be necessary not only to offer greater inducements but to dispel long-standing assumptions, both within and without the military sphere. We should have to change the way that the Army looks at itself, and also the way it is regarded by the outside world. While certain improvements have been made in the education and training of officers, none would seem to have gone far enough to fulfil the Committee's condition of being 'sufficiently striking' to attract attention and carry conviction—of an adequate change. Schoolmasters, in general, have tended to view with pained surprise any boy of scholarship standard who expressed the intention of entering the Army, and to deplore such a waste of his gifts. And in most public schools where an 'army class' existed it has not stood high in the estimation of the boys themselves, being commonly regarded as the refuge of those who have more brawn than brain. Only a few years ago a headmaster candidly told a soldier who was seeking his aid in improving the supply of officers: 'I only advise boys who would be quite impossible in any other walk of life to go to Sandhurst.' The effect of an opinion so widespread and long-standing has naturally been to keep the standard of recruitment low, and, naturally also, the opinion was extended rather than changed by the experience of the last war when the army absorbed the nation and the 'old boys' who came into the army for the duration of the emergency found themselves in subordination—permanently, and not merely while they were serving their apprenticeship to arms—to the low-rated 'army class' of their schooldays. Only a dynamic proof of professional efficiency could have altered such an old-established view—and that, in general, was hardly forthcoming.

In some ways the military profession, if it tenaciously maintained its claims to privilege while the war lasted, has been more ready than most to abandon its preconceptions. That progress is apt to be concealed by a habit of 'trade-union' loyalty which leads its members to deny publicly, often in tones of the utmost indignation, the faults they not merely admit but castigate privately—soldiers are rarely true to their better selves in public speeches. But since the war there has been a remarkable concurrence of opinion among the heads of the Army on the need to broaden the basis of military education, and although suggestions differ on the means of achieving this object, they all have a 'University' keynote. The old prejudice against officers who entered the Army through the Universities instead of through the Military Colleges has disappeared, and been replaced by a desire to obtain as many as possible. Under present conditions, however, the supply is limited; partly because of the greater cost to parents of this mode of entry; partly because the career has not been sufficiently attractive to young men capable of taking a good degree. Even now, the antedate given to University candidates is so limited that a man who has taken first-class honours starts at no advantage, even at a disadvantage, in seniority compared with the cadet who has passed through Sandhurst. Until this is changed we can hardly expect more candidates from the Universities, or those candidates to be of the best.

As an alternative there has been an effort to widen the educational basis of the Royal Military College at Sandhurst, and to remodel the system on university lines. Addressing the Headmasters' Conference in 1930, the Chief Instructor at Sandhurst frankly said on the subject of these changes:

'Warfare was becoming more and more complicated, requiring brains and ability of the officers, and we found that we had to build up the brains and personalities of the officers from the very beginning. We realized that in the Great War some of the greatest mistakes of officers were made in their dealings with civilians and in their lack of knowledge of civilians, and we realized that a great war needed broadmindedness on the part of its leaders.

'The old regime at Sandhurst aimed at turning out purely military specialists, and this was not what the Army or the public wanted. The curriculum which was going on undoubtedly deadened a boy's intellect and led his thoughts into narrow channels. A boy was asked to have an active mind when his body was really exhausted. He was never taught to think out things for himself. We made him spend hours taking his rifle to bits and still more hours putting it together again.

The Higher Education of Officers

'The Sandhurst curriculum has to be drastically over-hauled, and in the new curriculum we now try to give a boy the power of self-development.'

Where the object of old was to turn out a cadet who on joining his regiment would be a perfectly trained private soldier—it was even laid down that there was to be no attempt to train him as a leader—the aim is now to give him an idea of the elements of leadership and some practical opportunity of exercising it; weapon-training has been reduced to an outline knowledge, and general subjects increased in variety, while teaching in class has been supplemented by providing more time for private study.

Through these changes there has been a marked improvement in the educational value of a Sandhurst course. Yet the closer approach to the University system has tended to emphasize the gulf which separates the intellectual atmosphere of a military college from that which characterizes a university. It is easy to provide company officers who are good sportsmen, but difficult to find instructors who combine deep knowledge with the ability to create a thirst for it. It is still more difficult to develop the power of independent thought in an establishment steeped in the traditions of military discipline. Thus, despite the enthusiasm shown in pursuing this aim, the result has fallen short of the original hopes.

There has been, partly in consequence, a recent revival of the suggestion that the military colleges should be abolished and entry into the Army be entirely through the Universities. For this system to produce the required number of officers it would, of course, be necessary to subsidize the University course of accepted candidates. Even so, the cost would be an inconsiderable fraction of the Army budget, a fraction so small that if viewed with a sense of proportion it should not weigh against the prospective benefit. There is also the possibility of a shortened course, of two years, such as officers of the Royal Engineers already do at Cambridge after being commissioned—one recommendation of the Haldane Committee which has been carried out, with benefit. In that case the expense to the State would hardly be more than that of the present system, since the cost of Woolwich and Sandhurst works out at about £350 a year for each cadet, of which the parents as a whole bear only a third.

The trend of modern warfare gives ever-increasing point to this suggestion, as a University offers a broader educational basis and also more opportunity for specialized study, both of which are needed to meet the growing complexity of warfare and its tendency to be more and more influenced by non-military factors. Again, to make entry through the University general would help to diminish the difference of outlook, as distinct from a difference of ability, between officers who are likely to stay at regimental duty and those who may be employed in the higher direction of forces. Modern warfare demands an ever greater power of adjustment to new conditions; the effect of the higher direction may be paralysed unless the executants also acquire an increased degree of mental adaptability.

Another potential advantage of a general University entry might be in offering the means of fulfilling one of the most important recommendations of the Haldane Committee:

'It is desirable in every profession to have a foundational basis on which the insight of those who practise it rests. To change the metaphor, it is always helpful to the practitioner, old or young, to have a background for his reasoning against which he can set or estimate it. For the physicist, pure mathematics performs this role, for the student of philosophy, the history of past systems is the background against which he sets and estimates his ideas; for the physician, physiology and pathology give him what he needs of this kind, just as anatomy gives it for the surgeon. Is there any subject which can bring the study of military strategy and tactics into a relation with life in yet wider aspects in such a way as to illuminate that study, render it more interesting, and develop not only its significance, but the direction in it which must be looked for in new ideas?

'We believe that the study of military history in a wider and less restricted form than has hitherto been current in establishments for military education may do a great deal in this direction. The strategy of a particular nation must always be in large measure the outcome of its geographical conditions and of its history. Great Britain and the British Empire consist largely of possessions surrounded or in large measure bounded by the sea. Their military history has therefore been based on sea-power. This fact has exercised a dominating influence on British strategy and on British history. Apart from this history and the strategical necessities which it has disclosed neither the science nor the art of British warfare are intelligible. They require an intelligent and comprehensive study of history to bring out their meaning, and to guide the officer in his military studies. With France and Germany the conditions and the histories have naturally been quite different, and the study of them, while very valuable from a general standpoint, cannot take the place of that of British military institutions, and of the fashion in which with us land-power is conditioned by sea-power.'

Such a truly educative use of military history has not

proved possible under the present system. It demands, in the first place, the study of books which treat the subject scientifically instead of sentimentally: as history, not as a pleasantly flavoured fairy tale or an uplifting moral story. Books of the former kind are rare in this field; there has been little encouragement to produce them. It demands, in the second place, the development of a critical mind in the student; to this there has been even less encouragement. A few instructors, inspired by the university ideal, have done their best to bring it into the military colleges, but their effect has been overborne by the weight of authority —well-meaning but uncomprehending, saturated in pious traditions, and anxious lest discipline might be impaired or respect for superiors disturbed. Armies are temples of ancestor-worship. It is not necessary to depreciate the moral help they gain from this devotional practice in order to appreciate its mental hindrance in seeing the facts of experience clearly and gauging the trends of the future. So long as history is regarded as sacred ground, military science must remain where science as a whole was centuries back. It has not yet emerged from the Middle Ages. With a general broadening of outlook among those who are now rising to the higher places of the Army, there is hope of similar progress at the military colleges, but the latter is conditioned by the former, and we cannot expect it to be as fast as is necessary. It might be quickened if the process of education was moved to places where the desired atmosphere already prevails.

A suggestion of a different kind, but with the same aim of making the Army a career attractive to talent, is the creation of a special Staff Corps. It might be recruited from university graduates who had taken a good honours degree, forming an intellectual *élite* from which the higher direction of the Army could in turn be recruited—with the double advantage that they would have been trained from the outset for the work, and have escaped years of deadening routine. Such a system would enable better use to be made of the university route of entry than at present, without necessarily enlarging its scale. It would apply to the Army the long-tested method by which the Civil Service provides its higher, administrative class. It might be made more elastic by providing opportunity, for subsequent entry into the Corps, to regimental officers whose gifts had been late in maturing, or even to Territorial officers of outstanding military ability who had found, as not infrequently happens, that their natural hobby should have been their chosen profession. The creation of such a Staff Corps would enable permanent rates of pay to be offered sufficient to attract the ablest university products, and to keep them in the service—whereas, to-day, the ablest of the younger staff officers are being tempted to leave the service early by the slowness of promotion and the poorness of the pay in comparison with what men of their age and calibre can command outside.

The obvious danger in forming a separate Staff Corps is that its members might become out of touch with the problems and difficulties of the ordinary soldier, leading to consequent friction and to the issue of unpractical directions. But this danger already exists, and has long made itself felt, in the present system. To-day, perhaps more than ever, the gates of the Staff College control the level of advancement, and the 'p.s.c.' hallmark is a badge of separation. Moreover, nothing is more conducive to friction between the Staff and the Line than the fact that many an aspiring soldier ultimately finds the gates of the Staff College closed to him, and is filled with a bitter sense of having wasted twelve or fifteen years in a profession which now has no future for him. With a Staff Corps recruited direct from the Universities he would have a fair idea of his destiny from the outset, while being able to keep a hope of joining the elect, instead of, as at present, hanging under a fear of eventual disappointment.

To give members of such a Staff Corps an understanding of regimental conditions, and to prevent them losing it, it would certainly be necessary for them to do spells of duty with a unit at intervals throughout their career. Except at the outset this would merely be a continuation of the present system, with the nominal difference that they would be seconded from the staff to a unit, and the beneficial difference that their departure, for return to the staff, would be no cause of grievance to the regiment. They might also gain in experience by doing their spells of regimental duty with different arms, thus becoming better equipped for the direction of combined forces. The drawbacks of a separate Staff Corps are obvious; they tend to diminish, and the advantages to become more manifest, in reflection. Here I must confess that, for my own part, I have hitherto viewed with disfavour anything which might widen the gulf between the Staff and the regimental soldier, having seen so much of the troubles which arise under the present system. Thus when I originally referred to the old, if vague, suggestion for a Staff Corps, I had the half-formed thought that it would suffice to point out the drawbacks; it was only as I continued to think about it, and the possibility of utilizing it as a development of the university entry, that I began to change my view, becoming more impressed by its potential advantages. The ills are already inherent in the existing staff system; a higher extension of that system might lessen them while improving its value—on the principle of cure by 'the hair of the dog that bit him'.

Whatever the merits of these several suggestions for raising the level of military ability, it is well to realize that it will be a long time before their application can appreciably improve the situation. Even if any of them were adopted forthwith, many years would pass before the officers educated in such a fresh atmosphere would rise to the high places of the Army. During those years they would be affected by the successive layers of their seniors, and be passing on the effects to their juniors. Thus, if they rose to the top in forty years, it would be still too much to expect that in another forty years the atmosphere there would become as clear of traditional dust as their own had been when they left the university eighty years before. To gauge the implications of that time-lag is a check on optimism. Nor is it the only one. We may recognize the value of a university training as a means of broadening the mind, but we should avoid the mistake of overestimating the effect. If it raises a hope, it is by no means a guarantee of freedom from prejudice and the capacity to weigh questions impartially. An hour in some common-rooms would suffice to dispel such illusions. By contrast, some of the broadest minds have passed through the narrowest grooves. It is not uncommon to find less tolerance and less receptivity to new ideas in a man who has passed with the highest honours to the heights of the Civil Service or commerce than in a former schoolfellow who has barely scraped through Sandhurst. In the Army itself it is observable that the stoutest obstacle to progress is the *alpha minus*, cleverly orthodox, rather than the *beta plus*, more aware of his own limitations and so more ready to pause for reflection. The man is more than the system. The best system of education is no more than a help, although a bad one is a hindrance.

Thus, any of the suggested reforms that might be made in the education of officers are, at the most, only hopeful forms of treatment; they are not a solution of the problem —of developing adequate adaptability to the conditions of future warfare. This turns on the simple yet fundamental question of *attitude*. To cope with the problems of modern war we need, above all, to see them clearly and analyse them scientifically. This requires freedom from prejudice combined with the power of discernment and with a sense of proportion. Only through the capacity to see all relevant factors, to weigh them fairly, and to place them in relation to each other, can we hope to reach an accurately balanced judgment. Discernment may be primarily a gift; and a sense of proportion, too. But their development can be assisted by freedom from prejudice, which largely rests with the individual to achieve—and within his power to achieve it. Or at least to approach it. The way of approach is simple, if not easy—requiring, above all, constant self-criticism and care for precise statement.

It is easier, however, to find an index of progress, and consequently of fitness to bear the responsibility of exercising judgment. If a man reads or hears a criticism of anything in which he has an interest, watch whether his first question is as to its fairness and truth. If he reacts to any such criticism with strong emotion; if he bases his complaint on the ground that it is not in 'good taste', or that it will have a bad effect—in short, if he shows concern with any question except 'Is it true?' he thereby reveals that his own attitude is unscientific. Likewise if in his turn he judges an idea not on its merits but with reference to the author of it; if he criticizes it as 'heresy'; if he argues that authority must be right because it is authority; if he takes a particu-

The Higher Education of Officers

lar criticism as a general depreciation; if he confuses opinion with facts; if he claims that any expression of opinion
is 'unquestionable'; if he declares that something will
'never' come about, or is 'certain' that any view is right.
The path of truth is paved with critical doubt, and lighted
by the spirit of objective enquiry. To view any question
subjectively is self-blinding. There is nothing more astound-
ing, if amusing, than the way many a soldier, for example,
in his heated denunciation of some criticism of soldiers'
limitations, will prove out of his own mouth that it is at
least correct in his own case. So, to end on a lighter note,
I would suggest to my readers that they may learn something by watching how various soldiers, and themselves if
soldiers, react to this discussion of the problem of developing the scientific approach to military problems. And if
they are not soldiers, they may gain additional profit by
observing their own and their fellows' reaction to a critical
examination of their own profession.

PART III: MEASURES

N

CHAPTER XV

Combined Defence

The reactions of the services upon each other have been immeasurably increased by the advent of air power. So long as there were two services, one operating on land, the other on sea, the line of demarcation between their functions was comparatively simple to draw. It was only the edges that overlapped, and combination there was largely a matter of detail. Even so, our history offers all too many examples of friction on the border. In the highest sphere, that of grand strategy, there was certainly room for dispute over the respective allotments of money to Navy and Army; but in most countries geography tended to provide the answer to the problem. With some, naval interests were clearly paramount; with others, land defence was no less so. It is true that with some Continental powers, at certain periods in their history, desire for overseas expansion dictated a change of military proportions which frequently produced a division of effort. Those efforts have at least bequeathed a lesson, in the failure, as often through financial strain as through actual defeat, of the powers that have spent their substance in simultaneous pursuit of superiority on land and sea.

Combined Defence

It is a lesson that we might ponder to-day, the more so since we have profited in the past from others' disregard of it. If the experience has not lost its meaning, this is certainly more difficult to translate now that two have become three, by the addition of the air. The complications are more apparent than the solution. The danger is that complexity may lead to mere compromise—to an equalitarian distribution of effort and outlay instead of a necessary reconciliation of functions in the light of a guiding principle. The longer that the issue is postponed, the more uneasiness will grow as to whether we have the best insurance policy for our needs and for the premium we are paying. While recognizing the difficulties and drawbacks to any fusion of the Service Departments, the public may reasonably hope for further progress in co-ordination. And it will more readily accept the financial burden placed upon it if the proportions of our defence system are adjusted on a true strategic basis, and not merely perpetuating the somewhat haphazard reconstruction of the forces in the immediate post-war years. If the structure of our defence is to bear proof of architecture, a spirit of cooperation will not suffice; there must be a controlling mind. In the Services themselves there has been a marked evolution of opinion on this subject during the last few years. A Ministry of Defence may be the eventual end, but it is likely to come at the end—of a gradual process. It should come as the roof on a structure for which we have yet to collect the material—minds that can consider the problem of defence as a whole, unaffected by sectional ties of feeling and service. Meantime we should progressively strengthen the organs that we already possess. The recent publication of Lord Esher's Journals and Letters has been a reminder that, when the Committee of Imperial Defence was originally formed it had a nucleus of permanent expert members, and that the idea was then mooted of converting this body into 'a *joint* Imperial General Staff'. What was desirable a quarter of a century ago, when there were only two services, essentially different, is surely more urgent now that there are three, and with functions that are no longer separable.

Moreover, the outlay on defence needs to be considered as a whole from the point of view of its purpose. Upon this the question of 'adequacy' turns. Those who pin their faith for security to a policy of isolation based upon a self-sufficiency in armaments are apt to twist the facts of the situation into line with their argument. So, too, are the separate-minded advocates of a stronger navy, a stronger army, or a stronger air force. If these types of force can no longer be considered apart, neither can the general problem of defence be separated from the strategic conditions of the time, and of this country. Nor can we disregard the financial basis. It would be comforting to many of us if we could once again possess through the Navy the measure of security that we enjoyed of old. But even if the factor of cost alone did not remove it beyond the bounds of possibility, the intervention of air power would. It would be comforting if we could develop an air force strong enough to forbid any serious attack on this country, but even if the cost were feasible, the technical conditions promise no such complete guarantee, while it would not suffice to protect our supplies upon the oceans. The same line of reasoning applies to those who support the claims of the army to increased outlay without due regard to the other services. To attain a level of armament in all three spheres which would give us back our old security is impossible, technically or financially. Contemplation of these hard facts drives us, willy-nilly, towards admitting the wisdom of the policy of collective security. The question that remains is whether we can approach more nearly to 'an adequate standard of defence' and capacity to play our part in a collective system, out of the money we can afford—through a distribution of expenditure and service functions which may be more scientifically adjusted to the basic conditions of modern defence. This is, above all, a question of proportion—of classifying the risks and the needs in order of importance, and arranging expenditure accordingly.

To grasp our need of an 'adequate standard of defence' is easier than to gauge our actual needs. The solution depends on the problem. And this, unfortunately, is complicated by factors beyond any one nation's control—the scale and type of armament that others adopt, the technical development of weapons, the consequent changes in the conditions of warfare, and the reaction of these upon our permanent geographical conditions. Unless we have first taken the measure of these changes, more money may be money wasted. Combined with the general desire to develop our defences there has been widespread anxiety lest the immense additional expenditure now approved may fail of its purpose through faulty distribution. That anxiety is shared by many members of the Services. In face of past experience and present doubts something more than a bald official assurance is needed to convince the public that their money will be laid out on a forethoughtful plan instead of by mere compromise. To satisfy conflicting interests is not the equivalent of putting our defences in a satisfactory state. No worse delusion could be fostered. Merely to enlarge our 'building' without due attention to the new stresses and strains that it may have to bear is a policy of jerrybuilding. It is the conditions that should determine the design, and design which should govern expansion. The first step towards a satisfactory solution is a scientific analysis of the problem.

This brings us face to face with the question whether we have the means of conducting such an analysis and correlating its results. If we could clearly separate the spheres of the three Services, and separate these from non-military factors, it is conceivable that each might be able to calculate the effect, on its own powers, of changes in its own conditions. But the greatest of all modern changes is the growing inseparability of the three spheres: air power alone has ensured this, giving a new enlargement to the old service motto '*tria juncta in uno*'. The more that each sphere reacts on the others the more difficult it becomes for each service to gauge the probable effect of new elements, especially external elements, on its own problems. In the very nature of things there will be a tendency to put the maximum discount on the potential effect of the intruding elements and to adopt a maximum estimate of their own. Centuries of experience have shown that the fighting services in any country are instinctively conservative; there is no cause for surprise here if one remembers how much they depend on tradition, and the sentiment that springs from tradition, to sustain their spirit under stress. If that instinct has so often delayed their adoption of new means necessary to their own salvation, it is likely to operate more strongly in assessing those which tend to their own diminution. It would be too much to assume that the infusion of scientific instruments has suddenly made a complete breach with the past and produced a scientific habit of thought. Underlying any habit of thought, moreover, there is human nature. Men are more ready to sacrifice their lives than their livelihood: and to sacrifice their own importance often comes hardest of all. Here one is reminded of a pre-war episode when the adoption of the aeroplane was urged upon certain leading soldiers after M. Bleriot's early success. A natural doubt of its practicability was expressed: but still more natural was the subsequent remark, in accents of repugnance, that if it were to fulfil the inventor's expectations it would ruin the cavalry's function, and thereby end a great tradition. The narrower the orbit the more strongly do such instinctive forces work, holding back a newer generation who, if less in subjection, would take a broader view. Departmentalism tends to thought-tight compartments. For which reason any scheme of reform towards greater co-ordination, must take account of human nature, and have as its first aim to free the individual from departmental limitations.

Here is the shoal upon which our statesmanship of defence has run aground. The post-war calm delayed recognition of the danger that if a storm should arise the ship might break up. In detail, improvements were made in the working arrangements of the Committee of Imperial Defence. But in the means to achieve a scientifically calculated redistribution of our forces it was wanting. As a step in this direction a Chiefs of Staff sub-committee was created, so that instead of having to reconcile the separate opinions of the technical heads of the three Services, Ministers might receive their pooled advice. This sub-committee was mystically defined as being 'the Chief of a War Staff in commission'—a trinitarian notion which demanded more than human qualities for its fulfilment. It seemed to expect that at their occasional meetings these men, normally occupied with the cares of the Service in which they had been bred, would cease to be three and

Combined Defence

become one. It is no secret that the early history of that Sub-Committee was more productive of storms than of progress in co-ordination. Of later years there was an improvement on the surface. But scientific truth is not to be found on the surface. The members of the Sub-Committee seemed to have learnt the political habit of give and take, and had thereby been able to reach a measure of agreement. That was something gained. But it was a gain that might lead to greater loss when tested by the reality of war, which passes judgment with inhuman infallibility on what is obsolete.

The growing public anxiety was expressed in a series of leading articles, and a large accompanying correspondence, in *The Times* during the winter of 1935-36. This helped to bring the issue to a head. The demand for new steps towards the co-ordination of defence developed rapidly and was strongly pressed in Parliamentary debates.

In the first of those leading articles the question was posed: 'What is the best way to tackle this problem of co-ordination, so that calculation shall supersede compromise? There is no doubt that the advocates of a conjoint Ministry of Defence have grown immensely during recent years; most significantly, among the younger members of the Services. Dissatisfaction with the present palliatives is accentuated by knowledge of the friction that has continued beneath the surface, and by perception of the growing danger to which we are exposed by new technical developments. Ideas of possible organization range from a super-Ministry which should completely absorb the three existing departments to a small Ministry, superimposed, which should guide the Government in formulating a common policy and apportioning expenditure between the services. The larger proposal has certain theoretical attractions, but its practical drawbacks become manifest as the problem is more closely studied: apart from the immense task of reconstruction that would be involved it is well to remember that the efficiency of an organization is often in inverse ratio to its size. And there would be a real danger that the energies of the man at the head, and also of his asistants, would be so absorbed in grappling with the administrative complexities of the new organization that the purpose of its creation would be stifled. The urgent need in defence matters is not for more administrative activity, but for more thought—towards eliminating waste of force, waste of money, and obsolete methods.

'It is here that the more modest organization would be of inestimable value, having at its head a man who was largely free from administrative cares. He would need a joint staff drawn from the three Services and permanently at work on the broader problems of defence. Such a staff would no longer be difficult to find, since now for nearly a decade a number of picked officers from each of the fighting Services, as well as from the Civil Service, have yearly passed through the Imperial Defence College. But there is one essential condition, based on the human factor—that those appointed to this joint staff should henceforth be no longer dependent on their Services for promotion. That dependence, even more than intermittent attendance, is the root fault of the present joint committee. It is more than we expect of human nature that an officer should reach conclusions disadvantageous to his own particular Service if there is a likelihood that he may be subsequently penalized for taking the broader view. Here, indeed, is the crux of the problem of co-ordination. Once such a joint staff was created, its senior representative might take part in the meetings of the three Chiefs of the Staff as an additional, and more impartial, member. But since later training may not entirely counteract early association with a particular Service, it would seem desirable that the Committee should have as its chairman, and the joint staff as its head, a civilian. This must be a man who could devote his time to studying the problems of defence: and it would be a great asset if he was a man who had previously been a student of war in the broader sense. Whether he should himself be a Minister is a moot point. If a Minister he would, while freed from departmental responsibilities, have the advantage of being able to explain the proposed lines of defence policy in Cabinet discussion and in Parliamentary debates. On the other hand, it might not be easy for him to avoid impinging on the provinces of the Prime Minister and the three Service Ministers. Here again, it is wise not to overlook human nature. He would also be liable to disappear, owing to a change of Government, just when engaged in unravelling some tangled problem. And there would always be the danger that the post might be used to accommodate some Minister who did not fit elsewhere yet could not be discarded for political reasons. Moreover, the type of man who would be a good head for such a defence policy organ might not be equally suitable as a member of the Cabinet or as a Parliamentary spokesman. The balance would seem to incline in favour of appointing a man who was not, or at least would cease to be, an active politician: to serve for a definite term of years. But whatever doubt may still remain on this question, there can no longer be any doubt, in view of past experience and present problems, of the need for such a higher organ of defence with a whole-time chairman. Under its auspices, moreover, further combined organs might be developed. There would certainly seem scope for a joint Intelligence department: the present separate arrangements produce overlapping that is often inconvenient while leaving gaps in each Service's information that are potentially dangerous. Waste of effort is thus apt to be combined with want of knowledge—a false combination.'

The case for a change in the prevailing system was promptly supported by those who were able to speak with special authority. The step forward which led to the creation of a Sub-Committee of the Chiefs of Staff in 1923 had been taken upon the recommendation of the investigating Committee presided over by Lord Salisbury. Twelve years had passed and now, with added experience, Lord Salisbury pointed out where that step fell short of securing an impartial decision and scientific solution. Referring to the Committee of Imperial Defence, he declared: 'Where it breaks down is at the top.' Not merely impartiality but a thorough grip of the subject was needed in the chairman of such a committee. Because of its heterogeneous composition and the intricacy of the questions with which it had to deal, it was too much to expect that the Prime Minister could successfully add it to his other burdens. The reality, as Lord Salisbury pointed out, was that 'instead of the business of the Committee in his hands being a whole-time job it has only received the crumbs which the overwhelming other obligations of a Prime Minister can give it.' Lord Trenchard, who had served six and a half years on the Chiefs of Staff Sub-Committee, contributed the fact that only 'on rare occasions' were its meetings presided over by a Minister: it thus fell to one of the Service Chiefs to assume the invidious task of chairmanship while remaining the spokesman of his own case. 'I fear, that under pressure of work and other causes, unanimity has been too often reached by tacit agreement to exclude vital differences of opinion, to avoid issues on which such differences might arise, and to restrict the scope of the Committee's reports to matters on which agreement can be reached (as you suggest) by "give and take".' This candid admission lent a peculiar touch of irony to Lord Hailsham's claim, in the House of Lords the previous May, that the existing system had the advantage that the Government 'in almost every case gets a unanimous report from the three professional heads'. For it could hardly be of advantage to our security that vital issues should be thus shirked.

Two soldiers who had an intimate knowledge of the working of the sub-Committee, Lord Milne and Sir Ronald Charles, in a joint letter, strongly supported the case for a whole-time Minister of Defence. But they implied that he could manage without a combined staff, relying merely on the existing secretariat of the Committee of Imperial Defence. They also argued that 'the C.I.D. should formulate policy only; it is not within its province to dictate strategy, which is the responsibility of the staffs of the Service Ministries'—which prompted the reply that it was difficult to see how combined strategy could be produced by separate departments. Nevertheless, it was notable that their experience had brought these distinguished officers to see the need for a whole-time authority to reconcile any conflict of views between the Service chiefs over questions of defence policy.

The essential falsity of our existing position, in the sphere of defence, was already well known to those in touch with the services. There was recent experience here to provide a warning. The situation which arose in the Mediterranean a few months before had led numerous officers to see that organized plans were as essential as organized policy. When combined action is called for, and this will be normal in any major emergency, combined planning is necessary beforehand. Strategy, in the broad sense, cannot be left to the separate departments. This, indeed, had already been recognized by assembling a Joint Planning Committee to assist the Chiefs of the Staff Committee. But the results had not been sufficiently reassuring. They pointed to the need of a permanent 'plans' section as part of the new defence organ—not to supersede but to co-ordinate the work of the separate staffs. A comprehensive exploration of the different strategic problems that may arise, an assessment of their relative importance, and an estimate of the type of forces needed, is the proper foundation of any defence policy. Without a combined staff of adequate size, to study problems independently, a higher organ of defence was likely to forfeit much of its effectiveness.

While the conversion of public opinion to the necessity for a change may be traced to the palpable illogicality of the existing system, awareness of the facts had a no less marked effect within the services. More and more, their members had come to see, and to say, that efficiency of defence could only be attained through greater co-ordination. The extent of this conversion appeared the more notable when one took account of the very natural fear that such a change might adversely affect their own careers. Yet, significantly, it was rare now to find dissentients save among certain of the most senior members who, in any event, had only a few years to run. And even then, when seeking to discover reasonable arguments against the change, such as could be distinguished from instinctive objections were not easy to come upon. One or two, however, deserve mention. It was suggested that a civilian chairman would be seriously handicapped in thrashing out technical issues. But this argument seemed to over-estimate the degree of technicality which accompanies discussions on combined strategy—a sphere, moreover, into which many factors enter that are beyond the professional orbit of a soldier, sailor, or airman. But even if the difficulties were to be conceded, how was it possible to obtain the necessary impartiality in the chairman except by having one who was a civilian? Objection was also made to the idea of a permanent joint staff that it would set up a conflict of advice such as formerly prevailed in India between the Commander-in-Chief and the military member of Council. But this objection seemed to be based on a misunderstanding. For, as a further leader in *The Times* pointed out: 'the joint staff would not be an alternative source of advice to the trinity nominally embodied in the Chiefs of Staff Committee, but a means of helping the head of that Committee to reconcile any conflict in the views of the three separate services represented upon it. And the head of the joint staff would be the same person as the head of the committee. The joint staff would enable more scientific investigation of problems before the Chiefs of Staff Committee starts its discussion. It could also provide a superior means of gathering the data. For once such a joint staff is formed, further combined organs might be developed under its auspices.'

In another article late in January it was emphasized that: 'The measures actually required to secure an organic defence plan to which all the Services are contributory are neither grandiose nor elaborate. The step to be taken may not be the last step, but it should be a step in the right direction; one that will not have to be retraced. The guiding principle is "wholeness". To see the problem, and deal

with it, as a whole there must be freedom from sectional
cares and from sectional ties. It must be approached
without distraction of time and with detachment of view.
The more honest a man is the more he realizes his susceptibility to bias. Freedom from all bias is an ideal not easy
to attain, but we can go a long way towards it if we remove
the material ties which hinder a man in freeing himself from
it. So long as he has a reasoning mind, not unduly swayed
by sentiment, many a man can rise above the limits of his
sectional training if he is sure that he will not suffer for it.
And the more time he can devote to the broader issue the
more likely he is to see it broadly. Hence the foundation
of an effort to deal with defence as a whole must be the
formation of a combined staff. Its members must be free
from other cares during their service upon it, and they
must be assured that they will not be penalized for having
taken a broad view if they subsequently return to their
own Service. Those who have passed through the Imperial
Defence College in the past decade provide a field of recruitment for such a combined staff. That staff must have
a whole-time head, who will also be chairman of the Chiefs
of Staff Committee. These seems to be general agreement
that he should be a civilian, to ensure an impartiality
greater than could be expected, or at least would be conceded, to an officer hitherto connected with a single
Service. A broad view, a judicial mind, and a progressive
spirit are the combined qualifications to be looked for in
filling the post. Whole-time attention to the problem would
give such a man a better grasp of the basic qualities of each
of the Services than a man whose professional experience
is confined to one Service is likely to possess of the other
two. Enlightened by the detached studies made by his
staff, such a civilian head would be able to preside over

the discussions of the Chiefs of Staff, and reconcile their natural divergencies of opinion, more effectively than has been possible for a Prime Minister diverted by other calls and weighed down by a multitude of cares. If the ultimate decision would still rest with the Cabinet, the grounds of that decision would be far better analysed, clarified, and synthesized than ever in the past. To aid the process, this new organ should have the means to institute research and organize experiments: the cost would be small compared with the value and the ultimate economy.'

The pressure for improved machinery grew stronger with every week that passed, and at the end of February the Government announced that a Minister for the Co-ordination of Defence was to be appointed. He would deputize for the Prime Minister as Chairman of the Committee of Imperial Defence, and in supervising all its activities. He would preside at the meetings of the Chiefs of Staff Sub-Committee whenever he or they thought it was desirable. He would also—and this added a heavy burden to his responsibilities—be in supreme charge of the Emergency Supply organization and the Industrial Planning. At the same time the Joint Planning Committee of the three Services was to be increased by the addition of three permanent officers, graduates of the Imperial Defence College, and a whole-time secretary. Here was the nucleus of a joint staff—but a very small one in comparison with the scale of the problems that awaited exploration and solution. Also, its beginning was belated. This was made manifest in the Parliamentary debates which followed the fresh Government White Paper on Defence, and the new Estimates for 1936.

The Prime Minister dwelt at length on the reasons for rearmament, and on its industrial basis. But when he came to the organization of defence itself he did little to elucidate the ideas behind the rather vague outline of defence policy in the White Paper. He remarked that there had been criticism of it 'on the ground that it does not disclose our full plans'. But he merely added that it was necessary to 'keep the position flexible'. Flexibility is certainly desirable, and it is hardly to be expected that the Government should disclose, or fix, the plans in full detail. The White Paper indicated certain actual steps that were taken in each of the Services and also towards an organization. What it failed to make clear was whether there was a plan, even in a flexible state. And, if so, whether such a plan was related to actual problems and adjusted to new technical developments.

Mr. Baldwin spoke of the necessity of 'repairing deficiencies in each of the three Defence Forces'. The remark suggested a continuation of the habit of considering each separately instead of as a combined solution to a common problem. For deficiencies do not exist in a vacuum—they are necessarily related to a standard, and that standard to a problem. It is only by determining this that it is possible to estimate deficiencies. Owing to our geographical conditions, any major emergency we may have to meet presents a combined problem. This compels us to see how we can fit together the responsibilities of the three Services, and gauge how far the qualities of one may supplement the deficiencies of another.

There is more than a risk of wasted effort in building up our forces without clarifying our minds—as to how the different types of force react on each other, how they will fit the more obvious strategic problems, and whether a better fit can be obtained by a readjustment of proportions and duties. It is good to keep flexibility—but it was

Combined Defence

important that the Government should dispel any impression that they were merely perpetuating a fog.

In order to play our part in a system of collective security we have to be sure of our means of 'endurance', which depends at bottom on security of supplies. Food is the primary need, then raw materials. The public, which remembers the narrowness of our escape from the submarine danger, is aware that such a threat may be repeated in new and multiple forms. It wants some inkling of how the Government see a solution of this problem. It wants to be reassured that the Government have taken full account of the possibilities of interception—in relation to the geographical situation and to the technical means. Might the protection of the sea-routes be better fulfilled by a redistribution of the sea and air means of defence, so that the burden on each might be lightened? Also, how far could our dependence on food supplies from overseas be reduced by storage or development here?

Then come the problems of exerting pressure on an aggressor, in aid of our partners in any system of collective security. What is the best form in which our support could be given? This raises the question of whether we should contribute a field force or proportionately larger air support. Its answer depends on a number of factors, which demand careful evaluation. The public would have welcomed enlightenment as to whether the Government had reached any conclusions and what were their grounds. With such varied strategic problems to face, it would seem essential to classify them in proportion; then to determine what types of force suit each under present and near future conditions; then to see how far the several compounds can be blended into one general compound—and adjust the proportions of our forces accordingly.

Combined Defence

The cost involved in the programme which the Government have adopted is estimated as nearly £1,500,000,000 in five years—and this may be extended to march with foreign developments. It is a formidable demand. The nation will be ready to face it if convinced that the money is being well laid out, and that money is not being spent on types of defence that are of dubious value under modern conditions. But something more than a mere assurance will be needed to reassure the public. It would be a mistake to disregard the widespread uncertainty over the value of the different Services and arms. For years the public have been subjected to a bombardment of arguments concerning the effect of the newer means on the older—on 'bombs and battleships', on battle and blockade, on air attack and air defence, on gas and high explosives, and many similar questions. If these multiple controversies have done no more, they have disturbed the mind of the people and deepened their feeling that the methods of scientific enquiry have yet to be applied to the problems of defence. It would be vain to hope that this uneasiness would be stilled by burying discussion. Uneasiness is uncomfortable, but it is better than false confidence.

The experience of the last war, with its countless examples of misjudgment and obscurantism in high places, has left too deep a mark on the public mind to justify any expectation that an attitude of blind trust could be revived, even if it were desirable. Nowhere to-day is there anything approaching, for example, the unquestioning faith which the mass of the people reposed in the Navy before the war. Nor has post-war experience done much to strengthen the hope that the lesson has been taken to heart, or to cure the doubt of authority's capacity to look ahead and move with the times. The public memory is not so short that it forgets the deprecatory and even scornful attitude shown towards military mechanization only a few years ago, at a time when our pioneers had given us the lead in that field: it marks the contrast with the situation to-day when we are hastening to make up lost ground.

No large-scale programme can now be adopted without raising big questions of a broadly technical nature: and vital issues depend on their being satisfactorily answered. There are three general questions which stand out, each with a specific supplementary question of great importance. The first is how can we ensure the security of our supplies: its supplementary concerns the present and future value of battleships in the scheme of protection for the routes of supply. The second is how we can exert pressure on a hostile power: its supplementary concerns the value of a field force. The third is what combination of means, and what proportion between them, will yield the best value in proportion to the outlay: its supplementary concerns the value of the co-ordination arrangements for improving that combination and determining its proportions on a scientific basis.

On all these questions the Ministerial speakers were more successful in establishing the need for an increased outlay than in conveying an idea how it would be effective in attaining the object. When they came to the specific technical issues over which controversy has raged, they left—or rather failed to remove—the impression that the decision had taken form first and the arguments been polished up afterwards. Despite the tact and skill with which they handled their case, it seemed like 'a case' rather than the result of an objective inquiry. That impression was produced by the tendency to make their points without sufficient emphasis on the points that have been made in question of existing theory. Thus, when the Admiralty spokesman, Lord Stanley, came to the battleship question, he showed good promise by recognizing that beyond the long-standing critics of the battleship there was a great body of opinion which was 'honestly doubtful'. Yet his subsequent remarks became an argument against the critics rather than a weighing of the arguments for the help of honest doubt. He quoted from an account of the battle of Jutland a comment that, so long as the German capital ship was bottled up by the Allied capital ship Germany's naval forces were virtually impotent to do us harm, and declared: 'That shows only too clearly the value of battleships during the Great War.' If the verdict had been limited to the portion of the War preceding Jutland, it would have been more convincing. For we know only too well that the Germans thereafter turned their attention to an alternative means of naval action, and brought this country to the brink of defeat. Nine months after Jutland Jellicoe himself confessed that we had not 'anything approaching' command of the sea, saying: 'It is quite true that we are masters of the situation so far as surface ships are concerned, but . . . this will be quite useless if the enemy's submarines paralyse, as they do now, our lines of communication.' Even in the sphere of battle-fleet operations the new menace led the Admiralty to the conclusion that the battle-fleet ought not to venture into the southern half of the North Sea: it was an ironical reflection on the class-name of these 'Dreadnoughts'.

The menace may take a different form next time, but can we feel reasonably confident that the foresight will be more sure? In estimating the possible effect of flying craft, we should be careful not to risk flying in the face of history. There was too much 'complete confidence' on

Combined Defence

the part of the Admiralty spokesman, too sheer a declaration that all the critics of orthodoxy were 'entirely wrong' in all their ideas, to win the confidence of the great body of honest doubt. The real question, as Lord Stanley truly said, is not 'whether a bomb can sink a battleship' but whether new methods of warfare can prevent battleships from carrying out their traditional functions, and discount their utility. Yet his argument became concentrated on the narrower aspect, and only on parts of this. He emphasized that the battleship 'because of its size . . . can be divided into compartments by which the damage from explosion is localized'; but he did not remark that other compartments have to be flooded in order to bring the ship back to an even keel, nor evaluate the strategic loss caused by a return to dry-dock for repairs. Nor did he seem to have taken note of that weak spot which was epitomized by the former Director of Naval Construction, Sir Eustace Tennyson-d'Eyncourt, some years ago: 'The Achilles heel of all ships really is in the afterpart—the propellers, the shafting, and the rudder—and that I am afraid we shall always have with us.' Strategically, crippling may be as effective as sinking. Again, the assertion that 'defence always catches up with attack' overlooks the historical fact that it has often failed to catch up in time to save armies and navies, and the countries they are intended to protect, from defeat in the interval.

The time-factor in a more immediate form has an essential bearing on the second question, and its supplementary. In introducing the Army Estimates Mr. Duff Cooper made a sympathetic impression by his candid admission of defects and his welcoming air towards suggestions. But when he came to the question of having a field force he seemed to start with an assumption rather than with a question. He dwelt on the arguments in favour of it while in effect ignoring the main reasons for doubt. The first turns on the question whether any field force that we sent could arrive in time for the crucial opening phase of a war—which is generally expected by the Continental General Staffs to coincide with the opening days. The second turns on the question whether, once the initial surprise has passed, modern attack has a sufficient prospect of overcoming modern defence. Any forces we could send would be a trifling addition to those that a Continental country can provide for its own static defence; the potential value of ours is that, when modernly equipped, their longer training might enable them to play a part disproportionate to their size in a counter-offensive to eject an aggressor. But unless they can either arrive in time for the opening phase or have an adequate technical prospect of effective attack we ought to face the question whether our expenditure and our aid might not be better devoted to a larger air contribution.

Mr. Duff Cooper did not attempt to discuss these questions, but suggested that any Continental allies we might secure would not be content without the dispatch of a land force. That may be so. It is worth remembering Foch's answer of 1910 when Henry Wilson asked what was the minimum military aid that would satisfy France: 'A single private soldier; and we would take good care that he was killed.' Foch reckoned that this would suffice to draw the whole manhood of England into a Continental land struggle. The event proved him correct. But the experience raised a doubt of the practical wisdom of the course into which we were drawn. And reflection on the technical conditions of modern warfare deepens it. Today we have come to distrust the idea of embarking on

Combined Defence

mass warfare. Mr. Duff Cooper himself declared: 'The next war will be a war of machines, and men, save in so far as they serve to operate these machines, will be useless targets for the enemy.' Yet in another remark he seemed to invite a repetition of mass, and massacre, when he declared that our people 'will not be content to stand idly by and watch other countries fighting with their whole manhood'. A field force for the Continent may easily become the thin end of a 'mass' wedge. Here is another reason for weighing the question with care.

As with the battleship, doubt should not be confused with dissent. Many of those who have doubts of the battle-ship or of a field force would have been glad to have them dispelled. But for that they wanted better evidence that the Government had an open mind and was not wearing a made-up tie. They feel uneasy when departmental authority still shows the traits through which its judgment has gone wrong in the past. This brings us to the third question, and its supplementary. Does the appointment of a Minister for Co-ordination, without an independent staff, promise to provide the means of examining such major questions, and of determining any necessary change of roles and proportions between the services?

Early in the summer Sir Thomas Inskip, who had been appointed to this responsible post, gave an account of his activities during his first two months in office. He covered much ground, although he skipped over some of the most awkward places in a way that did not altogether satisfy the House—when the veil of secrecy is donned it is difficult to tell if the wearer's eyes are on the ground or in the air. Nevertheless, his discourse helped to give Parliament a fuller idea of the amplitude of our defence problems, especially in the sphere of supply, while he fostered hopes that the necessary measures were being considered to deal with them. Most welcome of all was the announcement that an investigation of 'the all-important question of food in war-time' had been undertaken, and that a sub-committee had been appointed 'to make the necessary arrangements for the food supply of the civil population'. For here is the basic condition on which the whole of our war-effort depends, and round which all strategic and munition questions revolve. A prime supplementary is the protection of merchant shipping, and it was encouraging to hear that this was now receiving attention: the ramifications of this problem are so immense, however, that it is well to realize the distance that may lie, and seem to grow, between investigation and solution.

Many of these defence problems cannot be dealt with, or even examined, as if they formed a compartment. Planning would certainly be simpler if only it could be treated like a card-index. Instead, it is like building a house of cards, in which, if one be unbalanced, the whole may collapse. Sir Thomas Inskip devoted the longest and most informative part of his account to a survey of the problems of war material supply, and it threw a revealing light on their interdependent nature. Yet these are simple compared with the strategic problems, which comprise so many uncertain elements, even in their technical aspect. Moreover, the details of the supply situation served to suggest how great a burden this lays on the responsible Minister and, consequently, how difficult it must be for him to find the time necessary for covering the still more complicated field of the fighting services. Because of its complexities, too, it would be hardly enough to remain content with covering the field. There may be places where the Service Chiefs find it difficult to reconcile their respective views, and the ability of the Co-ordinating Minister to assist them in achieving something better than a compromise solution will depend on his having the time to explore for himself the roots of the problem. It is possible, too—more than possible if history has any meaning—that the joint view may be out of joint with the truth. Here the Co-ordinating Minister may be the only check on a downfall.

We should never lose sight of the fact that the expansion of forces is not an end in itself, even within the military sphere. And there is need of a better assurance that the great issues of strategic policy are adequately grasped. If there is a doubt here, it has been fostered by a tendency on the part of ministers to talk as if strategy were outside their province. For this there is less justification than ever under the new conditions of war. There was no stouter upholder of the soldier's voice in strategy than Field-Marshal Sir William Robertson, yet his matured conclusion was that 'the real headquarters of armies in these days are to be found . . . at the seat of Government at home, and plans of campaign are, and must be, now analysed and criticized by civilian Ministers at the Council Table in a way quite unknown a few decades ago.'

Modestly as Sir Thomas Inskip has referred to his own powers, innate and conferred, he has been inclined to sound a note on behalf of others which was too assured to be reassuring—after the experience of the past century. Or even the past year. Thus, in regard to the Mediterranean emergency he spoke of 'the dispositions that were made with so sure a touch, and with such a remarkable anticipation of the course of events'. It was a statement that might well excite ironical comment in the Services, for it was certainly in remarkable contrast to the impression gathered by anyone in touch with them the previous autumn. To a considerable extent the troubles that arose were due to the scarcity of resources, and it is right to sympathize with those who, in Sir Thomas Inskip's phrase, had 'to make bricks without straw'. But it did not appear that some of the steps which were then and thereafter taken in haste had been adequately thought out beforehand. And thinking does not depend on a large increase in the Estimates.

In a previous speech Sir Thomas Inskip sounded a particularly true and important note when he made a plea for 'just a little quiet thinking'. The phrase has a wide application. Exception can only be taken to it on the score that what is required in regard to the whole question of defence to-day is a lot of quiet thinking. There is no cause to complain of the mental activity of the Service departments now: to use a phrase which seems to be becoming popular in them, they are 'starting hares' in all directions. The hurry and hubbub of the chase, however, are not conducive to quiet and deep reflection. It is not uncommon to hear officers complain that they are working to catch up time on schemes and plans which could, and should, have been worked out in the years of calm. The danger under these conditions is that while the plans may be sound in themselves they may be built on a shaky foundation—of false premises.

The basic problems of modern war are so big as to require years of study and the opportunity for such study. It is often overlooked that the different Service Departments provide few, if any, posts where study is possible in freedom from executive duties. Their staffs are kept busy with a multitude of immediate cares. Contrary to the popular idea, they work hard—too hard for study outside their direct sphere of responsibility. These Depart-

Combined Defence

ments have nothing that can be truly described as a 'thinking section', devoted to the comprehensive exploration of war, its conditions and developments with a view to a scientifically gauged forecast of the future. The need has been often urged, but never met. Even if it had been fulfilled, it would have been difficult to avoid a sectional view. The limitations of that view are being gradually overcome through the activities of the Chiefs of Staff Committee and the enlarged Joint Planning Committee, and since the summer a Joint Intelligence Committee has been added. But it is no disparagement of the good work now being done by those Committees to recognize that they can hardly fulfil such a far-thinking role. They have more than enough to consider in the abundance of immediate contingencies.

If the history of the last war has one outstanding lesson it is that the faults of execution, though not few, were small in effect compared with the faults of conception. These arose from a defective 'appreciation' of the problem. If there is to be a reasonable prospect of a better appreciation another time, when the problem will be even more complex, it is essential to provide the means. The services have their teaching colleges; they need a research foundation, recruited on the widest possible basis. Under the Minister for the Co-ordination of Defence there are to-day a number of busy working committees, but as yet no 'quiet thinking' detachment. Such reflection requires time, but there may still be time, if more be not lost.

CHAPTER XVI

Reflections on Defence

There is a fundamental truth in the statement that 'defence depends on foreign policy'—as the Leader of the Opposition pointed out in 1935 and the Prime Minister reiterated in 1936. There is further truth in the Prime Minister's qualification that it is not 'only our foreign policy that matters'; and that definition must be extended to embrace the 'foreign policies of all the other Great Powers'. But even this is not the whole truth. For if we exclude a policy of non-resistance, any security will depend on our judgment of technical factors as well as political factors. Foreign policy modifies and clarifies the problems of defence: it does not alter their nature.

To give a simple example—if all nations combined with the whole of their forces to take action against a single aggressor, their action would be unavailing if that solitary country found a technical means of cancelling out all their weapons. The actual situation is not likely to be so simple, but it is important not to overlook the military elements in the pursuit of political ideals. The value of our contribution to collective security depends on the effectiveness of our own security within that system, and this depends on a sound technical estimate. A country that does not contribute its share is an ineffective partner. A country that cannot stand the strain, because of some internal military flaw, is a defective partner—a weak 'prop' to any collective system. For this reason it is essential that we should carry out the most searching self-examination, in the light of modern developments.

It has been a national misfortune that in the past Parliamentary debates on defence have been diverted on to political issues, and that the broad technical problems which underlie any system of security have been too often ignored in the discussion of foreign policy.

'Adequacy'

The White Paper on Defence which inaugurated the Government's rearmament programme, after dwelling on 'the serious deficiencies' of 'our Defence Forces and defences', declared that unless these were repaired 'the country and the Empire would no longer possess an adequate standard of defence'. It did not, however, explain what was meant by 'adequate'. The use of such a term, without definition, suggested that the problem had received inadequate consideration.

To regain our old naval strength, relative to other fleets, would involve an immense outlay—and this would, almost for certain, have to be increased on account of the armament race that would thereby be stimulated. But, even supposing that we could stand the financial strain, we could not regain our old degree of real sea-power—owing to the changed conditions. We might be able to protect our ocean routes—given an adequate cruiser strength—

but could not rely on protecting the terminal ports, or the narrow sea approaches where those routes converge. Sea-power in the last war barely availed to guard our supplies against the menace of a handful of submarines, which were operating under most disadvantageous strategic conditions. To-day, the menace of the submarine is multiplied by those of shore-based aircraft and high-speed light craft (a line which several continental countries are actively developing). Estimated at the minimum, these new factors have seriously complicated the problem of safeguarding our supplies. Further, whatever doubt there may be as to the direct effect of air attack on ships, there can be little doubt that the new triple menace will have a serious indirect effect in cramping fleet and troop-ship movements—it is wise not to forget that submarine menace alone reduced the battle-fleet to a state of local strategic paralysis at certain stages of the last war.

When we turn from the Navy to the Army we are confronted with a much greater disparity relative to the armies of the other Great Powers. It may be possible to estimate the scale of forces that would be adequate to maintain order in the overseas territories, and to defend them against such forces as an enemy could bring across the sea or by long overland routes for an attack on them. But to gauge what would be 'adequate' for decisive participation in a continental struggle is beyond measurement. On the other hand, we have to reckon with the certainty that the greater our effort on land the more it will subtract from the maximum effort at sea and in the air—because, even if manufacturing resources were unlimited, a similarly increasing proportion of the sea and air forces would be absorbed in escorting, guarding, and assisting the operations of the army abroad.

Reflections on Defence

In the air, parity with neighbouring air forces would seem to be our definition of adequacy, and may be attainable. Yet the basic value of our strength is affected by several inherent handicaps. First, because of the fact that as a country to defend, this has the highest vulnerability of any—offering a more concentrated target and being more dependent on certain restricted arteries of supply. Then we have no continuous air routes; other air powers lie athwart our main lines of communication with the Empire. This fact offers a threat of interruption, and may hinder the rapid 'switching' in which lies one of the main strategic assets of air power. Thirdly, in air warfare, by contrast to land warfare, the defence is still inferior to the attack.

This survey may help us to measure the difficulties that surround the problem of 'an adequate standard of defence'. It also raises the question how far our system of defence suffers from the revival, in a new form, of the tendency among his opponents which Napoleon first exploited, and then ridiculed—that of 'trying to be strong everywhere'. There is a disquieting suggestion of the 'cordon system', with its weakness everywhere, in a defence policy that aims at attaining 'adequacy' in three defence forces.

Before committing ourselves to a rising scale of expenditure, with an indefinite end, ought we not to enquire whether we are getting the best economic value in terms of security from the forces as now organized? Here, on a higher plane, is the old question of quality and quantity.

Deficiency in quantity is largely a matter of comparison with the forces of other powers in the light of geographical conditions. It is easier to gauge correctly than a deficiency of quality: for although one can tell when particular weapons are wearing out or are surpassed by newer models, this is less important than the basic question whether the pattern and proportion of the defence forces as a whole is suited to the latest conditions of warfare.

National Vulnerability

A fundamental condition underlying the problems of defence is that security cannot be estimated purely in figures of armed strength. The strength of a country in war is not such a simple sum. There is reason in the French contention that any calculation of strength must take into account the resources of a country for war, as well as its forces. But even this sum, so difficult to work out, is too simple for truth. The measure of a nation's military strength depends on the measure of its vulnerability to attack no less than upon its forces and resources. This factor of 'vulnerability' has yet to be adequately appreciated, although it has grown immensely in importance under modern conditions, especially under pressure of air power. It affects all calculations of war, from the highest scale, of the comparative defence situation of countries, down to the effect with which particular weapons can be credited. The vulnerability of the target counts for at least as much as the power of the weapon—and possibly counts for more.

Vulnerability itself is a compound of factors. The relative vulnerability of a nation is affected not only by its geographical, but by its industrial, political, and even sociological conditions. The very industry that augments its strength for war may at the same time produce a counterbalancing degree of vulnerability. And the centralization of industry may counteract the growth of industry from a military point of view. Wise statesmanship would

Reflections on Defence

give as much attention to diminishing and dispersing the target offered to an enemy's forces as to developing its own forces. The preparedness of the people is no less important. As safeguards against air attack, for example, education and understanding count at least as much as concrete measure for the provision of shelters and masks.

To illustrate the effect of this condition, we may take the case of two imaginary countries. The first has, let us say, two thousand first-line aircraft but its industry is highly centralized, while its people have a high standard of living, and are largely dependent both for raw material and their food upon overseas supplies. The second country has only a thousand aircraft, but the targets that its territory offers are difficult of access or well dispersed. Then, of the two, the second might well prove the stronger in reality. Now, unhappily for us, our situation combines the disadvantages suffered by both these imaginary countries. By a great effort, at great expense, it is conceivable that we might rectify our adverse ratio of military force. Only in small degree, however, is there any remedy to our state of vulnerability. We cannot alter geography.

Anti-Aircraft Defence

The Territorial Army as a whole carries a greater responsibility than the citizen-force before the war, now that it is definitely the Second Line. But the men of the Territorial anti-aircraft units count for more than any other class of soldier, Regular or Territorial. They are the outposts of the First Line—both in the time and the nature of their role. For on them may largely depend the possibility of any field force being able to embark and the maintenance of the national activities upon which our war effort depends. And they must be ready for action earlier than any other part of the Army, before the normal processes of mobilization are under way.

These are factors which need to be realized by the public, and especially by the recruitable section. For instinct, reinforced by the military tradition, tends to associate soldiership with physical movement and thus lends most attraction to the arms of the service which move fastest and farthest. But reason, developing a sense of proportion, should make clear the outstanding importance of the duty which the Territorial anti-aircraft artillery and searchlight units undertake.

To emphasize this by no means implies an unreserved faith in the power of guns to defeat hostile air attack. Thanks to the development of new instruments, such as the Vickers Predictor, anti-aircraft gunnery attains results in practice which far surpass the experience of the last war. But it has to be remembered that the benefits wrought by these automatic means of calculation depend to a large extent on the aircraft maintaining its course, height and speed—as the target normally does in practice. Under war conditions, when the aircraft's first aim will be to avoid offering a target, and where the anti-aircraft personnel will themselves suffer tensions and hindrances that are not felt in peace-training, it would be rash to count on more than a fraction of the present percentage of hits. Moreover, the ever-increasing speed of aircraft and the development of new modes of attack complicate the technical problem to an extent which cannot be gauged.

To weigh the difficulties and avoid false confidence is not to discount the value of anti-aircraft guns and units. Rather is it an argument for hastening their development, and multiplying them. A doubling of numbers would promise more than a doubling of hits, and much more than a doubling of deterrent effect. As with aircraft themselves, the influence of anti-aircraft armament may be even more moral than material. And it is none the less important in consequence. If it was true in Napoleon's day that the moral was to the material as three to one, a study of modern war conditions suggests that the ratio now may be at least six to one. The moral effect of anti-aircraft guns works two ways: first, by the nerve-strain and disturbance it causes to the enemy pilots; second, by the comfort it brings to the population of the area which is threatened by air attack. One of my strongest impressions of the war is the difference of tone in certain districts before and after anti-aircraft guns were provided, even though these guns were not equipped with instruments that promised more than a fluke-chance of hitting the attackers overhead. Until a few guns were sent there were serious signs of a moral breakdown. The feeling of being able to hit back is an invaluable relief from tension. This is likely to apply more than ever to the critical opening days of a future war. And the chances of being able to hit back with effect seem, on the whole, to be improving—in the light of such actual experience as the recent Abyssinian and Spanish wars have yielded.

Totalitarian War

It is manifest that many soldiers are contemplating a vast expansion of the Army and its fulfilment by conscription, in the event of another war. That is a natural view on their part, although there is cause for doubt whether the technical trend of modern warfare as a whole is compatible with the effective use of large numbers. But, apart from this issue, they naturally desire the most powerful Army that can be provided by the country.

It is the statesman's responsibility to take both a wider and a longer view. He has to determine how far the maximum effort in one sphere can be reconciled with the needs of other spheres. He has also to look beyond the military victory, and to ensure that the steps taken for this purpose do not overstrain the fabric of the nation nor damage its future—so far as a wise economy of effort can avoid these risks.

The true aim of a nation in war is to quench the enemy nation's will to war with the least possible material and spiritual loss to itself. That is a modification, which has hitherto proved practical in our own history, of the Clausewitzian dogma of 'absolute' war. It would seem, however, that some ministers and their advisers believe it to be no longer feasible. The basis of such a departure from our historic practice deserves a fuller explanation than a mere assertion, or a single haphazard lapse, provides. The Minister for Defence dismissed our centuries-old tradition rather casually when he remarked in a debate on defence: 'There have been occasions when our contributions to some alliance have been defined as so many men or so much in subsidy, but on these occasions, if the war was lost and the interest involved was lost, there was no blow at the heart of England.' It is difficult to see how such an assertion can be applied to the struggle with Napoleon. It is refuted by the knowledge we possess of Napoleon's dominant aim as well as his plans for the invasion of England. So flimsy a historical argument arouses a doubt whether the case for accepting our commitment to totalitarian warfare as inevitable has received adequate reflection, and whether the other reasons are better founded.

For centuries Britain successfully conducted her wars on a limited basis, on land at least, whereas all her adversaries who pursued an unlimited policy ruined themselves. Experience showed that to seek predominance both on land and sea overstrained the Power which attempted it. How much more probable is such a consequence when the effort has to be spread over land, sea, and air. True concentration and economy of force lies in conserving effort where we can.

If we drifted into copying Continental folly in the last war, we should be chary of consecrating this lapse as a permanent basis of our policy. The older British tradition represents a theory proved by three centuries of practice. With it, too, is linked the British tradition of individual freedom, our most precious heritage, which will be immediately endangered if we accept the new foreign theory of totalitarian preparation for war. It would be the supreme irony of our history if we sacrificed this freedom in the process of preparing to defend it. It would be like committing suicide to escape a fear.

The Time Factor

In the renovation of our defences we have to catch up time in travelling a distance which other countries have already covered, and while they are still travelling on. In some ways, especially in the provision of the most modern equipment, there may be advantages in a late start. No country can afford to re-equip its forces on a large scale every year or two, so that when a process of re-equipment is complete the forces of that country are likely to have a qualitative advantage over those of countries which carried out their programmes when design was less advanced. But, as in the Derby, the timing of such a 'burst' is difficult, and, unlike the Derby, the post is movable. This condition increases the disadvantages of a country like ours, which is unlikely to choose the occasion for forcing the issue in an armed test. It is a matter of general recognition now that time was lost in repairing the deficiencies of our defences. That is a fact for which there was much excuse, and some wisdom—at least in the sphere of executive measures, as distinct from preparatory study. Even so, it would be hard to maintain, on the basis of recorded utterances, that Ministers made the deficiencies of our equipment, and the obsolescence of what we had, clear to the public until 1935. Or that they had taken full account of it themselves.

There is now an inescapable responsibility for ensuring that no further time be lost. This requires something more than an energetic execution of the steps already decided upon. It demands foresight—and the development now of such organs as are likely to be needed if an emergency should arise in the future. The organs should be mature before the growth of the elements which they have to organize; otherwise the process of absorption will outstrip the power of digestion, as in 1914. In some respects there are disquieting symptoms. We see the renovation and expansion of our defences in full course while their new means of co-ordination are only beginning to work. Why could not the organ have been developed earlier? The need has been urged for years: its admission was certainly belated. We were told of the inquiry into the battleship's powers of resisting bombs, and that the critics as well as the advocates were heard, yet it followed the initial steps of laying down the battleships. Surely it would have been better to hold such an inquiry at an earlier stage? These thoughts are bound to check a ready satisfaction with the improvements that have now been made. In Parliament various critics have urged the appointment of a Minister of Supply, a development towards which general opinion is moving fast. The scale of the task is so immense as to imply the need of whole-time attention. Yet the arguments might equally, and perhaps even better, have been based on the importance of allowing the Minister for the Co-ordination of Defence to devote his time to the co-ordination of the defence forces, and the study of their interlocked problems. So great is the complexity of those problems, so uncertain are many of their elements, so rapid is their development under modern conditions, that their study and treatment are more than a full-time occupation for the ablest of minds.

The time factor, in a fuller sense, governs the disposition of our naval forces; underlies the question whether we should prepare the dispatch of a field force to the Continent at the expense of other alternatives; dominates every calculation as to the effect of air power on land and sea forces, and on their bases of action. For thousands of years, since war began, it has been waged in 'slow time' —on land, at walking pace. An acceleration of pace began last century, with the development of the railway and the steamship. It became marked in the last war, when the motor was added, yet the misunderstanding of its meaning and the misapplication of its qualities helped to produce the paradoxical situation that mobility in particular elements had issue in a state of general immobility. During that war aircraft were only in infancy; since then they have

Reflections on Defence

multiplied in quantity, range, and speed. There is reason
to ask whether we have yet grasped the many-sided effect
on war in general when the operations of war are carried
out, on different yet conjoint planes, at speeds that vary
from three miles an hour to three hundred miles an hour.
Time and space, the basic elements in more strategic problems, have now become disturbingly variable. Any prospect of gauging the effect of such variables demands a co-
ordination of research and thought far more than anything yet attempted. Beside these problems that of material
supply is a simple matter. Moreover, while time can be
saved in the manufacture of material by the application
of more energy, the new problems of strategy may not
be solved by accelerated thinking. Time is needed for
the thought that is necessary. The only safe way of ensuring it is to increase the opportunity—by freeing those
who have to do the thinking on this subject from extraneous
cares, and by developing a real organ of thought without
further delay.

CHAPTER XVII

The Changing Army

The past two years have been marked by some definite steps towards the modernization of the Army. Hitherto the post-war period had seen much activity of ideas—there is abundant evidence that British military thought has for the first time commanded the attention of, and blazed the trail for, the armies of the world. That development of ideas produced in turn a growth of practical experiments in mechanization, tactics, and organization. But the experiments had less consistency and tenacity than the ideas— sometimes they were ill-planned; sometimes discontinued because of some contrary current, and then renewed after a needless loss of time and experience. Meantime the Army as a whole went on almost unchanged—in a pattern that might serve for Imperial policing—with some improvized help from motor transport—but became ever less suited to the conditions of modern warfare. So long as money was lacking, and no foreign danger was on the immediate horizon, the authorities preferred to postpone modernization in order to keep intact the number of men and of units. They might have reorganized the Army on a smaller scale and newer pattern; but this alternative course was hindered by the system of financial control, by the Cardwell system, by mistrust of what the 'politicians' might do with money thus saved for re-equipment, and by a natural reluctance to embark on changes of uncertain issue. On the existing scale of units, the margin of money available for new equipment was inevitably small. Experiments continued, but no serious attempt to apply their results was feasible until an increase in the total money became likely.

That change of prospect took place in 1934. The sum available for 'warlike stores' had declined from £2,250,000 in 1925 to less than £1,500,000 in 1930, then returning by degrees to its old but still inadequate level. For 1935 it was doubled—being raised to £4,500,000 (out of total estimates of £43,500,000). Although nearly half of this had to be devoted to the replenishment of ammunition reserves, the balance enabled considerable progress to be made in providing units with mechanized transport and other up-to-date equipment. And this in turn helped the Army to derive more practical value from its tactical and structural experiments. The most important one introduced in 1935 was the trial of a new infantry organization. The 6th Infantry Brigade at Aldershot was remodelled to consist of one mechanized machine-gun battalion and three rifle battalions, which thereby became more handy in action while being augmented in power through having a light machine-gun in every section—or fifty-two in all. The man-power of the battalion was to be somewhat reduced, if not as much as the requirements of mobility and the potentialities of the new armament suggested. The transport was entirely mechanized; not a horse was left in the brigade, the officers' chargers being replaced by light cars. The trials of the brigade proved very instructive, and paved the way for a general infantry reorganization.

The Changing Army

But the small tractors used in this brigade were surpassed in several respects, not least in cheapness, by the four-wheeled 15-cwt. Morris trucks with oversize tyres which were issued later in the year to the 5th Infantry Brigade and other units. Experiments with the armoured machine-gun carrier were revived, and the 7th Infantry Brigade on Salisbury Plain was used for this purpose. They afforded convincing evidence of its value, and the general adoption of this most useful auxiliary is expected when an improved machine has been developed. As a light machine-gun the Czechoslovakian 'Bren' was adopted, and arrangements made for its production here, to supersede the war-time Lewis gun. The Army also heard that it was, at last, to be equipped with anti-tank guns: two types were adopted— one a 'hand gun' and the other a heavier weapon, but both have a penetrative power much higher than those formerly tried. With the mechanization of the infantry mortars, the task of giving close support to the infantry was handed over to this weapon, in place of the light howitzer. At the same time, the artillery support, and its fluidity, were increased by the conversion of the 'light' (formerly 'pack') artillery brigades into additional mechanized field brigades. The cavalry were also the subject of an experiment in mechanization, a squadron of the 3rd Hussars having their horses replaced by a new type of light motor vehicle, capable of travelling across country, and from which the men could jump out instantly.

The progress of the Army was thus mainly directed towards improving the general mobility of the older arms —in contrast to the latest trend abroad, where efforts were being made to create a number of 'mechanized' divisions in the full sense, basically composed of armoured fighting vehicles. In the British Army the one Tank

Brigade continued in existence, but was not yet completely equipped with up-to-date light tanks and had no
modern medium tanks. During its brigade training in
August it gave evidence of fresh progress in wireless control and in the art of moving in a state of controlled dispersion; and it was learning to free itself from the fetters
of transport. During September it was split up and used to
represent the battalions of infantry tanks, one to each
division, which were now projected. This was a development upon which opinion was somewhat divided and uncertain, although there was general agreement as to giving
the infantry some form of armoured support.

The Territorial Army was still left waiting for any
general modernization of its equipment or organization,
but it was given an increased responsibility in the defence
of this country against the danger of air attack. Part of the
new anti-aircraft units required for this purpose were to
be formed by the conversion of existing infantry units. A
number of battalions in London were already converted to
anti-aircraft artillery or searchlights before the end of the
year, and as a consequence the 47th and 56th Divisions
were merged into one, as the London Division. The general
strength of the Territorial Army continued to dwindle
during the year, although its quality on the whole improved. But there was now a prospect of more liberal
treatment, which promised to react beneficially on its
recruiting problem.

In the Regular Army, too, there was certainly room for
more generous conditions, not only in the treatment of
the men but in dealing with the promotion situation in the
commissioned ranks. The Stanhope Committee wrought
some improvement, but its results hitherto have disappointed expectation, and shown that more radical

The Changing Army

measures are needed to relieve the existing congestion, to remove the glaring inequalities of the existing system, and also to reduce the age-level in the senior grades—which might prove dangerously high if war came, especially a war of rapid movement.

Among events of 1935, the Royal Review, held at Aldershot on July 13th in celebration of the King's Jubilee, provided an impressive spectacle and also a piquant contrast between old and new types of unit, and movement. In September Army Manœuvres were held for the first time since 1925, and only the second time since the war. They, likewise, provided a piquant contrast as well as much-needed practice. In these, two army corps were pitted against each other, and 'Westland' achieved a signal success. Its commander, Sir Cyril Deverell was chosen as the next Chief of the Imperial General Staff, to succeed Field-Marshal Sir Archibald Montgomery-Massingberd in April 1936. There was also a new Secretary of State for War, Mr. Duff Cooper having taken over the office from Lord Halifax, who had temporarily held it after Lord Hailsham's departure earlier in the year.

At the end of the year came the announcement of the first really large steps in Army reorganization since the war. One was the conversion of twenty-eight battalions into mechanized machine-gun units, so as to form 'new model' infantry brigades composed of three rifle battalions and a machine-gun battalion. Another was the mechanization of eight cavalry regiments and the creation of a mechanized Mobile Division formed of two mechanized cavalry brigades—instead of one, as originally proposed —and the Tank Brigade. Each of these cavalry brigades was to consist of one light tank regiment and two motor cavalry regiments, equipped with the new vehicles speci-

ally designed for easy dismounting. At the same time the
cavalry brigade in Egypt was to be converted into a
mechanized formation consisting of an armoured car
regiment, a light tank regiment, and a motor cavalry
regiment.

No horsed cavalry brigades were to be kept. The divisional cavalry regiments, however, were to remain horsed.
For the Indian Army authorities were still reluctant to
allow the five British Cavalry regiments serving in India
to be mechanized, although there were twenty-one Indian
Cavalry regiments—a total which many modern soldiers
had come to regard as disproportionate to their value. So
long as this attitude persisted the consequence was that,
under the Cardwell system, five regiments at home had
to be maintained on a horsed basis to provide reliefs for
those stationed in India. It meant that, as the five at home
provide the protective mounted troops for the Infantry
divisions, these would be at a disadvantage compared with
those of the Continent, where mechanized reconnaissance
groups had already been created.

The increasing range and rapidity of the moves that
armies may make, especially with their tanks and other
mobile troops, necessitates a corresponding increase in
the range and rapidity of protective reconnaissance.
Horsed cavalry are incapable of providing this, with the
result that infantry who have to depend on the divisional
cavalry regiments for their protection would be exposed to
serious danger if pitted against a modern army.

The mechanization of the cavalry had been decided
on in preference to their reduction and the expansion of
the Royal Tank Corps. If this was rather hard on the
newer arm, which had borne the burden of developing the
means and methods of mechanized warfare, it ensured the

preservation of the Cavalry tradition, general and regimental. Some doubt must remain, until experience proves the contrary, as to the ability of horse-minded soldiers to become mechanically minded and to get as much out of their machines as a corps who are natural enthusiasts for machinery. But the mechanization of the cavalry was at any rate in significant, if somewhat ironical, contrast to the fervent declarations of continued belief in the value of cavalry which the spokesman of the War Office had made in Parliament only two or three years before. Cavalry, if viewed with a sense of reality, have been ghosts on the battle-field ever since they were reduced, by modern fire, to dismounted action as a normal course on meeting opposition. And now that any kind of troops can be moved in motor-vehicles, the distinction between cavalry and infantry is becoming artificial, except in the case of cavalry who are converted into armoured car or light tank regiments. These alone retain the basic historical characteristics of the cavalryman—*the man who fights mounted*. The tankman and the airman are the true heirs of 'cavalry' in their mode of action.

Early in 1936 further decisions were taken towards the modernization of the infantry. They involved the complete mechanization of its first line transport, horse-limbers being superseded by the new 15-cwt. Morris trucks, while even the officers' chargers were to be replaced by light cars or motor cycles.

There was also a decision on the new organization. The rifle battalions were to be similar to the experimental pattern tried out the previous summer, with a light machine-gun to each section of seven men—providing fifty-two light machine-guns altogether in the battalion, as well as a platoon of four mechanized mortars. The machine-gun battalions were to be somewhat different to the experimental pattern tried out with the 6th Infantry Brigade in 1935. Instead of three machine-gun companies with a total of thirty-six guns it was now to have two companies with a total of thirty-two guns.

The apparent reduction of the machine-gun strength would, however, be offset by a gain in protected mobility. For these companies were to be equipped with low armoured vehicles from which the gun can be fired. With three companies there was a tendency to distribute them in a stereotyped way, one to each rifle battalion: an 'un-economic' tendency which was accentuated by the fact that the guns had to be dismounted for firing. The new organization would be a check on this tendency, encouraging a swift concentration at effective points. There is far more value in thirty-two 'mobile pill-boxes' than in thirty-six machine-guns which are carried two to a vehicle and have to be exposed, together with their personnel, in dismounting the guns for action.

The anti-tank company was to be reduced from four platoons, each of four guns, to three platoons. The intended issue of a portable anti-tank rifle diminished the need for so many of the larger weapons—which will be two-pounder quick-firing guns hauled by a specially designed truck.

A new addition to the battalion was a mechanized scout company, of three platoons; this was to be equipped with fast vehicles of the truck type with light armoured protection—thus enabling them to push forward swiftly in reconnaissance without the excessive caution engendered by the fear of running into a sudden hail of bullets. One great advantage of adding a mechanized scout company to each machine-gun battalion was that every infantry brigade would be able to provide its own rapid reconnaissance over a wide area. And that value was not likely to diminish even if the divisional cavalry were mechanized. For modern armies have to work, and soldiers to think, no longer in terms of head-on contact on a narrow front, but of covering an area against which a mobile foe has a 360-degree range of approach.

In addition, troop-carrying companies were to be created as part of the Royal Army Service Corps, equipped with motor coaches or lorries sufficient to move the men of a whole infantry brigade. There was to be one of these troop-carrying companies for each infantry division. Their provision promised to increase the mobility of the infantry, while further increasing efficiency by economizing energy. Hitherto the value of the mechanization of first line transport had been curtailed by the fact that the bulk of the personnel still had to march.

Another important decision was that the divisional artillery would be mechanized. This prospective change was assisted by the fact that a much cheaper means of artillery traction than the light dragon had now been produced, and had proved satisfactory in operation. The heavy, the medium, and the Army field brigades had already been mechanized, but the divisional field brigades had remained horse-drawn, thus being a handicap to homogeneity and efficiency.

Less favourable comment was aroused by reports that the General Staff were proposing to increase the infantry strength, by raising four new battalions—it was understood that an addition of fourteen battalions had originally been considered but abandoned because of the difficulty of obtaining enough recruits for the infantry even at their existing strength. While it was recognized that the garri-

sons of certain key areas overseas might well be strengthened, criticism of the proposal was based on the fact that
out of some forty-five battalions already in India, no less
than twenty-six were devoted to internal security duties of
a dispersed kind for which they were overarmed, besides
being less suited to it than a specially raised police or
gendarmes would be, while thereby their own proper
training was retarded.

In March the new Army Estimates were published.
From the Secretary of State's accompanying memoran-
dum it appeared that they only provided for the continuation of the programme adopted a year before—not for
the further steps foreshadowed by the Government's new
White Paper on Defence. Even so, they showed double
the previous year's increase; rising by a further £4,176,000.
The increase was also more evenly spread, and the impression left by a survey of the Estimates in detail was that
the opportunity had been taken to treat all aspects of
Army expenditure on a rather more generous scale, rather
than concentrating merely on its re-equipment. Mechanization accounted for only two million pounds of the total.
Nearly half of this was due to the replacement of horsed
limbers by trucks in the infantry first line transport. The
provision for tanks and other track vehicles was actually
less than the previous year. There were other rather puzz-
ling features. Although the policy of mechanization had
been adopted, there was practically no reduction in the
sum to be spent on remounts. The total of horses and mules
were still over twelve thousand, being reduced by barely
fifteen hundred. The Equitation School at Weedon was
still to be continued, although training only thirty-eight
pupils a year at a cost of over £20,000. By comparison
with this the Tank Corps Schools dealt with an average

of five hundred and fifty pupils for a mere £46,000. It was to be observed also that only £37,000 was allowed for the Mechanization Experimental Establishment, and that no increase was shown in its slender staff of ten officers. The possibility of savings through mechanization was suggested by the fact that an increase of £16,000 in motor fuel was offset by a reduction of £57,000 on forage. Another curious discovery was that the sum allotted for lectures at Sandhurst amounted to the munificent total of £20 a year—which did not suggest much aid towards the excellent idea of developing the Royal Military College on University lines.

With the advent of the new regime in the spring there were marked changes of policy apart from an acceleration of programme. Many of the questions of reorganization were re-examined, and although this imposed a delay fresh conclusions emerged later in the year. The decision was taken to mechanize the whole of the cavalry, in order to ensure that the divisional cavalry regiments had adequate mobility to perform their function of reconnoitring ahead of the infantry, who themselves may now advance much faster by being carried in motor convoys. The mechanized cavalry brigades, too, were to be remodelled so that armoured troops would predominate, instead of unprotected motor cavalry who might be easily held up. Furthermore the new infantry brigade fell out of favour, before it came into force. It was thought to be too bulky, while also not allowing enough flexibility within the divisional organization. General Staff opinion has veered towards the plan of a brigade of three battalions. Each of these would be rifle battalions equipped with the new light machine-guns. The machine-gun battalions—now to number twenty-six—are to become divisional and corps troops. The division itself will probably have two of these battalions, embodying the mechanized machine-guns and anti-tank guns required for the support and protection of the division as a whole. Another idea, following the Continental trend, is to provide a divisional reconnaissance element, strong in automatic weapons and mobility, which should be capable not merely of discovering the enemy's whereabouts, but penetrating his screen and probing his dispositions, besides seizing points ahead of the advancing columns.

The new model organization—with its three infantry brigades of smaller size and its heavier infantry weapons under divisional control—is expected to improve manageability and to diminish road congestion, while allowing a more flexible power of concentrating extra fire support at the vital points. This accords with the principle already adopted with the artillery, wherein the artillery permanently allotted to the division is kept on a minimum scale, while its potential support is on a maximum scale. Just as the increased proportion of 'army' artillery enables the divisions which have the harder nuts to crack to be heavily reinforced for the moment, so the infantry brigades can be treated similarly in giving them machine-gun support in accord with their need.

The reorganized rifle battalions, divested of their heavy machine-guns will consist of four homogeneous companies, each with twelve of the new Bren guns. The new infantry organization constitutes an official recognition of the growing value of the light machine-gun in modern warfare compared with the rifle. It has raised the question whether the rifle should be discarded. But it will be some time still, unfortunately, before the new Bren guns can be produced in sufficient quantity to equip the infantry on the scale already approved. Until that stage is reached it would be premature to discard the weapons we actually possess even though their value is shrinking. Moreover, while the Bren gun is a light weapon of its type, it weighs twenty-one pounds without the tripod, compared with the nine pounds of the rifle. When its much increased expenditure of ammunition, and the weight of the magazines, are taken into consideration, the total load imposes a definite brake on the mobility of the infantry section. Thus its full value can only be reaped in so far as mechanized means of transport can be developed to lighten the strain of pre-action movement and the burden of ammunition supply. If the new organization is not likely to be the last step, most soldiers feel that it is a good first step towards increasing fire-power while maintaining, and even improving, mobility.

This interim period is, however, a time for thinking—so that the next step may be a longer stride still towards what one may call 'economic fighting-power'. Recognizing the limitations of the rifle as a factor in modern battle, some soldiers consider that it is now only of use for hill warfare and sniping. Others who agree with them in principle would not go so far. A rifle can be a deadly weapon in the hands of a man who is both an expert shot and skilled in the use of ground: it can be used, and one has seen it used, most effectively in stalking hostile machine-guns. Yet to concede its value as a fine weapon in expert hands does not affect the basic point. For we cannot expect the bulk of the men who are recruited for the Regular infantry to attain the necessary expertness. It is a still more improbable assumption that the mass of the Territorial Army, or the men who are hastily raised in war, will become experts. Thus there is a strong case for re-examining the foundations of tactical power in the light of modern conditions.

The Changing Army

It is uneconomic to send into action more men than can contribute effectively to the issue. More men merely mean more loss without compensating profit. If it were not for ammunition supply one man would suffice, and two would be ample, for handling each light machine-gun: as mechanized means of carrying ammunition on the battle-field develop so the uneconomic call for more human carriers will disappear. Here it is not without significance to recall that in the Palestine campaign Lawrence, a most expert rifle-shot, came to discard the rifle for a stripped light automatic as his personal weapon—his camel served as the carrier, enabling him to make the Lewis gun a one-man weapon. To send into action, as at present, seven men with each light machine-gun is certainly uneconomic as a general rule. Two would be enough where extra ammunition can be brought up easily in a carrier; even where it could not, three men to aid the light machine-gunner could carry as many magazines as the present six men if they were relieved of their encumbering rifles. For close quarter fighting an automatic pistol would suffice: a 'gangster' gun might perhaps be still better.

There are many occasions in war when 'economic tactics' would suggest that only two men should go forward with the section's light machine-gun; the others being kept under cover, to go up later. In certain conditions— for example, at night and in other forms of obscurity, an increase of man-power in proportion to weapon-power is desirable. Even here it is questionable whether the present scale is not uneconomic. A smaller section would be less of a target, while its higher controllability would add to its effective strength. Moreover, the apparent reduction would be further offset by an increase in the number of units.

The Changing Army

It is at least worth reflection whether we cannot here find the means to a solution for one of the chief military problems of to-day—the unmanageable size of the division, and, on a lower plane, of the battalion. In the past both fulfilled a definite tactical conception: owing to the dispersed method of fighting now enforced by modern fire, as well as other factors, both have become distorted. The battalion was a unit that could, in a true sense, be handled by its commander: it is now becoming impossible to 'command' in battle.

To reduce the size of the division by having two infantry brigades instead of three would be an awkward step in several ways: it would restrict the range of tactical combinations and cramp the possibilities of manœuvre. To reduce the size of brigades, as the new organization does, is a better way. But it may not go far enough unless the size of the battalions, also, is diminished. This might best be achieved, as suggested earlier, by reducing the size of the basic sub-unit—the infantry section. Against the tactical advantages of this step may be urged the disadvantages of having too large an 'overhead', since it would be difficult to reduce the headquarter wing proportionately. The solution might be to transfer to the brigade a considerable part of the administrative work that is at present performed by the battalion. It would tend to save money, and save time for training. Although it may sound novel, it is in accord with the underlying current of evolution. And the 'economic' possibilities, both tactical and financial, deserve exploration.

CHAPTER XVIII

The Brakes on Recruiting

In addressing a conference of the Press at the War Office recently the Adjutant-General to the Forces emphatically declared: 'I do not believe in an ostrich-like policy. If a thing is a fact, why not say so?' This is a wise attitude in all human affairs, as history has shown so many times that mankind's failure to learn this lesson is the strongest evidence of its incapacity to profit by experience. To pretend that troubles do not exist is the surest way to help them grow to the point where they are dangerous, and may be incurable. The lesson has a particular application to the recruiting problem. It would hardly be possible to proclaim the need of recruits more insistently than has been done during the past year. The zeal shown by the recruiting authorities could hardly be surpassed. Yet the fact remains that these efforts have not merely failed to remove the shortage, but that the shortage is increasing in spite of them. That fact shows that appeals will not suffice. Something more practical is required to give the Service itself a new and greater appeal to potential recruits. Publicity can play an important part, but it only has a lasting effect when the picture it conveys is justified by the

The Brakes on Recruiting

reality. Exerted prematurely or misleadingly it carries the risk of a recoil.

For too long there was a tendency to look for the cause of the trouble outside rather than inside the Service, and to cast the responsibility mainly on pacifism. This had the effect of delaying necessary enquiry into the real causes, and their rectification before either the shortage or the risk of war developed to their present proportions. It is somewhat ironical to reflect that a year or two ago, when pacifism was more prominent and the need less urgent, there was less difficulty in obtaining recruits than there is to-day. But it would not be true to say that the type of recruits even then was as good as the conditions of modern warfare require. And now the improvement in employment outside has naturally made the men who are required more reluctant to join the Army under the existing conditions of service.

The fact that the other Services have found no difficulty in obtaining the much increased number of men they needed has served to show that there is no lack of young men who are willing to join the Services wherever service has an adequate appeal. Meanwhile the present regime at the War Office had been making widespread enquiries among the Army at large which have contributed to a clearer view of the problem. Significantly, the Government's spokesmen have since admitted that pacifism has little or nothing to do with the problem, and have already announced certain measures that are being taken to make the Army more attractive. Welcome as these are, they hardly go far enough, so that it may be worth while to set out in detail the results of an independent investigation of the problem.

The existing checks may be grouped under four heads—

The Brakes on Recruiting

conditions of service, conditions in the service, conditions of foreign service, and conditions after service. The first turn mainly on the scales of payment, and the unfortunate difference between expectation and realization. A promise of fourteen shillings a week clear—with food, clothes, and other needs, as well as pleasures provided free—does not seem bad, if hardly enough to attract the type of man required for a skilled professional army. But the man has hardly enlisted before he learns the inexactness of the inducements held out. He is promptly compelled to pay for a host of small items, varying with the regiment he joins— among them such things as shoes for physical training, regimental cane, regimental buttons for his overcoat, regimental history, mug, cleaning materials, pressing his uniform on issue, labels for bed, blankets, socks. This initial total comes to fifteen or sixteen shillings—and although some regiments help him a little out of regimental funds, others add further items. On top of this he finds, even while at the depot, monthly stoppages from his pay for such items as athletic subscriptions, library, rifle club, haircutting, washing, regimental journal. When stoppages have been deducted, the soldier is fortunate who is handed more than ten or eleven shillings over the pay-table.

It is certainly interesting to compare these facts that confront the soldier with a leaflet that was issued to the representatives of the Press, entitled 'Some Interesting Facts'. It was there stated: 'On enlistment he receives a complete outfit. . . . Gym kit is provided.' Another promise that has a subtle flavour runs: 'Organized games are a part of Army life and all men have an opportunity of taking part. The cost of upkeep of the grounds does not fall on the soldier.' Since nothing causes more sense of grievance than the fact of false promises, would it not be

wiser to tell the prospective recruit, with the honesty that
is the best policy, that he will receive 'fourteen shillings
a week less certain deductions'. It would be better still
if all that he really needs was provided for, or his pay
raised proportionately.

There is another rub in the statement 'He has free food.
Three good meals a day are served in dining halls.' For
the inadequacy of the food has been one of the soldiers'
strongest complaints, especially the fact that they had to
buy their own suppers. Of late years, a number of regiments have managed, by good administration, to provide
suppers for the men, but even now this is by no means
universal. The country should be a little more liberal in
what it provides for feeding its Army.

While there may be no need for a considerable all-
round increase of pay, proficiency should be better re-
warded than at present, if the level of efficiency is to be
raised—this discrimination in favour of the good soldier
is desired by the men themselves. At present the grading
is too gradual; the fully trained man in his fourth year of
service only earns a shilling a day more than the raw recruit.

The conditions in the service call for improvement in
many ways. I have heard good regimental officers declare
that when they go round barracks they wonder that any
man enlists. Such an opinion may overrate the badness of
barracks compared with the housing conditions that can
be found in some of our great cities, but it does not overrate the shock that often awaits recruits who come from
decent homes. They must read with a smile, if they can
screw one up, another of the 'interesting facts' in the leaflet
already mentioned:

'He is housed in well-lit and ventilated rooms. He is

provided with a bed and bedding and a clean issue of bed linen each fortnight. Baths with hot and cold water are available at convenient hours.'

Who would imagine from this that they will find large barrack-rooms often so badly illuminated that men cannot see to read, which drives them to spend their evenings out? Or that many of these rooms are so ill-heated by an antiquated system of fires that in cold weather, even with all windows closed, they never get passably warm? Central heating would make an immense difference to the comfort of men who have to make their homes in barracks, and would also ensure hot water for shaving. Again, 'bed' is a euphemism for the present iron cot, with its unyielding slats, and its bolster filled with wood shavings which make it almost as hard as resting one's head on a brick. The ordinary army hospital bed is cheap, and its general issue in place of the iron cot would be a boon to the soldier. Some day, too, a country which wants to attract a good type of man may even think it worth providing pyjamas. It would be cleaner and smarter than sleeping in their shirts, and even an old-style sergeant-major might admit the improvement when he got over the shock.

No one is likely to disagree with the desirability of a smart appearance by day—and when walking out after the day's work is over. But few serving soldiers have any desire to see full-dress brought back again, while the privilege of wearing mufti, although valued, is regarded as having its drawbacks, especially on foreign service. When young, and with a natural pride in themselves, they like to be recognized as soldiers—but as workmanlike soldiers. In consequence the permission to wear blue has been much appreciated. The drawback has been that the soldier had to buy it for himself, and it is good news that the Government is now to provide it. But the men do not want it to be so drab as some generals have insisted in excessive zeal for uniformity. With true regimental pride they want it to bear some of the regimental distinctions, and a coloured stripe down the trousers according to the arm of the Service. Many of them would like it to have a roll collar, and to wear collar and tie, as the Air Force now do.

In barrack-life generally there are still too many restrictions and vexations which are out of tune with the modern spirit, and with common sense. Guards and roll call at night are among them, and in a number of stations they have been dropped for some time. Church Parade is an old grievance—as a parade. Off duty the soldier should share as far as possible the normal rights of the citizen. Many improvements and relaxations have been made in recent years, and progressive commanding officers have gone still further than the official recommendations—with beneficial results. Most regimental officers now agree that the system of passes is quite unnecessary. Yet until recently a man could not leave the station without a pass showing his destination—so that if his girl wanted to be taken to some nearby town, and then changed her mind, preferring another, he could not meet her wishes. All that is really needed is a permanent pass marked 'Reveille to reveille when not on duty'—and that merely as a safeguard against the inquisitiveness of the Military Police. If a pass is marked with a fixed hour of return it tends to make the soldier stay out longer than he would if he were free.

On duty, discipline has become much more sensible in recent years, although in some units the punitive element is still too prominent. No pacifist can do as much harm as

245

a bullying and foul-mouthed N.C.O. Where he exists, he is a bad advertisement for the Army in attracting the youngsters of to-day who are most of them only too eager to learn, if intelligently taught. And the more the officers are in touch with the men the better a unit is likely to be. Apart from such faults in the methods of discipline, there are two more general causes of complaint which tend to hinder recruiting. One is the state of obsoleteness in which the Army's equipment, and consequently its training, has been left for so many years. No keen youngster is stimulated by the feeling that he is training for the last war—and the boys now growing up are the sons of the infantrymen of 1914-1918. They have heard enough to put them off the prospect of a repetition. Passchendaele still sticks. The other general cause of complaint, and disillusionment, is the way that the soldier's time is still wasted in duties that have no serious relation to training for war. 'Fatigues' are, above all, a fatigue to the soldierly spirit—and their effect is worst when coal fatigues and similar drudgery are inflicted for weeks on recruits who join their battalions eager to learn what soldiering means. There may be no escape until we revert to General Maxse's post-war scheme for employment companies to perform such military household duties and set the active soldier free for training. Even then, other waste-pipes of time and enthusiasm will need attention. Brass-polishing and cleaning still play too large a part, and even so the result seems to be counted less than the time that is expended in such ways. Everything that engenders a sense of futility, of activity without adequate purpose, reduces a man's self-respect and resourcefulness, and thereby impairs his value for civil employment later.

The conditions in the service, however, are a less concentrated grievance than the conditions of foreign service. When men enlist, for seven years with the colours, the form that is given them has a footnote to the effect that, if the exigencies of the service require it, they may be held for another year. In practice, this enforced extension has become normal—and it is felt all the more because it prolongs the time they have to spend abroad. Parents of potential recruits, as well as the youngsters themselves, dislike the thought of a five-years absence, and are naturally aggrieved when they find that it becomes six. To make it worse, when they at last reach home, they are apt to be discharged almost at once, and find themselves 'on the streets'. Thus the sense of broken promises, which was implanted in the first weeks of their service, is renewed at the end.

It may seem a pity to enumerate all these deterrents at a time when recruits are so badly needed. But the men who have served know them—and naturally spread them in recounting their experience. It is more important that they should be known to those with whom the remedy lies. For so long as they are unremedied the prospect can hardly be improved by recruiting appeals, and there will be a serious danger of the supply drying up at its source. Thus there is good reason to accept the Adjutant-General's admonition: 'If a thing is a fact, why not say so.'

Possible remedies for the first two classes of adverse conditions have already been discussed. The third could be met if men were given long leave after three years' service abroad, and enabled to obtain a really cheap passage to England. Otherwise the foreign service system must be so reorganized that the tour abroad does not last more than four years, except for units which may be specially recruited for the purpose. The fourth condition

The Brakes on Recruiting

—that of a future for men after they leave the service—requires that they should have six or nine months at home before their service expires, while there should also be an extension of the system of vocational training.

The Secretary of State for War was happily inspired when he declared in a recent speech that the removal of causes for a sense of injustice should be the guiding principle in any treatment of the recruiting problem. And he enumerated a no less desirable corollary when he laid down, as 'a not impracticable ideal', the aim of guaranteeing 'to every man who joined the Army and left it at the end of his period of service with a good character that he should pass straight from the Army into a good job'.

CHAPTER XIX

The Territorial Army—Its Strength and Weakness

A tour of the camps of the Territorial Army is an experience that remains refreshing despite repetition: it is natural to ask oneself why. It can hardly be due to the training, since from year to year this has varied little and most of it is necessarily concentrated on small detail. Moreover, the evolution of methods has been almost as slow as the provision of new equipment. The tonic effect must come not from method or matter but from spirit—from renewal of contact with a force of men who themselves, as one comes to realize, gain a renewed charge of vitality from this annual spell under canvas. That the officers achieve this may seem rather perplexing when one sees how they expend it—in guest-nights, on top of field exercises, that run on almost to the next morning's parade. It would seem a miracle that they last out the fortnight, but spirit triumphs over body with a good margin to spare: and the bracing effect on the spirit obviously continues. Camp blows the cobwebs out of the soul. And anyone who visits these citizen-soldiers in camp is unlucky if he does not get something of the same feeling. It is bound to have an effect on the impression that the

249

training makes, tending to disarm criticism. The value of camp to the individuals who attend is so manifest that, at the time, it is apt to check the question how far it is serving the larger purpose for which it is intended.

But in reflection that question must be faced, and answered. Standards must change, and be raised. Much of the controversy over the last war is due to the difference of the standards which are applied to its military issues. The men who held responsibility feel that they did their best, and credit their friends similarly. What was done, except for the mistakes of which they are conscious, thus becomes their standard, in weighing the leadership shown during those years of struggle. But the historian should judge it by a higher standard—allowing for the actual conditions, yet taking account of past experience, he must ask whether what was done was the best that could have been done. Likewise in examining the present state of defence, the ultimate standard is whether it is adequate to the need. The need depends on the problem, and even when this has been estimated as well as possible, finance and other considerations set limits to the scale of force. In regard to quality there is only one safe basis—whether it is as good as it can be. Criticism must be true to this standard.

During the years of comparative international tranquillity that have passed it was natural to apply an easier measure to the Territorial Army. The primary need was to sustain the spirit that kept the force alive, under a cloud of public indifference and a 'cutting' wind from Whitehall. Now the atmosphere here has changed, following the hot winds that are blowing from the Continent. The importance of the Territorial Army is better appreciated, an encouragement is taking a more definite form. This is being reflected in the state of the Force.

Its Strength and Weakness

By comparison with the past the Territorial Army, as seen in camp, shows a general improvement. After shrinking for years, its strength is now rising. Camp attendances last year had increased more in proportion, and this is really a sounder guide. The type of man in the ranks is on the average, at least in the South, better to-day than in the earlier years of my experience. The young officers, especially, are often superior. Training has definitely improved both in interest and, as a natural consequence, in standard. No units stand out as some—like the 4th Northamptons—did nine or ten years ago, nor do I think any are tactically so advanced; but the average has reached a higher level. Among the contributory causes are the greater thoroughness of pre-camp instruction, the development of instructors through increased attendance at courses, and the more systematic organization of exercises in camp. Here, again, I have not seen any formation which organized its training quite so thoroughly as, for example, the East Midland and the Norfolk and Suffolk Infantry Brigades did, in their different ways, in the past; but such pioneering work helped to give an impetus to methods of training which have a widening influence and are reflected in the general progress that can be observed to-day. It has been helped by the increasing assistance given by the whole-time soldiers to their part-time comrades, and has received a noteworthy reinforcement by the appointment of Regular brigade-majors. Keen and up-to-date in knowledge, the benefit they have brought is generally acknowledged.

Everywhere fuller use is being made of what the Army spells T.E.W.T. and appropriately calls 'tute'—the tactical exercise without troops—as a foundation for the different operations that are practised. The training, too, shows more sign of adaptation to the conditions of modern warfare; where many units did no night training at all, and few did it more than once in the fortnight, most of them now go out once each week—to acquire the instinct and practise the technique of movement in the dark. In view of the growing importance of obscurity as a cloak from modern weapons this may seem a small proportion of time to spend in preparation, but it is not easy to ask more broken nights' sleep of men whose spell in camp is often their only holiday of the year. Daytime offers scope for learning concealment from the air as well as the art of using cover in the tactical approach; if both these arts are hampered by the tendency of Territorial camps to be located in rather bare parts of the country, for non-military reasons, there are signs of definite progress in them. It has gone along with a general improvement in the section-leading. This, to me, was the feature of last year's camps, for the handling of the sections, the little fighting groups, has been a specially weak spot in the Territorial Army during the past decade.

Now, however, one must apply the higher standard. The foreign situation compels us to face the question whether the citizen force is up to its greatly increased responsibility in the scheme of national defence, taking due account of the probable conditions of a modern war. Judged by this standard the Territorial Army as it exists to-day is far from justifying contentment.

Its deficiency of strength, which is still nearly twenty-five per cent below the authorized figure, is the least of its deficiencies. For my own part, the more I explore the tendencies of modern warfare the less importance pro-portionately I attach to mere numerical strength. Indeed, the use of the armed masses which were seen in 1914 are likely to be more danger than value to the country which attempted to mobilize them to-day. But that consideration hardly applies to our land forces. Their scale is so small in comparison with continental levels that the difference between present and authorized strength would not appreciably affect the strain on communications. Nor would the full number necessarily count for much more in the field than the present numbers; our trust has to be placed in quality, and an improvement here might easily outweigh the mere addition of 40,000 men. So long as an establishment is fixed, the failure to fill it is apt to have a lowering effect on quality. The sense of being short is insidiously depressing; the desire to fill up leads officers to take in men of a lower grade of intelligence and physique than is desirable. When it is realized that this 'vacuum pressure' has been operating for nearly a generation, it may help to explain why comparatively few of the pre-war Volunteer and Territorial type are found in the ranks, which, in the infantry, are almost entirely recruited from what before the war was the militia class. Even so, a large proportion appear to be physically inferior to the pre-war militiaman or special reservist. For, if I am correctly informed, the number of Territorial infantrymen who try for enlistment in the Regulars only to be rejected for some physical defect is high.

This physical factor is serious, since the present trend of warfare demands an increasingly athletic type of infantryman. Even more does it require a higher level of intelligence. The improvement that has been noticed recently in the type of man recruited for the Territorial Army does not go nearly far enough. The artillery and engineers naturally get a better type than the infantry, but even this is not good enough. It would only be fostering a delusion to suggest that, in general, the men of the Territorial Army to-day are mentally and physically equal to the tests of present-day warfare—by the standard of true need. Nor are the bulk of the men in the Regular Army. But the Regular's qualitative deficiency can be reduced by careful physical and educational training, while the length of his service allows time for him to absorb military training more gradually. The Territorial needs to be of a higher type originally—physically as good as and mentally better than the Regular at full development—because he has to learn the soldier's technique so much quicker. Is there any hope of bridging the gap between what is and what is needed? None, so far as I can gauge, unless the Government take steps of a larger span than the concessions given last year, beneficial though these have proved.

To place the main responsibility there is not to overlook the part that the employers and the military authorities must play in clearing the path for a better entry. The attitude of both has changed much, for the better, but there is still room for improvement. It would not be difficult to point out ways in which the military authorities could make service attractive to a higher type of man— and officer. There is plenty of scope for modernizing the training; for increasing interest and sense of actuality; for eliminating archaic details which bore the intelligent civilian by their obvious irrelevance to present-day warfare; for abolishing restrictions, sanctified by custom, which irritate the self-reliant citizen. Again, since the quality of instruction largely depends on a well-furnished mind in the instructor, it might be well worth while to encourage the Territorial officer to nourish his military ideas on something less constricted than the manuals. The average

Its Strength and Weakness

Regular reads less than the student in most other professions, but he reads a lot more than the average Territorial officer. The latter has become more proficient in technical practice than the old Volunteer, but he has become regulation-bound.

To attract a higher type of officer, it is essential to give further scope to those who prove their ability. For the sprinkling of tactical and technical enthusiasts are the salt of the citizen-force. A larger proportion of brigade commands and similar appointments should be given to Territorial officers, and the time is long overdue for the War Office to fulfil the promise implicit in a post-war addition to the Royal Warrant and make one or two Territorial major-generals. Such an action would be a deserved tribute, and a tonic. More definite advisory representation at the War Office is also desirable.

Moreover, the promising young officer should receive wider encouragement as well as the mature commander, and this want undoubtedly coincides with the country's need for a larger number of potential staff officers. In several other armies now the non-professional officer is given opportunities to qualify for staff appointments. Apart from the need for such a reserve there is a risk of reviving an old sore if the staff jobs of the national army should have to be reserved for Regulars while the civilian soldier was merely allowed to keep the fighting. Even to-day, there is a needless cause of irritation in the way that Territorial officers whose services are recognized by a C.B. are given it in the civil, instead of the military division, like the Regular. In general, the heads of the Army have been more active in showing sympathy than in removing causes of grievance. The citizen soldier has good reason to appreciate the spirit nowadays shown by

Regulars, senior and junior, in their contacts with him; he could still wish for more imagination.

But the bigger responsibility lies with the Government, if the state of the Territorial Army is to be adequately improved. They have the power, at no cost, to give better recognition to the services rendered by Territorial leaders and supporters, as well as greater incentive to employers. They also hold the purse-strings, and the financial factor bulks large in the Territorial problem. At present, the employer, especially the small one, who releases men for training, often suffers a loss by so doing. And the Territorial officer is often out of pocket. It may be undesirable to pay a premium for public service, but it is for the Government to consider ways of compensating actual loss thereby caused.

With the rank and file, money is even more important in its bearing on the problem. The hope of adequate progress depends on adequate provision. This does not necessarily demand a rise in direct payment to the man. It is true that the marked improvement in training last year can be traced to the larger number of 'drills' that were done, and this in turn to the increased inducement offered to N.C.O.s and men. But to draw the higher type of man that is necessary into the ranks, I am inclined to think that the 'indirect approach' would be more promising.

Better clothing is needed. Some of the khaki suits that are issued to Territorials would lower a tramp's self-respect. Khaki shirts should be an issue, not a luxury for units or men who care to pay for them. I find, too, a widespread demand for a jacket with roll collar, so that collar and tie may be worn with the shirt—this has gone far to enhance the aircraftman's self-respect. For the evenings a suit of blue is keenly desired, and should be provided.

Better food is needed, and a good evening meal: the type of man who is wanted is accustomed to this. At present some units supplement the normal fare out of their pockets, and the effect is reflected in the type of men they are able to attract. In others, the men themselves contribute, and only the type who can afford it are taken. But what is to-day the exception should become the rule.

Again, now that the Territorial soldier is asked to undertake a greater liability, it is worth considering whether he should not be covered by some form of insurance against loss of employment, if the Territorial Army has to be mobilized. The possibility of this is a deterrent to men who have made a good start in a civil occupation.

In the training sphere, too, the attraction as well as the efficiency rests with the Government in one important respect. Lack of modern equipment is a serious check on interest, especially in the man who thinks. The Territorial Army at exercise in recent years has looked too much like 1914 to convince the keenly enquiring youth of this generation that, by joining it, he would be going far to fit himself for playing a part in modern war. He may be mistaken, but that has been his impression. There is too much make-believe, and too many substitutes. There are as yet no tanks, no mortars, no proper mechanized transport in the Territorial Army. It has not even gas-masks. When the necessary equipment is provided it is likely to have an effect not only on the attraction of service but on the interest of the training, and thereby cause a second wave of appeal to the type who are needed. For methods are apt to fall into a rut, and ideas become stagnant, when the range of tools is limited and their pattern unchanging.

The Territorial Army

The pattern of the organization also is too static. The infantry body is out of all proportion to their supporting arms. This tends to obscure the purpose of the Second Line, which needs clearer definition. The Air Defence and Coast Defence units know what their role is in emergency. The members of the ordinary divisions need a clearer picture to stimulate their efforts. It is not easy for them to conceive how these twelve divisions in their present form will fit into the scheme of a future war.

The Territorial Army to-day can be summed up by saying that it is going on as well as can be expected. But that is different from being really fit—as fit as the conditions and war risks of to-day require. A realization of the danger should be a spur to the kind of men who are wanted, but it would be unwise to rely simply on this—and it is only part of the problem. Until the Government and the War Office have done all they can to remove its 'internal' handicaps and increase its appeal, it will be premature to look wider for the cause of the present deficiency.

CHAPTER XX

The Volunteer in the Car—An Army Motor Reserve

====

With the progressive mechanization of the Army, in itself the inevitable sequel to civil changes, there is an assured and growing need for a large reserve of motor-trained and motor-minded men. Only through the existence of such a reserve can the Army be expanded or even maintained, in the event of a fresh national emergency.

This need is unaffected by any conflict of opinion on the practicability of mechanized forces in frontier regions of the Empire where we may be called upon to wage small wars. For, like the Territorial Army as at present composed, such a reserve would only be called upon in case of a 'great war', and by universal admission a war of that kind would be of a far more mechanized nature than the last. Even the last was mechanically transformed between 1914 and 1918. Whatever the future of the continual competition between armour and armour-piercing weapons, all movement of troops and transport is likely to be on a mechanical basis. This result, the reflection of civil conditions, is inevitable if only because of the continued decline of horse usage and horse-breeding—

259

The Volunteer in the Car—

although motors are taxed and horse-breeding is subsidized.

Despite this unmistakable trend, no organized motor reserve exists. A vast reservoir, however, is available. For effective utilization in emergency, preliminary organization is essential. First, in order that the authorities may be able to classify the personnel according to their technical competence and earmark them for appropriate functions. Secondly, in order that the personnel themselves should be able through an understanding of military conditions to fit smoothly into Army organization. With such a foundation it will be far easier to develop in emergency the additional military knowledge for turning motor-trained men into efficient members of mechanized units. Even without the addition they will be ready to serve in transport and message-bearing duties, for which the need is always greatest in the first weeks of a crisis.

As an insurance against emergency and a framework for the possible expansion of the Army we now maintain as a 'second line' twelve Territorial infantry divisions. Yet it is recognized, as a result of 1914-18 experience, that ordinary infantry soldiers can be quickly trained by intensive methods, and that the rank and file of these divisions are primarily of use as a means of giving officers and N.C.O.s practice in imparting instruction and handling troops. In contrast a mechanized army requires as a second line not only a cadre of officer and N.C.O. instructors, but a body of men already acquainted with motors and able to take their place in the ranks of mechanized units. On the outbreak of an emergency it will not be possible to develop *ab initio* both their military and mechanical training, and of the two the latter is more difficult. But motor-trained men could soon be turned into efficient motor machine-gunners and members of tank and armoured car crews.

There is a source, still untapped, from which they might be obtained. The country has many thousands of motorists and motor cyclists of military age, most of whom belong to the great motoring organizations and are thus readily accessible. Many, too, are members of motoring and motor cycling clubs of a 'sporting' type. Pursuit of their hobby tends to develop in them the most valuable military qualities—nerve, decision, judgment, dash, sense of direction, knowledge of country, habit of and skill in map-reading. But the bulk of this youth, having grown up in a motoring age, feel a distaste for soldiering of the old 'foot-slogging' type. Allied to this is often a distaste for the customary forms of military training and discipline, which they regard as archaic and unintelligent, as well as too closely akin to the petty restrictions of school life. If they are to be grafted on to the potential military strength of the country they must not be parted from the machines that are their hobby. And it is also advisable that the military system, in so far as it is applied to them, should itself be attuned to the modern outlook.

From such a class the bulk of Volunteers and Territorials were recruited before the War. To-day this source of recruitment is largely running to waste. The loss is not merely material but moral. Lack of touch between the youth of the country and its military forces tends to dampen spirit and interest in the defence of the nation. Although the personnel of the present technical units are often of a high type, their growth is restricted by the heavy demands made upon their time and the specialized nature of their training.

To provide a suitable and adequate reserve for the

motorized Army of the near future it would seem wise, therefore, to tap more widely the pre-war Territorial classes, now the motoring community, and to adapt the service required of them to the normal conditions of the day. The prospects are the better because there have been definite manifestations of a widespread desire among young motorists and motor cyclists to link their hobby with military defence. Some years ago there were informal discussions on the subject in which the late Sir Henry Segrave and other prominent motorists took part, together with soldiers, Regular and Territorial, to whom the idea appealed. It may be worth while—as a basis for thought —to outline a scheme which was evolved during those earlier discussions.

Enrolment, as in the Volunteers, should replace enlistment until mobilization; and there should be two categories:

(a) Those who merely enrol on a general register as willing to serve in case of emergency, but wear no uniform and perform no duty in peace. Members of this category might, however, be attached to units of category (b) when desirous.

(b) Those who enrol as active members.

Each category would be classified in two sub-divisions, the first consisting of those who are purely drivers; the second of those who can also pass a test of mechanical knowledge, theoretical and practical. Active members would undertake:

(a) To pass an elementary course of instruction in the rifle and machine-gun, merely sufficient to understand firing and safe handling. They would be allowed, if willing, to attend a full course of Territorial Army standard.

(b) To attend a minimum number of outdoor motor

exercises, which would be held on Saturdays or Sundays during the spring, summer and autumn. (It is suggested that the annual minimum might be five.) The exercises should take the form of strategic and tactical reconnaissances, communication tests, mobile machine-gun schemes, and strategic movements.

No compulsory camp would be held. But members might, at their own wish, be attached to Territorial Army units in camp or to Regular units during the annual exercises. Motor duties would include carrying messages, staff officers, or machine-guns. During such attachments petrol should be supplied from Army sources. There is no need to stress the value to the staff and umpires of such increased means of communication as these attachments would provide.

Pay would be issued only during such attachments, and then at ordinary Army rates. Uniform would be provided for active members only. Arms and equipment would not be necessary. Members would use their own cars or motor cycles. A small annual compensation would be paid for this. It might take one of two forms:

(*a*) The remission, by arrangement with the Treasury, of half the annual licence in the case of active members of the first sub-division, and the whole duty in the case of those qualified for the second sub-division. This method of compensation would seem to be the most attractive to the class of recruits that are desired, not least because it would be a token of Government recognition of the national value of the scheme. Moreover, it might tend to enlist parents as active recruiting agents.

(*b*) If, however, such an arrangement proved impossible, an equivalent grant should be paid to motor cycle members and a larger grant to motor car members, although

The Volunteer in the Car

not necessarily so large a grant as under arrangement (*a*).

It is a matter for consideration whether, in addition to this compensation for wear and tear, a small petrol allowance should be paid for week-end exercises. The moral basis of the scheme is that no compensation be paid for members' personal service or time, except during attachments. The class to whom the scheme would appeal will serve for the privilege of fitting themselves for the defence of the country, and the interest they are likely to get out of such training.

Units of the Motor Reserve should be raised under the auspices of the Lords Lieutenant of counties, with the advice and assistance of the national motoring organizations and local motoring clubs. For convenience they would be administered by the Territorial Associations, who would co-opt representatives of the clubs. The units would not, however, form part of the Territorial Army, although they might be affiliated to the county regiment or to the Royal Tank Corps.

While the details of any such scheme are, obviously, open to adjustment, the underlying idea gains force from recent occurrences, and the need has become more pressing with the rapid extension of mechanization in the Army. Small as was the cost involved when the project was originally put forward, it was an additional cost at a time when the Territorial and Reserve Forces Vote was being cut down. Then it proved an insuperable obstacle. The objection can hardly hold to-day. The idea has since been carried into effect in certain Continental countries and developed on a great scale—which strengthens the case for its revival here.

PART IV: FORECASTS

CHAPTER XXI

The Last War and the Next

═══════════

If some countries announce their schemes of rearmament as a regretful necessity, while others announce it in tones of martial pride, a feature common to all is the air of confidence that the measures are technically sound. They all appear satisfied that the fact of rearmaments is equivalent to efficiency. Is such confidence justified? Past experience hardly supports it, and the doubt is increased by the complexity of the conditions which surround any future war. Any reasonable man must hope that war will have no future: but a reasonable man must know that reason plays small part in human affairs. And experience does not lend much encouragement to the hope of no more war.

'What will the next war be like?' 'Will it be anything like the last?' These are questions that, in the present state of apprehension or resigned curiosity, are almost daily hurled at anyone who is a student of the grim branch of knowledge which is sometimes called the science of war. Such a description is far too flattering—the neatest comment upon it that I have seen was one by Rebecca West to the effect that: 'before a war military science seems a

The Last War and the Next

real science, like astronomy, but that after a war it seems more like astrology.'

Those who have progressed furthest in exploration realize that its scientific study has barely begun. They will also be the least inclined to venture upon detailed predictions. Confident prophecy is best left to generals, who as a class have a traditional fondness for it, and as prophets have no reputation to lose. We have only to recall some of their prophecies that stand on record.

If there was one feature of the half-century preceding 1914 that would seem impossible to misjudge, it was the increasing advantage of the defensive, due to the growing power of infantry firearms—first the magazine rifle and then the machine-gun. An obvious corollary was the limitation placed on cavalry action. The American Civil War, as it advanced, made these new factors plain. It was not to be expected that European generals would profit by this second-hand experience, since the great Von Moltke dismissed it as no more than 'two armed mobs chasing each other round the country, from which nothing could be learned'. But the Franco-German War, despite its brevity, demonstrated at Gravelotte and elsewhere the same change of conditions. Nevertheless in 1883 we find the German protagonist of the 'Nation in Arms', the future Field-Marshal von der Goltz, declaring that 'the idea of the greater strength of the defensive is a mere delusion'. The Boer War might surely have suggested a doubt of this dictum, yet in 1903 the future Marshal Foch, already acting as the official mould of French military ideas, committed himself to the confident prediction that 'any improvement in firearms is bound to strengthen the offensive'.

He at least had not been a participant in any real test,

but the future Field-Marshal Haig, called upon by the Royal Commission, when fresh from the South African battlefields, to give account of the light that he had gained, was confident that 'cavalry will have a larger sphere of action in future wars'. His forecast might have been more intelligible if he had been thinking merely of mounted troops, which had been necessary to cope with Boer mobility. But he showed that his mind was fixed on the cavalry charge by the stress he laid on mounted *action*, and he confirmed this subsequently by the severe measures he took to curb the tendency to turn cavalry into mounted riflemen.

His view was shared by the military authorities of all the Continental Powers, with the result that in 1914 Germany, France, Russia, and Austria each deployed over a hundred thousand cavalry. With what result? The French relied for their information mainly on their cavalry, but, as has now been officially related: 'This immense mass of cavalry discovered nothing of the enemy's advance . . . and the French Armies were everywhere surprised.' The most important effect that the German cavalry achieved was that, by their reckless destruction of telegraph lines everywhere, they did much to paralyse their own command during the advance into France. The Austrians' advance was 'preceded by a great mass of cavalry'; their official history records that most of them never came within sight of the enemy, owing to their horses being disabled through sore backs. They at least were luckier than those who did make contact. For since the Russian cavalry stayed behind, the remaining Austrian cavalry bumped into the Russian infantry; poor shots as these were they did not fail to hit such a target, and the Austrian cavalry came back with nothing to compensate their heavy casualties.

The Last War and the Next

This cavalry prelude was overshadowed by the drama that followed, when the main armies clashed, but it was perhaps the hugest farce that has ever been enacted in a theatre of war.

The generals were no more fortunate in gauging the possibilities of newer instruments. Not many years before 1914, when the attention of a member of the British Army Council was drawn to a note on the development of aircraft, he endorsed it thus: 'We are no nearer the solution of the conquest of the air than we were in the days of Montgolfier's Fire Balloon.' A more comprehensive disbelief in change was expressed by General Sukhomlinov, the Russian War Minister who warned the instructors at the Staff College that he could 'not hear the words "modern war" without a feeling of annoyance. As war was, so it remains; all these things are vicious innovations.' Sukhomlinov was disappointed of his ambition to command the Russian armies in the war, but he could at least content himself with having helped to ensure that they marched blind and little better than armless to the slaughter.

Different in form, but fundamentally similar in nature, was the assurance of the French Commander-in-Chief, Joffre, when on August 6th, 1914, he serenely declared: 'It may be concluded that the Germans are executing a plan of which we have knowledge.' Hence it was with ample confidence that he launched his forces eastward into Lorraine, and into a trap, while the Germans were sweeping through Belgium.

If the German Command thus scored an initial surprise, they threw away the advantage through an over-confidence that verged on intoxication. They told the Austrians that if the French Army took the offensive they counted on attaining a decision 'on the 21st day of mobilization', i.e. August 23rd. If the French Army stayed on the defensive behind its frontier defence, they might take a week longer to achieve a decisive victory. They would then transfer their forces to the Russian front where they 'should arrive on the 41st day of mobilization'. The decision had not come when August 22nd came, although that day the French, advancing blindly, ran into the advancing Germans in the Ardennes, and were thrown back. Although mauled, they slipped away. Yet the German Command was sufficiently persuaded that the decisive victory had already been won that, on the 25th, it began transferring forces to Russia from the right wing. By the time this reached the Marne, it was much weaker than the forces opposing it. And on the 41st day of mobilization, September 11th, it was in full retreat!

The decisive turn had come with the penetration of the British Expeditionary Force into a thirty-mile gap between the two German armies of the right wing. This gives an ironical turn to the fact that the German Command had rebuffed the offer of their Navy to interfere with the shipment of the British force, saying that 'it would be of advantage to settle with the 160,000 British at the same time as the French and Belgians'.

The blindness of generalship, especially towards new developments, was not cured by sharp contact with reality —partly, perhaps, because that contact was at secondhand. The German machine-guns had paralysed movement on the battlefield for months when Haig, resisting a proposal for increasing the British strength in these weapons, remarked that: 'The machine-gun was a much overrated weapon and two per battalion were more than sufficient.' Called upon for his judgment, Kitchener conceded that four per battalion might be useful, but anything 'above four may be counted a luxury'. Long before the war ended, there would be a scale of more than forty heavy and light machine-guns per battalion—but that was due to the foresight and forceful pressure of a civilian minister, Mr. Lloyd George.

Military myopia likewise prevailed when means were mooted to overcome the defensive barrier formed by the hostile machine-guns. When the project of building tanks was submitted to the British Engineer-in-Chief in June 1915, he icily remarked: 'Before considering this proposal we should descend from the realms of imagination to solid facts.' Eight months later, when the first tank performed in front of Lord Kitchener, his comment was: 'A pretty mechanical toy.' 'The war', he added, 'would never be won by such machines.'

Most of the generals were confident that it would be won long before such unnecessary aids could be produced. They had been equally confident from the earliest months, and they remained so despite constant disproof.

On September 13th, 1914, General Wilson, the right hand of the British Commander-in-Chief, unwisely noted in his diary a conversation he had had with the guiding brain of the French: 'Berthelot asked me when I thought we should cross into Germany, and I replied . . . in four weeks. He thought three weeks.' That very day the Allied armies were held up on the line of the Aisne, where they remained for the next four years.

The following June, Poincaré, the French President, pathetically complained to Kitchener: 'Joffre and Sir John (French) told me in November they were going to push the Germans back over the frontier; they gave me the same assurance in December, March, and May. What

The Last War and the Next

have they done? The attacks are very costly and end in
nothing.'

Lest it might be imagined that these optimistic forecasts
were merely, if rashly, uttered to encourage ministerial
morale, one must record a few more prophecies in which
the generals indulged in their own circle. Thus, in
November 1914, Sir John French asserted that all the
hard fighting of the war was over; in January 1915, he
expressed the opinion that the war would be over before
June; in February, Joffre said that it would be over by
July; in March, Haig felt sure that the Germans would be
wanting peace before the end of July; in August, he
declared that he would not be surprised to see the enemy
give in by November, and that in any case they could not
go on after January 1916.

When it came to preparing the great offensive of July
1st, 1916, Haig and his chief executive, as the British
Official History records, 'impressed on all, at conferences
and other times, that the infantry would only have to
walk over and take possession of' the enemy trenches. The
actual attack on July 1st was a complete failure on the
greater part of the front, with a loss of 60,000 men in a
single day.

At the end of 1916, continued disappointment led to
the replacement of Joffre by Nivelle, who planned a great
offensive for 1917, declaring: 'We shall break the German
front when we wish.' When his executive subordinate,
General Micheler, reported that the enemy were building
a new third line of defence out of reach of his artillery,
Nivelle lightheartedly retorted: 'Don't be anxious, you
won't find a German in those trenches; they only want to
be off!' He confidently asserted that he would break
through the Germans' first two positions 'with insignificant

273

loss', that in three days at most his armies would be in open country, beginning the great pursuit to the Rhine. The offensive was duly launched and at nightfall had progressed about 600 yards instead of the six miles anticipated in Nivelle's programme; its continuation on subsequent days did little more than increase the loss to a total of 120,000. The chief effect was to strain the morale of the French troops to breaking-point, producing a dangerous series of mutinies in the attack-sickened army. It was crippled for the rest of the summer and had to be nursed carefully for the rest of the war.

Notwithstanding the paralysis of his allies, Haig told the British Cabinet in June 1917, that 'if the fighting were kept up at its present intensity for six months Germany would be at the end of her available man-power'. By such assurances he gained a dubious sanction for his own continued offensive at Ypres. On August 21st he reported to the Government that 'the time is fast approaching when Germany will be unable to maintain her armies'. On October 8th, arguing for permission to press deeper into the Passchendaele morass, he declared that the enemy might collapse 'at any moment'. With obvious doubt, as if making a concession to pessimistic politicians, he prefaced his view of 1918 prospects with the remark: 'Even if they hold out until next year.' But even if they did, and were able to transfer troops from the Russian front, he did not contemplate any serious check to his offensive. Not by a single word did he suggest the possibility that the Germans might take the offensive. As late as January 7th, 1918, when he came home to see the Cabinet, he expressed the opinion that the Germans would not attack. But on March 21st, they refuted his prophecy, by breaking through his front to a depth of nearly forty miles.

The Last War and the Next

If the series of crises that followed were retrieved, and the scales of the war turned, by the arrival of American reinforcements, it was the pressure of sea-power that undermined Germany's resistance and ensured her collapse. This fact lends significance to the French Command's pre-war estimate of the help that the British Navy would afford. Colonel Repington, the military critic, had written in *The Times* that it was 'worth 500,000 bayonets to the French'. General Wilson, the strategic brain of the British War Office, retorted that 'our Navy was not worth 500 bayonets.' After consulting the three leading French soldiers, he wrote: 'Castelnau and Joffre did not value it at one bayonet . . . Foch is of exactly the same opinion.'

This catalogue of misjudgment by the highest professional opinion should serve as a warning for the future. It should be engraved on the walls of every War College. Even if it does not cure the habit of prophecy among military chiefs, it should make us wary of accepting dogmatic assertions, especially where novel developments are concerned. But there is a further lesson. Such a catalogue goes far to show that Rebecca West was right, and that military science is 'more like astrology'. Perhaps that conclusion is rather hard on astrology.

There is, doubtless, a science of war; but we are a long way from discovering it. Apart from the mere technique of utilizing weapons, what passes for 'military science' is hardly more than the interpretation of conventions nurtured by tradition and warped by sentiment, patriotic and professional. Sentiment and science are incompatible, but this truth has yet to be accepted in the military world. Only two years ago Field-Marshal Sir Philip Chetwode, the Commander-in-Chief in India, reminded an audience at the Quetta Staff College of Marshal Saxe's verdict two centuries ago: 'Custom and prejudice, confirmed by ignorance, are the usual foundations of the so-called science of war.' Sir Philip Chetwode added that this applies still. If his 'military testament' should shake the complacency with present knowledge which tends to make any profession a mere profession of knowledge covering unexplored depths, it may prove not the least, indeed the greatest, of the services he has rendered.

But can we expect that any man's words, however forceful, can strike off the fetters forged by centuries of custom, and riveted by human concern for career, as well as by discipline? Few men, even of such calibre, would venture to be so candid until their careers were complete. And then, too often, their confessions will be pushed aside with a shrug of the shoulders, and the slighting comment: 'He's only a retired soldier.' The time factor dominates war; too appropriately, it rules the profession of arms. There is perhaps none where the dicta of the man in office are accepted with such uncritical deference, or where the termination of an active career brings a quicker descent into careless disregard. Little wonder that many of them are so affected by the sudden transition as to cling pathetically to the trimmings of the past, and so to justify the stage and printed page caricatures of their class, caricatures which evoke the mirth of audiences blind to the tragedy. Yet a proportion of such men use retirement as opportunity for reflection, and there is much historical evidence to show that from this section has come more accurate prognostication of future warfare than from the reigning occupants of the seats of authority. The philosophic historian may deduce that truth emerges as ambition recedes.

It is not correct to say that the trend of warfare is im-

The Last War and the Next

possible to gauge—at least of warfare hitherto. Marshal Foch was making an appropriate confession rather than a scientific statement when he declared in 1926: 'The military mind always imagines that the next war will be on the same lines as the last. That has never been the case and never will be.' One can well understand that in retrospect the war looked different to him from anything he had ever conceived, or prophesied of it, beforehand. But the conditions that dumbfounded him and his fellows were only the climax of an evolutionary process which they could have detected, but did not. Every war for half a century, since 1861, had made it plainer. Other minds did perceive them.

M. Bloch, a civilian banker of Warsaw, gave a remarkably accurate diagnosis of their essential elements in his *War of the Future*, published on the eve of the twentieth century, before he had even the data of South Africa and Manchuria to confirm his deductions. There were also military minds, if these belonged to bodies not in the seats of authority, that foresaw the coming stalemate and pointed out its chain of causation. Captain Mayer, the French military critic, was provoked by Foch's fiery advocacy of the offensive to predict, only too well, the siege war that would engulf generals who were dreaming of mobile war without the means of mobility. He was boycotted for his audacity. So was the eminent military historian, Lt.-Colonel Grouard, when he turned from the past to the future, and forecast in 1911 exactly what would happen if the French Command adopted such a plan as they did, in 1914. And, as we have seen, the British military critic, Colonel Repington, had a far wider grasp than either the French or British General Staffs of the factors that would influence the issue of the war.

The Last War and the Next

While the trend of the future in the past could have been gauged—and was, by those who could study it in detachment—it has become far more difficult to foresee the course of the next war. Apart from the immense development of weapons since 1918, so many of the innovations of 1914-18 are still unassimilated. The military corporation, indeed, is in a state of acute indigestion.

In 1914, the armies marched to the battlefield on foot as they had done for centuries. The only difference was that they were taken part of the way by rail, and that their reserves could be switched from one flank to another by that same mechanical means. The main effect of this change was that such large numbers were vomited on to the roads beyond railheads as to impede their own manœuvre, while a supplementary effect, due to more rapid switching, was that an enemy's manœuvre could be more easily blocked. The war gave a tremendous impetus to the growth of mechanical transport, both road and roadless. Motor lorries multiplied by the thousand, but this acceleration of movement only improved the capacity of supply; it did not markedly affect strategy since it could not alter the immobility of fighting troops who had already been driven, by the machine-gun, to bury themselves in trenches. The possibility of moving at 30 m.p.h. was of little avail to soldiers who had been reduced by a tactical obstacle to 0 m.p.h. To resurrect movement in face of fire, the fire-support of the attackers was developed by multiplication—of guns—and by addition—of new weapons, the light machine-gun, the mortar, the grenade, together with gas, smoke, and flame-projectors. Some of them contributed to defence as much as to the attack, and none of them succeeded so far as to revive a war of movement.

Eventually the roadless armour-clad machine, known

as the tank, was introduced; this went further than any
other means to overcome the machine-gun obstacle, and
by German confession proved the most important military
factor in the final phase of the war. But the end came,
after a gradual withdrawal, before the tank had been
developed far enough to produce more than a local
acceleration of movement. In the army that retired, and
in the armies that followed it up, a mass of motor vehicles
were mingled with a greater mass of horsed vehicles. It is
a question whether movement as a whole could have been
much quicker even if the machine-gun brake had been
lifted. Retardation may have averted confusion. On the
other fronts—Bulgarian, Turkish, and Austrian—the brake
was less effective, with the consequence that the new air
weapon found gorgeous targets. And under its blows the
retreating armies dissolved in chaos.

The post-war armies are left with this necklace of
novelties, now much developed in quantity and quality—
so much developed that calculation of the effect, if war
should come again, is more difficult than ever. And the
force of tradition has led them, at the same time, to keep
their old tools. There has been no scientific redesigning of
the structure of armies. Modification has come mainly by
accretions due to imitation. Not as a reorganization inspired by a sense of proportion and guided by a revalua-
tion. In most of the armies horses are still mingled with
motors, unarmoured road-bound vehicles are linked with
tanks, the cult of the bayonet is wreathed around the use
of automatic firearms and gas. Soldiers may go into action
at any pace between 3 m.p.h. and 30, while from overhead
they may be attacked at 300 m.p.h. Is it not possible, even
probable, that when these differing rates of movement are
added together the sum may be zero?

The Last War and the Next

The Navies of 1914 showed a greater advance on the past than the armies. They were also less tested. Battleships and cruisers were the natural heirs of the old wooden ships of the line and frigates, but through steam and armour they had been so transformed that their properties were difficult to gauge owing to the paucity of naval actions since the mechanized age of naval warfare had dawned. With the invention of the torpedo they had been confronted with a new menace, at first projected by the torpedo-boat—to which the destroyer, developed as a counter—became a successor. If the new weapon had a certain likeness to the old fireship, it had much wider possibilities. These were increased by the advent of the submarine, while the movement of fleets suffered a fresh restriction by the development of mines. It was more difficult to estimate the change of conditions because of the controversy that raged round the torpedo. The conflict of enthusiasm and prejudice produced an atmosphere in which scientific study was suffocated—if it was ever possible among a class who were men of action and had never been educated in a scientific way of thought. The natural result was a compromise by which the maintenance of the existing order was mixed with concessions to the new idea.

Destroyers were added to the battle-fleet, but were tied to its protection rather than applied to an offensive role. As for submarines, at the outbreak of war in 1914, Germany had only twenty-eight, and by 1917 little more than a hundred, out of which only about a third were operating at any particular time. Yet, even apart from their deadly action against commerce, the effect of their latent menace to battleships was such that by the summer of 1916 the British naval authorities were agreed that the

Grand Fleet must be kept out of their reach. To quote the British Official Naval History they had 'so restricted the movements of a fleet of super-Dreadnoughts—each one of which could steam several thousands of miles without refuelling—that the waters opposite one-third of the eastern coastline of Great Britain, and about half of the North Sea, were outside its zone of effective action'. The Germans' paucity of submarines led in turn to the self-imprisonment of their fleet when the available submarines were wanted for the new unrestricted campaign against merchant shipping. The farcical result was thus reached that 'for the future the two great battle-fleets could but lie inactive, watching one another across a kind of "No Man's Sea", where attack and defence were concerned only with transport and commerce'. This direct action against the supplies upon which Britain depended for her existence was carried so far that by the following spring she was in sight of collapse before the danger was brought under control—through the introduction of the convoy system—which in turn depended on the additional destroyers provided by America.

This near-fatal menace was created by a comparative handful of submarines, operating under most disadvantageous geographical conditions, and in waters guarded by 3000 destroyers and light craft—odds of 30 to 1 against the submarines.

When these facts are weighed, they seem to impart a somewhat low gravity, and illogicality, to the voices of those naval authorities who, ever since the war, have been proclaiming the ineffectiveness of the submarine and the undiminished sovereignty of the battleship.

Moreover, the single menace offered by the submarine has now become a threefold menace—below the surface, above the surface, and on the surface—through the development of aircraft and of high-speed light craft. Battle-fleets may still be safe and supreme well out on the oceans, but their primary strategic purpose is to secure their country's coasts and ports. Although it is important that a country's merchant ships and transports should be able to sail the oceans safely, such safety will not suffice if they are sunk as they approach harbour. It is in the narrow seas and within reach of coasts—where most of the naval battles of history have been decided—that aircraft, light craft and undersea craft have their opportunity. It may be more than an opportunity; a supremacy, indeed—but there are too many incalculables for anyone to gauge this before the test comes.

It is clear that the value of a battle-fleet is now much restricted, while it is by no means clear that the necessity of having one, for powers that need to use the oceans, has in any way diminished. The burden of defence has increased while the security afforded has decreased. Instead of speaking of the 'command of the sea', we can only refer to the 'conundrum of the sea'.

The evolution of war at sea, as on land, has been towards multiplicity of means and complexity of methods. Simplification is not yet in sight. Moreover, the complexity is augmented by the increasing dependence of the fighting forces upon industrial resources. As a consequence, all the countries are developing schemes of economic mobilization, as a necessary foundation for their military, naval, and aerial mobilization. But this economic mobilization introduces numberless new factors that complicate strategic plans, while it is liable to dislocation by the new types of military pressure that are simultaneously evolving—especially that of air attack. Are the problems of future

The Last War and the Next

warfare becoming too complex for solution, at any rate by strategists who have been professionally trained to prefer simple solutions and traditionally nurtured in a preference for familiar means?

Reflection on these conditions suggests that there is only one safe prophecy about the next war—or that the safest prophecy is—that it will prove a greater muddle than the last. That it will begin in confusion and end in chaos. It is not that generals and admirals are incompetent, but that the task has passed beyond their competence. Their limitations are due not to a congenital stupidity—as a disillusioned public is so apt to assume—but to the growth of science, which has upset the foundations of their technique. They are like men who cling to their little wooden huts in an earthquake. The only way of salvation would be to get out in the open—to survey the problems in complete detachment and from the widest point of view.

But a scientific habit of thought is the last thing that military education and training have fostered. Perhaps that is an unalterable condition, for the services might hardly survive if they parted company with sentiment—if the bulk of their members detached themselves from the loyalties which are incompatible with the single-minded loyalty to truth that science demands.

CHAPTER XXII

A German View of the Next War

The director of Germany's military effort in the last war, General Ludendorff, has recently set forth his ideas on future warfare, and his creed of national life in preparation for it. He seeks to expound the doctrine of 'totalitarian warfare' which should be the natural accompaniment of the Totalitarian State. Addressed to his countrymen, his message deserves attention by other peoples. It also requires examination by scientific students of war.

He opens with a heavy attack on the theories of Clausewitz which, as he emphasizes, were the foundation on which the German plans in 1914 had been built. Clausewitz, who had died nearly a century before, moulded the minds of the leading soldiers and statesmen, not only in Germany but throughout Europe, during the generations which led up to the World War. Since then his theories have suffered some searching criticism, especially from Anglo-Saxon analysts, for their tendency to make policy the servant of strategy, and strategy little more than a strait lane to battle. The theoretical extravagance of Clausewitz's idea of 'absolute war'—'violence pushed to its utmost bounds'—was contrary to common sense. To use force without limit and without calculation of cost may be instinctive in a hate-maddened mob, but it is the negation of statesmanship. Germany's exhaustion in 1918 was the natural consequence of this delusion. The conductors of her war-machine, less wise than Bismarck, did not know when to stop; they went on until they tumbled into the abyss.

Although cause and effect here seem so clear, Ludendorff is still unable to see it. Through his coloured glasses the fault of Clausewitz's teaching is not that it lent itself to such extremes, but that it did not go far enough. It allowed policy too much importance, not too little. As typical of Clausewitz he cites a passage concluding: 'The political goal is the end, and warfare is a means leading to it, and means can never be thought of without a certain end.' To Ludendorff this is old-fashioned nonsense. The totalitarian principle demands that in war a nation should place everything in its service; and, in peace, at the service of the next war. War is the highest expression of the national 'will to give', and politics must therefore be subservient to the conduct of war.

It becomes clear that the main difference between Clausewitz and his successor is that the latter achieves what seemed unthinkable to the former, and 'thinks' of war as a means without an end—unless making the nation into an efficient army be considered an end in itself. This is hardly so new as Ludendorff appears to imagine. Sparta tried it, the and end of her existence lies two thousand years back.

With the aim of developing the nation for war, of creating a super-Sparta, Ludendorff's first concern is to ensure 'the psychical unity of the people'. For him 'the Christian faith, and the life shaped by it, are the prime causes of a national breakdown in the totalitarian war'. This faith must be replaced by one 'built on racial convictions, where life is rooted in an affined knowledge of God peculiar to itself': to put it in simpler words—a belief in a purely German God. From this will spring a healthy nationalism in which all women will accept that their noblest task is to bear vigorous sons to 'bear the burden of the totalitarian war', and all men will develop their powers for that purpose: in short—to breed, and be bred, for killing. The other positive suggestions which Ludendorff offers towards this problem of creating psychical unity boil down to little more than the age-old prescription of suppressing everyone who expresses, or even entertains, views contrary to those of the High Command.

The next need insisted on is for a sound and self-sufficient national economic system suited to the demands of totalitarian war. Ludendorff thus seems to realize that military power rests on an economic foundation. Yet, curiously, when he dwells on the crippling difficulties suffered in the last war, and gives striking evidence of the effect of the Allied blockade, he does not see how this reflects on his belief that wars are decided by battle between the armies. For the only point of praise which he can give Clausewitz is that 'Clausewitz only thinks of the annihilation of the hostile armies in battle'. To Ludendorff this remains 'an immutable principle', although it is a theory which has rarely been borne out in practice during the century since Clausewitz died. Happily for Ludendorff he is not troubled by historical facts when they present obstacles to his faith.

Let us now study his picture of the way that the totalitarian war will be waged. It should open without a declaration of war—lest the people of the nation which

A German View of the Next War

declares war should feel any guilty sense of being the aggressors. Within a few hours of the decision to make war, air, land and sea striking forces must reach their full war readiness. The rest of the air force and navy will complete their mobilization by the second day; and the rest of the land forces, a few days later. Hostilities will have already begun with the despatch of the mechanized divisions near the frontier to force an entry into the enemy country. On the seas the surface and submarine attack on the enemy's commerce will coincide with this opening stroke. 'The focusing point of the war now lies in sending air formations to gain air superiority over the enemy, to strike at the advance of the enemy's army by rail and otherwise, and also at aerodromes. Air battles will ensue.' It may be worth while also to bomb important industrial towns. Within forty-eight hours or less, the navy should sail to seek decisive battle with the foe. 'The main land advance' may begin a little later, because of the masses that will have to be brought up—and these will have to come by rail since motors will be inadequate to carry the numbers. 'There is no doubt that by the end of the second week of war operations will be in full progress everywhere.' Battle will follow battle till the enemy is finally crushed, or till reserves of men and material run out. 'In the wars waged by continental countries the decision lies on land.' The air force must first be used to help in beating the opposing army; only then will the army be able to act 'with its air force' against the enemy country in rear.

Land, air and sea action all have in common the fight to bring about a superiority of fire over the enemy. Nevertheless this will not suffice 'to bring about the annihilation of the enemy'. 'The final decision on land will lie in the fight of man against man, tank against man, or tank against tank'—how a tank can destroy a tank, any more than a warship can destroy a warship, except by fire, Ludendorff does not explain. For him, the land battle is still a process in which the infantry is helped forward by artillery, machine-guns, mortar and tank support until it 'overwhelms the enemy in a man-to-man fight'. Furthermore, 'attack is always the deciding factor in battles' Army battles with army, supported by aircraft; navy battles with navy, supported by aircraft; and 'in air battles air squadrons fight one another'. All movements should lead to battle; mechanization simply quickens the rush to battle.

Ludendorff has no moral objection to striking direct against the enemy people. 'The demands of totalitarian warfare . . . will ever ignore the cheap theoretical desire to abolish unrestricted U-boat warfare.' And aircraft will now combine with submarines in sinking every vessel which tries to reach the enemy's ports, 'even vessels sailing under neutral flags'. Likewise on land a time will come 'when bombing squadrons must inexorably and without pity be sent against' the people in the enemy country. But on military grounds, which are the ruling considerations, that time should normally be delayed until the battles have been won.

Ludendorff declares that technical means are becoming ever more important, yet clings to the old belief that strength lies in numbers—'it is a fact that "victory goes to the big battalions".' Hence 'the totalitarian war demands the incorporation in the Army of every man fit to bear arms'. He admits that the conditions of war require the fighting man to be increasingly individualistic, yet assumes that this is compatible with the strictest discipline, and fails to reflect that the Totalitarian State is hardly the

soil in which such individualism can flourish. He has a
welcome for every new weapon and instrument, but rarely
appears to consider how they may affect each other. He
conveys no clear picture, and seems to have none himself,
of the different factors of war in relation to each other. His
message would seem to be—multiply every kind of force
as much as you can, and you will get somewhere—but
where, he neither worries nor wonders. The one thing on
which he is really clear is that 'the Commander-in-Chief
must lay down his instructions for the political leaders,
and the latter must follow and fulfil them in the service
of warfare'.

What is offered in return for this claim to unlimited power
for the military chief, this demand for a blank cheque on
the resources of the nation? A faith, certainly—if it requires limitless faith to swallow it. The main articles of
Ludendorff's creed might be phrased thus: 'I believe in a
pure German God, the maker of the German nation in
arms; and in the Commander-in-Chief, his only son and
representative on earth. I believe in the almighty power of
numbers; in battle, as the means to winning war; in
attack, as the means of winning battle; and in the hand-
to-hand fight as the ultimate means of overcoming the
enemy's resistance.'

While it is clear that Ludendorff's faith is built on the
traditional military theory, despite his sweeping repudia-
tion of the theorists, and that it is essentially derived from
the past, it is difficult to find solid support for it even in
past experience. It is easier to find the wars where battle
did not prove decisive than where it did. Take the first
great war of modern history—the Thirty Years' War.
There were many battles in which one army was virtually
destroyed, yet none had any decisive influence on the

struggle. The mutual exhaustion had such effect, however, and made so deep an impression on military thought, that for nearly two centuries the average general was chary of fighting battles at all, while even the great ones took care only to fight when, by chance or by strategy, the dice were loaded heavily in their favour—when, as Saxe said, there was 'all imaginable reason to expect the victory . . . without trusting anything to accident'.

There was a change when Napoleon came on the scene. A Corsican, not a Frenchman; a supreme careerist, not a true patriot; he was unchecked in pursuing his ambitions by any sense of responsibility for the ultimate welfare of his country as apart from himself. If his dreams were boundless, he took short views, since his horizon was his own life-span. Time was always against him; and he needed quick results. Now, whatever be the difficulties of winning a war by a battle, it is the quickest means—*if* it can be achieved. Hence Napoleon's predisposition for this means.

In adopting it, too, he was helped by new assets. First was the newly introduced organization of the army in independent divisions—whereby, instead of being a single body, it grew limbs—with which it could grip the enemy at one point while it struck him elsewhere. This made it easier to force a battle on the enemy, to take him at a disadvantage, and to concentrate strength against weakness—while hindering the enemy's concentration. Another asset was the new mobility. The revolutionary armies could no longer maintain, or be maintained by, the old elaborate supply system. They had to find a new and flexible system; they had to secure their supplies where they could; they had to learn to live sparsely and march light. The troops themselves could not be kept in the old stiff-drilled formations, nor restrained to a slow pace for the sake of symmetry. But they could cover the country much faster than their opponents, and made rings round them on the battlefield. A further asset was the new artillery method—of concentrating fire rapidly against key-points; of disorganizing the resistance by this blasting fire before the assault was launched.

But even in Napoleon's hands, unlimited battle ultimately proved an unlimited liability. The military splendour of the Napoleonic age fixed the worship of battle like a yoke round the neck of soldiers. Yet the later Napoleonic wars were not decided by battles. Napoleon destroyed the Spanish armies only to find his trouble beginning. And it was not by battles that the Spanish guerillas undermined his power in Spain, and started his general ruin. Napoleon beat the Russian armies, but he did not beat Russia. The Russians wrecked his army by avoiding battle until Generals Hunger and Winter could get to work, and his real downfall was consummated in 1814—when the Allies sealed his fate by swooping on Paris while he was trying to tempt them to meet him in battle.

The American Civil War saw plenty of battles—and Lee's failure to win a victory at Gettysburg certainly damped the hopes of the South. But it was Sherman's back door entry into the South, his strategic march through Georgia and the Carolinas, which undermined the will of the Confederacy by an attack on their supplies and the morale of the people.

The last war was filled with battles, yet the most that the historian can fairly say is that they were a contributory factor—one of many—the main factor in the collapse of Germany being economic pressure. On this point there is Haig's own confession, at the end of October 1918:

A German View of the Next War

'Germany is not broken in a military sense. During the last weeks her armies have withdrawn . . . in excellent order.' The Allied armies were exhausted and needed to be reorganized before they could follow up. But Germany was broken internally by hunger, sickness and despair. Her breakdown developed directly from military disappointment, from the depression which spread when her own offensive in the spring failed to bring the victory that Ludendorff had promised. But the foundations of her resistance had been undermined by the Allied blockade.

The abortiveness of battle as a means of winning wars can be traced to the declining power of the attack to overcome defence. This condition was due to the growing power of modern firearms, and had been long in evolution. It was first manifest in the American Civil War, where it came to be a standard calculation that one man in a trench was equal to three or four in an assault. In Europe the wars of 1866 and 1870 brought fresh evidence of the paralysing influence of fire, although the brevity of both wars tended to obscure it. Nevertheless, after the second, the winning strategist of those two wars, von Moltke, drew the conclusion that his victory could not be repeated, and enunciated the lesson that: 'As a result of the improvement of firearms, the tactical defensive has acquired a great advantage over the offensive. . . . It seems to be more advantageous to proceed to an attack only after having repelled several attacks by the enemy.' His warning was lost on his successors. Their optimistic view, as expressed by von der Goltz, was: 'The idea of the greater strength of the defence is a mere delusion.' The optimism was shared in France where, near the end of the century, the future Marshal Foch coined the axiom that 'any improvement in firearms is bound to strengthen the offensive'—and proved it to his own satisfaction by specious arithmetic. British experience in the war against the Boers showed the fallacy of such assumptions, but was merely regarded in Europe as evidence of the frailty of the British attacks. Then came the Russo-Japanese war which foreshadowed nearly all the factors which upset military calculations in 1914—the paralysing power of machine-guns, the hopelessness of frontal attacks, and the consequent relapse of the armies into trenches. But military optimism was even more impregnable—to the assault of facts. To ardent soldiers war was unthinkable without successful attack, so that they were able to persuade themselves that attacks could succeed. The delusive basis of that faith was quickly exposed when the World War began, and was made clearer still when the trench deadlock set in—for four years. And it is significant that the only great battles which had far-reaching results before morale had broken down were those which took the form of a counter-stroke after the enemy had spent himself in vain attacks—the Allied victories in the first and second battles of the Marne, the German victories at Tannenberg, Gorlice, and Caporetto. Yet none of the commanders at the outset, and hardly any later, showed remembrance of Moltke's advice, or were willing to delay their own offensive dreams until they had dispelled the enemy's.

The historical basis of the belief in the hand-to-hand fight is equally false, and it reacts on the belief in numbers. For a century the military manuals of Europe had continued to emphasize the decisive importance of physical shock, echoing Clausewitz's dictum: 'The close combat, man to man, is plainly to be regarded as the real basis of combat.' The French doctrine of 1914 fervently declared that the object of all attacks was 'to charge the enemy with the bayonet in order to destroy him.' (That idea would still remain in the British manuals until 1924.) Something might be claimed for it if the emphasis had been on the psychological effect of a close-quarter threat, but the time and attention devoted to bayonet-training showed that the bayonet-fight was regarded as a reality. Yet even in the eighteenth century a practical soldier like Guibert had remarked its rarity, while Jomini was but one of a number of witnesses of the Napoleonic battles who said that, except in villages and defiles, he had 'never seen two forces cross bayonets'. Half a century later Moltke would point out the fallacy of the French assertion that their victory at Solferino had been won by the bayonet. In 1870 their troops were to pay heavily against Prussian fire for this delusion among their leaders, yet Boguslawski records that in actual fact 'bayonets were never crossed in open fight'.

Only in conditions where shock was a practical possibility could the theory of massing superior numbers be effective. It was difficult to adjust it to conditions where one man with a machine-gun might count for more than a much larger number who were advancing upon him with the bayonet. As the capacity to make such an adjustment proved to be lacking, the formula of victory became merely a formula of futility—and death. The fallacy was proved most emphatically of all by the Germans against the Russians; by their superior weapons and technique the Germans utterly discounted the vastly superior numbers of their Eastern front opponent. There the 'big battalions' merely made big cemeteries, burdened their own communications to breaking point, and bankrupted their own country's power, yet the lesson is largely lost on the man who directed the German forces. After twenty years for reflection he resuscitates these delusions for application in another war.

A German View of the Next War

Nevertheless we should be unwise to ignore them, and to accept instead the popular assumption that the next war will be waged in the air with the contending powers each seeking to destroy the enemy's capital and bomb the people into surrender.

It is worth while to approach the problem of future warfare along Ludendorff's path, not because his idea of the result is likely to prove real, but because it shows what is likely to be attempted. It is a guide to the outlook which still prevails among many of the military chiefs of Europe, to the persistence of obsolete conceptions along with new weapons, and to the consequent confusion of military thought. The general trend of the rearmament race now in progress fosters this by piling up numbers and by feeding the military chiefs with more means than their minds can assimilate. Ludendorff's is a fair representation of what may occur at the outset, if not in the issue, of a future war.

Mechanization has given the general staffs a new ground for belief in mobile warfare—the picture to which armies always revert in peace-time—along with a renewed confidence in the speedy success of their own attacks. Prolonged as was the resistance which the military authorities everywhere offered to the idea of mechanization, now that they have embraced it they build expectations on it which dumbfound a sober and long-standing advocate of this inevitable evolution. In many countries they have burst out into prophecy that trench-warfare is a thing of the past, and that the wars of the future will be fought and finished with a quickness hitherto unknown.

For the initial movements mechanized troops certainly offer a great advantage over those who have to march on foot or be brought forward by rail. This is the more important because of the growth of new fortifications along

the frontiers; the prospects of an invasion will obviously
be handicapped if the enemy is given time to man these
with the reserves that become available on mobilization.
Thus there is little doubt that the new mechanized divisions which the European armies now possess will be used
in the first hours of war with the aim of penetrating the
enemy's frontier and opening the way for the subsequent
general advance. All the general staffs are trending towards this new picture, in which the first phases of a war
are fought out by the mechanized part of their forces actually available, instead of waiting, as in 1914, until the main
strength of the army has been assembled.

But there is reason to doubt whether this mechanized
spearhead will produce the decisive advantage which is
sought. The chances are against this, unless the enemy is
not only taken unaware but is himself unmechanized. For,
in the first place, obstruction is the natural antidote to the
power of delivering mobile strokes which mechanization
has revived. By utilizing rivers, canals, and railways as
barriers, by demolishing bridges and blocking defiles, the
defender may go far to nullify the new menace. Moreover,
mechanization itself enables the means of obstruction and
demolition to be moved more swiftly to any threatened
spot. And the defenders' mechanized troops, having less
risk of being checked by hostile obstructions, may be
switched to meet the danger faster than the mechanized
attackers can develop it. Despite the apparent advantage
that mechanization has brought to the offensive, its reinforcement of the defensive may prove greater still.

While the prospects of this initial stroke by the mechanized forces are slight, they are bright compared with those
that await the main masses of the European armies. Even
if these come close enough to strike, what ground is there

for expecting that they will make more impression on the defence than in the last war? The main weapon that then stopped them was the machine-gun: there is now a far higher proportion of machine-guns, light and heavy, in all armies. The weapon on which the attackers mainly relied to overcome the defending machine-gun in the last war was artillery: there is far less artillery now in all armies than in 1918. Even if this could be increased to the war-time scale, it is a weapon that, when used in mass, tends to block the path of the infantry it is trying to help by plough-ing up the ground. It acts as an automatic military brake. Furthermore, it increases the encumbrance by the mass of transport required to supply its heavy appetite for shells. Armour, in the form of the tank, proved a better means in the last war of helping the attack forward: but armour used in a direct assault against organized defence would now seem to have lost much of its value, through the great and widespread development of armour-piercing weapons —there are now highly efficient anti-tank machine-guns, and even rifles, as well as guns.

There are greater possibilities, as I have elsewhere suggested, in the skilful use of obscurity as a cloak to the attack. Fog, natural or artificial, and darkness are the best antidotes to the defensive machine-gun. The risks of ob-scurity are mainly those of confusion; they are certainly less than those of annihilation, by machine-guns with a clear field of fire; and they can be much reduced by training. The superiority of highly trained troops over normal troops is much more pronounced in the dark than in daylight. Such a level of training, however, is difficult to attain during peace-time in mass armies raised by con-scription.

But the greater question that affects these mass armies

is whether they will ever reach the battlefield. Their approach must be made by roads and railways; they will crowd these arteries which now, for several hundred miles back, lie under the menace of air attack. Their immense demands in food and ammunition supply require a continuous circulation along these arteries; thus the strain and the susceptibility to interruption are maintained all the way back even when the armies themselves have passed on. To gauge what might happen it is worth studying the process of mobilization and assembly in 1914. Despite all the care and effort devoted to its machinery there were hitches which caused serious trouble, and threatened worse. Yet in 1914 there was no interference from the enemy such as is certain to-day through the intervention of air-power—from bombs on the bridges and rail junctions as well as on the trains and marching columns themselves; probably also from mustard gas sprayed over the roads, stations, bivouacs, and supply depots. There is no need to assume that the devastation will be as overwhelming as popular imagination and air enthusiasm picture. The complexity and delicacy of the process of mobilizing and moving forward an army is such that a mere touch, or series of touches, may well suffice to cause its collapse. The larger the army, and the more its mobilization process is speeded up, the more susceptible it will be to dislocation, because the greater will be the congestion of all the traffic arteries.

If the opponent should employ mustard gas, the paralysis of war is still more probable, for in the fighting zone mustard gas is most effective as a defensive blocking agent; it constitutes the most impassable, if invisible, barrier to advance, especially advance by armies composed of infantry; while in the rear zone it is essentially a dislocating agent, upsetting administrative arrangements and traffic circulation. But mustard gas is not essential to produce this stagnation. Machine-guns and demolitions should suffice to stop an advancing army; air bombs acting on inherent congestion behind should suffice to prevent it remaining where it has stopped. Blocked in front, the mass army is likely to break down in rear. If the maintenance of such armies is straining the resources of the nations in peace, in war the attempt to use them threatens national bankruptcy.

The attempt to seek victory in battle at sea has hardly more promise. Here again there is no need to imagine that the battle-fleets will be bombed to destruction. If the battle-fleets of the last war were deterred from meeting each other by the menace of the submarine and the mine, how much more likely is such a paralysing effect now that to these weapons are added the new dangers introduced by shore-based aircraft and torpedo-carrying speedboats—the little 'sea-sleds' which are fast multiplying in many navies.

As for battle in the air, here at present is a sphere where the offensive is superior to the defensive. But that offensive need not take the form of striking at the hostile air forces; it is simpler, far simpler, than it has ever been on land, to strike direct at the sources of the enemy's power without first breaking through his shielding forces. The spaces of the air are so vast and the speeds of aircraft are becoming so high that it is a waste of effort to fight when it is possible to slip past. Faithful to military tradition, some of the air forces, especially when under the control of conventional soldiers, may set out to defeat their aerial opponents; but, if so, they stand to lose the war while they are pursuing the battle.

A German View of the Next War

For, coincidently and subsequently, economic pressure will be in progress in all its varied forms—as even Ludendorff foresees. With the growth of social and industrial organization, economic targets have proportionately outgrown military targets, and they have become more sensitive as the latter have become less vulnerable. The complex web of a nation's commerce and industry, its administration and supply, can be easily torn. Externally the flow of its supplies can be more easily reduced to stagnation now that its trade routes are exposed to attack from shore-based aircraft and other new agents of interference.

Military wisdom now lies, not in amassing armies, but in diminishing national vulnerability. This is a compound of factors. The very industry that augments a nation's strength for military action may produce a counterbalancing degree of vulnerability. And the centralization of industry may counteract the growth of industry from a military point of view. Every means of reducing and dispersing targets, and also of decreasing their sensitiveness, should be studied and sought. The preparedness of the people is no less important. As safeguards against air attack, for example, education and understanding count at least as much as concrete measures for the provision of anti-aircraft weapons and shelters. A sturdy individualism based on a regime of reason and freedom, so long as it does not relapse into inertia, may withstand the shocks better than the emotionalism bred by totalitarianism, with its insistence on mass psychology and incessant appeal to mass sentiment. The self-reliant individual, capable of thinking for himself, has a better chance of adaptation to the unexpected. And the one certainty about modern war is that it is more uncertain than it ever was.

A German View of the Next War

Compared with to-day, it was simple to make military calculations in 1914; yet nearly all the calculations went astray—and the favourite failed. To launch a war nowadays, as remarked in an earlier chapter, is like backing a horse that has never run, and whose breeding even is unknown. If calculation ruled the rulers, they would surely abstain from aggression. But ambitious and warlike rulers are apt to prove the most hardened of gamblers. Napoleon is their patron saint—and there never was a worse case of obstinate self-delusion than his triumphal assurance on the march to Moscow. His kind may still produce gamblers of that kind. But they carry their own antidote so long as they concentrate on building armies for battle, and thereby burden their war organization with a weight it can no longer safely bear. There might be more reason to fear them if they were to develop a new art of war aiming at paralysis rather than annihilation, and operating by multiple pressure without combat: a super-guerilla warfare aimed at the sources instead of at the face of the enemy's armed power, and striking at the greatest number of points—economic, political and psychological —over the widest area, without offering a target or coming to a clinch.

CHAPTER XXIII

The Abyssinian War—and its Bearing on Future Warfare

The main lessons of this war, as now clarified by post-war evidence from both sides, have been briefly discussed in Chapter III; also their bearing on the question of future warfare. The course of the war did not run according to common expectation, and the situation after the first three months of war encouraged such excessive confidence in the Abyssinians' capacity for resistance that the dramatically swift ending of the main campaign tended to magnify the impression of surprise in the public mind. The Italians themselves have admitted that they had not foreseen the plight in which they found themselves at the end of 1935, nor such rapid and extensive success as ultimately crowned their efforts. Yet it was a war where the determining factors and conditions worked out, on the whole, in a way remarkably true to their calculable properties. That fact is an encouragement to those who believe that there is value in applying what is called the scientific method to the study of war, and that by its use it should be possible to gauge the general current and the local eddies with reasonable accuracy—instead of seeing their effects as the sport of accident and oppor-

tunism, and submitting fatalistically to the opinion that
every new war must find us unprepared for its conditions.
. If the study of war in the past has so often proved
fallible as a guide to the course and conduct of the next
war, it does not imply that war is not suited to scientific
study, but that the study has not been scientific enough,
in spirit and method. Looking back on the past it would
seem hardly possible that the authoritative schools of
military thought could have misunderstood as completely
as they did the evolution which was so consistently revealed throughout the wars of the nineteenth and early
twentieth centuries. Reviewing the record of error it seems
only capable of explanation by the conclusion that their
study of war was subjective, not objective—that they went
to military history to find texts for their sermons, instead
of facts for analysis. That conclusion has been strengthened
by experience in trying to estimate the probable course
of the Abyssinian War. Here the conditions were so
peculiar, and the unknown factors so numerous, that few
students could hope to treat the problem with the measure
of apparently assured knowledge that was available in
recent European wars. It remained to be seen how far
the margin of error could be minimized by examining the
coming war purely as a problem, without preconceptions
and preferences, guided only by a general understanding
of recent trends in the evolution of warfare. For my own
part I had to attempt such an estimate in the early summer of 1935, and it may be of interest because of the bearing on the question just discussed, to reproduce the bulk of
it, as it appeared in *The Times*, before passing on to discuss what actually happened. The retrospective view can
thus be compared with the prospective.

The Abyssinian War—

Prospect

'From a military point of view, the Abyssinian problem may be focussed in a single word: "Adowa". Perhaps more exactly, in a phrase: "The memory of Adowa." I do not refer here to the part played by the memory of this thirty-nine-year-old defeat in fomenting Italian irritation and increasing determination to attain results that will wipe out the memory. That factor lies in the political sphere, even though it may find expression in the military.

'The military bearing of "Adowa" lies mainly in its effect upon the attitude and action of the Abyssinians. If it came to a test, would they prove to be intoxicated by that memory of victory over the Italian forces, and imagine that 1896 could be repeated in the conditions of 1935? Would they, in that intoxication, fail to realize that their best hope of successful resistance lies in playing the guerilla game steadfastly from the outset?

'The Abyssinians' most serious danger lies in the possibility that they would, in false confidence, or under the sting of a loss of territory, assemble in mass to oppose the invaders near the frontier. In that case they would offer a promising target to the bombs of the Italian aircraft, and in some areas to the thrusts of mechanized forces. They might even be tempted into launching attacks in vain gallantry against the Italian machine-guns. Ondurman might be repeated. The student of military history appreciates how easily, with a little cunning, the Sudanese might have made things awkward for us in the advance to Khartoum. Instead, by excess of courage they played into our hands, and, by their massed advance in daylight, offered themselves up as a sacrificial demonstration of the effect of fire-power. At the worst, more tactical sense is to be expected of the Abyssinians—but fire-power has developed more in the past thirty years than any improvement in tactics can overtake. The only chance for the ill-equipped nowadays lies in guerilla tactics. Information from some sources makes it doubtful whether the Abyssinians have realized this essential truth, and are of a mind to act upon it. Adowa may prove stronger than reason.

'If the Abyssinians should be so unwise as to present a target to modern weapons, the consequences of a crushing disillusionment are not easy to predict. Its ripples might spread wide. When considering the possible effect of concentrated air bombing on such an unacclimatized people, one recalls the reaction which the Arabs suffered, on the other side of the Red Sea, when they first made contact with artillery fire during the Revolt in the Hejaz against the Turks. The shells which exploded among them were nothing compared with the weight of explosive that the Italian aircraft could drop upon the Abyssinians to-day.

'The Japanese have shown in Manchuria how air bombardment may pave the way for the advancing troops, serving as a longer range and more flexible substitute for the artillery barrage of the last war. It is likely that this method will be the Italians' strongest card, with tanks as a secondary agent, in forcing the evacuation of points where a prolonged delay might otherwise be imposed. But the further the advance progresses and the less the defenders offer a target, the greater the handicap in obtaining the full effect of these new tools.

'If the Abyssinians were wise enough to adopt guerilla methods from the outset, one does not envy the Italian commanders the problem that they would be called on to solve, especially if they aimed at the complete subjugation of the country—and such a country, topographically. The rugged plateau with its towering escarpment might be likened to the medieval castle of a giant's dream. Approaches are few and difficult, being fortified by nature with successive moats and barricades, while the communications of an advancing force would be as hard to safeguard as to create. "Air-pressure" on the defender's keep would not offer the promise of effect that this new form of the rear-attack holds out in other parts of the world, even in similarly de-centralized and unindustrialized states. Addis Ababa, the capital, is over four hundred miles distant from the Italian bases in Eritrea and stands over 8000 feet above sea-level; as a bombing target it would thus seem to be well out of reach of present service aircraft. The air problem might be diminished as the Italian land forces advance more deeply into the country—but the further they go the harder may become their military problems. The effective subjugation of a country largely depends on having targets that can be effectively smitten. Here, targets will be few unless the Abyssinians carelessly offer them. And nothing is more nerve-wracking for an army of occupation than the intangible ubiquity of a guerilla foe who is operating in his own country with room enough to play that game.

'But it is far more difficult to change to guerilla methods after a shattering reverse. Here is the risk that the Abyssinians run in remembering Adowa too well. It is true that the Spaniards succeeded in making such a change against the Napoleonic armies, after their own regular forces had been smashed. But they had Wellington to support them and, by his intervention, gained time and space for their guerillas to sprout throughout the countryside. And that successful change of method was achieved more than a century ago; nowadays, air-power and mechanization tend to accelerate the exploitation of victory over a congregated force, and jeopardize the chances of rallying the survivors to harass, where they cannot directly resist, the invaders' progress. Moreover, the nerve-shock of a new weapon is apt to have the deepest echo among a primitive people.

'Such knowledge as we have of the forces and equipment of the Abyssinians strengthens the impression that it would be foolish for them to embark upon an imitation of modern warfare. The number of "regular" troops of whom the Emperor might dispose are not likely to amount to more than forty thousand, and although levies amounting to more than half a million might be available to oppose an invasion that threatened the heart of the country, such quantities would have little value except for guerilla warfare, even if the miracle of keeping them supplied could be performed. The modern Abyssinian artillery is said to include only some three batteries of "75's". Beyond this, it is made up of a number of "elephant-guns" and a hundred or more ancient pieces. Mortars, like aircraft and tanks, may be counted on the fingers. Machine-guns probably total about three hundred, with double that number of automatic rifles—the Arab Revolt showed the essential value of these for guerilla warfare even, and an increase is certainly one of the Abyssinians' most urgent needs, together with adequate ammunition.

'The time the Ethiopians have had for training may not prove altogether an advantage, if one may take as having any general application some recent reports as to the well-drilled state of these troops. That type of training runs the risk of paralysing their natural fighting instincts and leav-

ing them a paralysed target. Primitive man knows how
to fight with cunning, but if you put him through a long
course of drill one may do no more than develop "tactical
arthritis". To counter the modern weapons of their
assailants the Ethiopians do not need similar heavy
weapons, any more than they need European drill, but
they certainly require an adequate quantity of light
machine-guns and small-arm ammunition. These are the
material foundation of guerilla tactics against a modern
army, as Lawrence of Arabia diagnosed and demonstrated
a generation ago on the other side of the Red Sea.

'By contrast, we may reckon that modern armament
will give to the Italian troops a fighting value much
greater than their actual numbers. The extent of these is
not certain, but a short time ago it was reported that there
was one white division in Eritrea, with the equivalent
of three native divisions, and another white division in
Somalia together with a native division. It is probable
that about a hundred thousand men have been despatched
from the Mediterranean, and although the shipments have
dwindled recently, during the bad season, it is likely that
the numbers would be increased before operations open.
A division in Sardinia has been standing by for some
time. The Italian forces are said to include a considerable
quantity of tanks and mechanized transport, as well as
several hundred aircraft.

'In estimating the possible courses which the Italian
forces may adopt, much depends on their object. If they
are aiming at the conquest of Abyssinia, the decisive
invasion would, in normal expectation, be made from
Eritrea. In this case, a main advance from Massawa southward upon Magdala, to bring the Abyssinians to battle,
might be accompanied by a flank advance from the southern

corner of Eritrea upon the rear of the defending forces. If there is no base in this corner capable of maintaining large forces, the route itself is more suitable to the movement of mechanized troops than along the difficult direct route of advance through the precipitous country between Massawa and Magdala.

'This combined advance from Eritrea might well be preceded by a further advance on the southern borders of Abyssinia, executed by the Italian forces in Somalia. It would serve to draw off the Abyssinians' attention and forces, especially if the threat went far enough and was direct against Harar, the Emperor's own province.'

The kernel of my 'appreciation' was packed into a nutshell by a Canadian caption-writer who put these headlines on an interview I gave his newspaper on September 4th:

'ADOWA ILLUSION MAY DECIDE WAR
SAYS STRATEGIST
Mass Attacks Will Mean Annihilation for Abyssinians
Liddell Hart Predicts.'

In that interview I also suggested that the Italians might find scope for their aircraft, apart from the normal military functions, in supplying their advanced columns as well as in a progressive demoralization of the population behind the enemy's front.

Retrospect

The invasion began on October 2nd. The main Italian forces, three army corps, moved southwards from Eritrea as expected. On the 6th after a short advance they captured Adowa without meeting serious opposition. The Ethiopians, following the wise admonitions of the Emperor, continued to show a promising restraint in checking the impulse to attack which 'the memory of Adowa' might have caused. The Italians began to suffer trouble with their communications and a pause of some weeks occurred. Short advances took place on the Somalia front in the south, and also from the southern corner of Eritrea, but were slow to develop further. Air bombing, however, began to produce some ominous symptoms of nerve-strain in the interior, despite the unfavourable conditions in which it had to operate—the wild nature of the country and the scattered population. The detachment of Dejasmatch Gugsa and other minor chiefs was a further symptom, and score, showing that the Italians were seeking to smooth the path of their strategy by fulfilling the old Roman maxim 'divide and conquer'.

Early in November the Italians resumed their southward advance, and on the 6th captured Makale, some eighty miles distant, again without meeting resistance. They then began to widen their penetration westward to the Takkaze River. If the Ethiopians were still showing a more than expected power to hold themselves in check, they had failed to develop real guerilla activity in harassing the advance. This was a lost opportunity, since the Italians suffered growing difficulties over the problem of supplying their forces. The scale of those forces accentuated the congestion of the inadequate communications. If the Ethiopians had been endowed with even a small air force they might at this time have precipitated an Italian disaster by attacking the narrow and scanty routes of supply on which the Italians depended. In the south General Graziani's forces captured Gorahai on the 5th, a coup in which they effectively used the 'air barrage' method to overcome the defenders before the attack was launched. But the exploitation of this advance broke down, and the pursuing forces had to fall back.

Stagnation set in everywhere, and the initiative passed to the Ethiopians, who at last began to develop a modified form of guerilla counter-pressure. Circling round the Italians' far-extended flank, in mid-December—a few days after the Hoare-Laval proposals had been formulated —they regained the crossings of Takkaze by surprise and pushed some way towards Aksum. A week later Ras Seyyum recaptured part of the Tembien and thus began to threaten the Italians' hold on Makale. They have since admitted that the effect of these moves made their whole position precarious. The timely intervention of the Italian aircraft did much to curb the immediate danger, but the worrying pressure was renewed and extended.

Thus when the New Year opened the Italians' military situation was not an enviable one. Contemplation of it led a large body of opinion in Europe to count on it worsening, and overlook the permanent elements of weakness which underlay the Ethiopians' situation. There was inadequate ground for such optimism so long as the Ethiopians lacked the means necessary for an intensive guerilla campaign, and until they also demonstrated their aptitude for it.

In mid-January the campaign took an ominous turn. Emboldened by Italian passivity, Ras Desta's forces pushed forward to the Somalian border near Dolo. If this was a potential threat to the flank of the Italian line of invasion from the south, it exposed the Ethiopians to a counter-stroke in an area where the terrain was favourable to tanks. General Graziani seized the opportunity, temporarily shifting his axis, and struck at the target thus offered. The tanks appeared in the Ethiopians' rear, their resistance collapsed, and the victory was followed up by a 240-mile pursuit to Neghelli. The following week the Italian forces in the north launched an offensive in the Tembien to relieve the pressure on the position at Makale. The Ethiopians met it with a counter-offensive in which partial success was purchased at heavy cost. It provided disquieting evidence of a new tendency—to make mass charges in face of machine-guns. The 'memory of Adowa' was asserting itself, dangerously. The Ethiopians were blunting the edge of their own forces. Marshal Badoglio noted that after the failure of these repeated attacks the Ethiopians, 'discouraged by their heavy losses, a shortage of ammunition, delay in the arrival of reinforcements and food supplies', had lapsed into a state of passivity. In consequence, he decided that he could safely take the offensive south of Makale, having now straightened out his communications.

Ras Mulugeta's forces awaited the assault and thereby exposed themselves to a concentrated artillery bombardment. After being blasted by high explosive, their position at Amba Aradam was encircled and overrun under cover of a thick fog—a fresh example of the benefit of the 'attack in obscurity'. By reckless counter-attacks the Ethiopian leaders had merely increased their losses and sapped the confidence of the men who were thus thrown against machine-guns. The Ethiopians lost some 20,000 men compared with 800 on the Italian side. Marshal Badoglio left the pursuit to his aircraft, and delivered a second stroke against the Ethiopian forces in the Tembien, followed by a third against the forces in Shire. As was inevitable, machine-power overcame an ill-equipped opponent who rashly accepted battle—and who each time did most of the attacking. Through this departure from common-sense strategy the Ethiopian forces had suffered a severe shaking, which was intensified by incessant air attacks. In following up their strokes the Italians made use of aircraft to overcome the brake of supply—the army corps on the right received its entire supplies by air in its advance to the Takkaze. By the beginning of March the Italian forces had regained the whole wedge of territory originally occupied in early November, and had extended it some twenty miles farther south, to Amba Alaji. This formidable position was abandoned by the Ethiopians without a fight. According to Italian accounts air action prevented the enemy making a stand there, while Ethiopian accounts say that the position was handed over to the invaders by the arranged desertion of the Gallas and other tribes; the two accounts are not necessarily contradictory, for the causes may have been supplementary.

In his attacks Marshal Badoglio had profited by using wider tactical frontages, so that the enemy's attempted counter-moves were baffled and repelled by an extended fire-screen. The evidence of the enemy's discouragement also inspired him to widen his strategical front. A force from the southern corner of Eritrea advanced 120 miles across the Danakil desert and occupied the Aussa territory; its escorting aircraft fed it with supplies besides covering it against surprise. On the extreme western wing, near the Sudan border, other forces advanced across the Setit and pushed on south, towards Gondar. This important centre was captured by a motor column of 5000 men with 500 lorries, which, after a preliminary move of 150 miles through Eritrea territory, advanced 220 miles into enemy country in twelve days.

Even so, the Italians, in five months of war, had only covered a quarter of the way to Addis Ababa. More than three hundred miles lay ahead, filled with great obstacles of nature which had incalculable delaying power if they were defended with resolution blended with discretion. Although the ever-threatened advance on Harar succeeded, by its mere threat, in detaining in the south a large proportion of the best-equipped Ethiopian forces, the Emperor sent considerable reinforcements north to make up the losses recently suffered, and he went up to Lake Ashangi himself to take command. Thus, when time and space factors were weighed, the chance of the Italians reaching any decisive result before the rains turned on the questions whether they could revolutionize the situation by some new means, or whether the Ethiopians would commit fresh folly.

In March the Italians adopted the widespread use of mustard gas, which they had shipped to Eritrea in large quantities and had already tried occasionally in earlier months. Naturally, they avoided using it in battle or laying it on their own direct line of advance, where it would have been a hindrance to themselves; but there was ample scope for its effective employment in covering their flanks and communications against hostile counter-moves, as well as in demoralizing the enemy's reserves and his people behind the front. The effect of this new weapon on a primitive race who had no protection was dramatic—the nerve-shock being greater than the physical damage. It is worth recalling that when the Germans first introduced gas into warfare, in April 1915, the French African troops were completely demoralized, streaming away in panic. Mustard gas naturally appears to have magic proportions, since the victims may be stricken without the slightest warning, merely through traversing a belt of ground which has been sprayed with the liquid some time earlier or through touching someone else who has a splash on his clothing. Although it is a disabling rather than a lethal weapon, and the deaths from it were relatively few in the European armies, the death-rate may be very high with unprotected troops and where no remedial treatment is available.

The rapid decline of Ethiopian morale which followed the repulse of their massed attacks and the advent of the gas campaign made it seem hopeless to await the Italians' advance or to rely on harassing operations against their flanks and communications. The Emperor was impelled to abandon wise strategy and adopt the desperate measure of launching his forces at the end of March to the assault of the Italian position at Mai Chio, south of Amba Alaji. The result was fatal, and could hardly have been otherwise. In their repeated attacks during the day of March 31st the Ethiopians had some 8000 men killed—more than a third of the attacking force. Next morning a fresh attack early was merely delivered to cover their retreat, which soon degenerated into a rout under the pressure of the air pursuit.

The collapse of this suicidal offensive was followed by the collapse of the Ethiopian army's will to resist. Thus the path of advance on Addis Ababa was suddenly cleared. There were many positions on the way where a comparatively small body of determined troops with machine-guns might have checked a multitude of assailants. But they were left open to the Italians, whose problem was now simplified, and reduced, to the organization of a triumphal march along a very rough road. This was largely a motorized march covered by a far-ranging barrage of aircraft.

The Abyssinian War—

On April 9th the Italians began their advance on Dessye, with the Eritrean army corps of some 18,000 men. It was fed mainly with supplies dropped by parachute during its march of 120 miles, covered in six days. Meantime Marshal Badoglio organized a force of 20,000 men, half Italians, half native troops, with a large convoy of lorries, to carry out the further advance on Addis Ababa. This picked force was brought up after the capture of Dessye and, leaving there on April 25th, it pressed forward in three columns by different routes, to reach Addis Ababa on May 5th. The invasion had been begun with a mass of over 300,000 men; the decisive advance, along the final three-quarters of the distance to the enemy's capital had been carried out by a severely pruned and newly proportioned spearhead composed of 20,000 men, some 2000 motor vehicles, and part of the 500 aircraft which had by now been concentrated in the war zone.

In the south Dedjasmatch Nasibu's army still offered a stout resistance on an entrenched line south of Sasa Baneh, showing the difference which even a trifle of modern equipment could make. Successive Italian attacks were repulsed for three days, but the lock was finally forced on April 18th with the aid of air bombardment. Graziani's advance was then again held up by the mud, and Sasa Baneh was not occupied until April 29th, after another stiff fight. With the Italians here on the offensive, the disparity of loss had been less marked than in the north; their casualties had been some 2000 compared with the Ethiopians' estimated 5000. But with the flight of the Emperor resistance had lost its point, while Nasibu's forces disintegrated under air pursuit once they were driven into the open. Thus the Italians' continued advance on Harar was a procession delayed only by the weather.

and its Bearing on Future Warfare

The machine had triumphed—over the man. The Lion of Judah had been crushed between the upper and nether jaws of Italy's mechanized forces. This reflection epitomizes the course of the Abyssinian war. It is no denial of the qualities of skill and courage which were called for, and displayed, in the handling of the modern weapons with which the Italian forces were equipped. There were stout-hearted men in the ranks of the invaders and in the command posts: without the power of resolution and endurance no deep advance into such a wild country would have been conceivable whatever the superiority of weapon-power. And back in Rome there was a human dynamo, charging the battery with an electric current. Yet when the fullest credit is given, apart from the moral issues, to these human factors, we are left with the basic fact that the decisive difference was produced by the war-machine.

The facts of the campaign point unmistakably to the conclusion that mechanization in the broad sense was the foundation on which the Italians' military superiority was built, while aircraft, the machine-gun, and mustard gas proved the decisive agents. The machine-gun on the ground for shattering the enemy's attacks, and the machine-gun in the air for exploiting its recoil. Mustard gas as an invisible and disheartening screen against interference and also as a spreader of panic at a distance. Aircraft as a super-mobile cavalry arm, and as a means of giving the ground forces a mobility, through elasticity of supply, they could not otherwise have attained; also as a distributor of disintegrating propaganda. If the Ethiopians played into the enemy's hands by providing him with targets, it should also be realized that with the advent of aircraft the chance of conducting successful guerilla warfare has been much impaired, as was foreseen by that supreme

317

The Abyssinian War

exponent of the art, T. E. Lawrence. It counters the guerilla's mobility by superior mobility. Yet, as it was, by trying to fight like an army the Ethiopians gave the air arm its opportunity to show its power in land warfare—for paralysing the action, and destroying the strength, of armies. It was thus a warning to the armies of Europe, and to those who still place their faith in mass of man-power.

CHAPTER XXIV

Would Another War End Civilization?

The question posed in this chapter is regarded by many as being not even a question. Thus Mr. A. A. Milne in his recent book, *Peace With Honour*, which ably exposes so many irrational assumptions of the past, says: 'Is it not *absolutely* certain that another European war would mean the complete collapse of civilization?' Any qualifying effect of the question mark is offset by the emphatic italics. And a little further on the question mark even is dropped: 'If we are on the eve of another Armageddon, then we are on the eve of the destruction of the world. That is absolutely certain.'

Conscious of temerity in facing such certainty, I still stick to my question mark. While recognizing the possibility that Mr. Milne's prediction may be justified, I can see reasons why it may not. Even if it is fulfilled I am inclined to think that the effect will come in an indirect and unexpected way rather than in the direct fashion that most publicists suggest—that it will come through the paralysis, not through the destruction, of civilization.

Here is the typical picture that the publicists paint. There is striking agreement between them—is it perhaps

Would Another War End Civilization?

because, lacking time for prolonged research, they each
copy one another? On the declaration of war, or anticipat-
ing it, the enemy's air-fleet appears over the capital. The
city is deluged with bombs, usually poison gas bombs, and
within a few hours it is a city of the dead. Millions have
been suffocated. With certain variations of embroidery
that pattern is continually repeated.

In *Cry Havoc* Mr. Beverley Nichols summons expert
witnesses, apparently furnished by his news-clipping
agency, to confirm the veracity of such a picture. Lord
Halsbury is quoted as saying: 'Mustard gas is the most
deadly of known gases. In an area, say, Richmond to
Barking, and from Finchley to Streatham (i.e. covering
most of Greater London) an effective lethal dose would
be only forty-two tons. In twelve hours every man, woman
and child in that area might fail to live.' Mr. Nichols
adds in comment: 'Since one R.A.F. bomber can now
carry two tons of bombs, twenty planes could now do this
work very easily.' This sounds appalling, until one remembers that mustard gas proved the *least deadly* of gases in
the last war, although the most widely disabling. The
death-rate among casualties was less than four per cent.
Its outstanding effectiveness lay not in killing, but in
hindering and upsetting military plans—it was a first-class
nuisance.

More weight attaches to the verdict of Thomas Edison,
who is quoted as having said: 'There is in existence no
means of preventing an aeroplane flotilla flying over
London to-morrow and spreading over the millions of
Londoners a gas which would asphyxiate these millions
in a relatively short time. From twenty to fifty aeroplanes
would be amply sufficient for the purpose . . . London's
population could be choked to death in three hours.'

Would Another War End Civilization?

A French physicist, Professor Langevin, is said to have stated: 'A hundred aeroplanes, each carrying a ton of gas, could cover Paris with a gas cloud twenty metres thick. This could be done in an hour and if there were no wind Paris would be annihilated.'

Even retired soldiers have voiced this view. Thus Lieut.-General von Altrock, of the German Army, has declared in the *Militar-Wöchenblatt*: 'The population over a large area may expect destruction at any moment. The next war will take the form of mass murder of the civilian population rather than a conflict between armies.'

Yet there are some notable witnesses who have ridiculed these alarming forecasts, and it is significant that they tend to be of higher scientific standing than the prophets of woe. Thus Dr. Freeth, who is chief research chemist of Imperial Chemical Industries, remarked at a meeting of the League of Nations Union that: 'The amount of nonsense talked about poison gas is beyond belief.' He pointed out that the most deadly gases could not be used in war—because of some simple catch. Carbon monoxide was one of the most dangerous. Every day omnibuses and cars were giving off large quantities. Yet, even when a mass of vehicles was held up in a narrow street, there were no casualties—because of the ventilating powers of the atmosphere. Carbon monoxide had a molecular weight of 30, while nitrogen had a molecular weight of 28 and oxygen of 32. 'So if carbon monoxide were let loose, in a very short space of time it would be knocked about and dispersed by the molecules of the air which had, for practical purposes, the same molecular weight. That was why people are not killed in rows in Bond Street.'

The first gas used in the war was chlorine: 'its effect depended on perfect atmospheric conditions at the right moment', combined with an unsuspecting and therefore unprepared enemy. Once its surprise effect had passed its value was at an end.

'The really killing gases were light', Dr. Freeth emphasized, 'and consequently easily dispersed by the molecular power of the atmosphere. All heavy gases were more or less immobile and could not move quickly. The only really useful military gas was mustard gas—and mustard gas was not a gas at all, but a heavy oil, made of alcohol, sulphur and chlorine.' Owing to its prolonged effect it might dislocate traffic for several days until it had been dispersed. But it did not spread rapidly, and if it fell on wet porous soil it decomposed.

'Chemical warfare had got such a hold on the imagination of the civilian population that the main danger was psychological.' The actual danger could be largely countered by precautions. 'If in a gas raid a man could keep his head sufficiently to close the windows, put out the fire, and wait until the properly constituted authority had dispersed the gas, he would be reasonably safe. If he had no duty to perform, and simply got into a bath, smoked a pipe, and laughed, he would be practically completely safe!' Clearly, there was a whimsical touch in this last piece of advice, but it served to correct the other extreme of prognostication, and to emphasize that understanding is the best safeguard.

A broadly similar view has been expressed by Professor J. B. S. Haldane, although he has emphasized that the disabling potentialities of poisonous smokes as well as of mustard gas were not fully developed in the war. The reason is significant not only in its reflection on the military outlook but as a guide in speculation on the future. For Professor Haldane revealed in *Callinicus* that the use of

Would Another War End Civilization?

mustard gas, which the Germans eventually introduced in 1917 (with most upsetting effect on the British Passchendaele offensive), was suggested by a British chemist to the military authority concerned with such questions. The General immediately asked 'Does it kill?' He received the reply: 'No, but it will disable enormous numbers of the enemy temporarily,'—whereat he said: 'That is no good to us, we want something that will kill.'

The trend of Professor Haldane's conclusions was that 'if our anti-gas measures are sufficiently neglected, the consequences may be very serious'. But he was as outspoken as Dr. Freeth in rejecting the alarming picture of 'the wiping out of the population of whole cities' by gas bombardment.

Where experts differ it is difficult for the objective-minded enquirer, even though he be a student of war in general, to decide where the truth lies. But I have been impressed by the fact that the claims made for gas are least among the active chemists engaged in gas research whom I have met—their measure of unanimity is such that one might suspect that it was due to 'trade-unionism' save for the fact that they agree, not in exaggerating, but in diminishing the importance of their own speciality.

What we can deduce, I think, from this controversy is that the vulnerability of the target counts for at least as much as the power of the weapon—and possibly counts for more. To that deduction, and its meaning, I shall return later.

But the feature which most strikes one in reading the forecasts of future horror, of cities blotted out in an hour, is the scant attention they pay to those who will direct the attacks—the military chiefs. By a curious self-contradiction, the very publicists who are most scornful of the military mind will take for granted that these air and gas attacks are directed with diabolical craft. They allow no credit to the profession of arms—not even the credit of having resisted throughout history every new development that has enhanced the terrible power of armed force. Yet they credit it with the overwhelmingly swift and decisive strokes of their imaginative picture.

It is left, however, to the General Staffs to conduct war —and their picture is very different to that drawn by the publicists. For the most part, it is still the picture of 1918 painted with the renewed confidence of 1914 upon a canvas of 1814. Right in the foreground stand the armies—not the air forces. As in 1914 the million-strong armies advance to battle—with each other. They are preceded by mechanized spearheads, but the bulk of the armies still march, partly through force of tradition, and partly because they are so large that mechanical transport only suffices to move their baggage and auxiliaries. Their aim is the Napoleonic one of destroying the enemy's army, and their leaders cling to the dream of riding the whirlwind in Napoleonic style. They are still intoxicated by the offensive idea, for the sobering effect of the chilly blasts of 1914-1918 has been overcome by fresh draughts of pure martial spirit. The true soldier's thirst is unquenchable. Whatever disillusionment he meets, he is always sure that things will go right next time.

Certainly, in the background of his present picture some unpleasant spectres hover. Aircraft and tanks are among them. Gas and smoke, moreover, confuse the outline in a mildly disturbing way. It is admitted that all these newer elements may affect the issue, but they are primarily viewed as aids in destroying the enemy's army, and their possible inconvenience to one's own is shunned so far as possible, like other displeasing thoughts.

Would Another War End Civilization?

Thus there is ground for the assumption that however a next war may develop, the war plans at least may be on familiar lines, and the opening moves may be according to pattern—the pattern that past wars have traced. This may be no more than a continuation of what 1918 witnessed, or, at most, what 1919 held in store.

Such a view runs counter to a prevalent popular assertion—that every war is utterly different from the last. No fallacy is more confidently stated as fact—like all catch-phrases this is hard to overtake once in its stride. Yet the truth is that history, even modern history, shows a gradual evolution in the character of wars. The paramount conditions of warfare in 1914 had governed the Russo-Japanese war a decade earlier, and had been clearly foreshadowed in the American Civil War half a century before.

This gradualness of evolution has owed much to the stout resistance which the military profession has always offered to novelty. The impetus of science in the nineteenth century did not suffice to storm these ramparts. The obstruction that the tank had to overcome on paper before it took the field in 1916 is well known; less familiar is the fact that it might have been available before the war began. There was Mr. de Mole's tank, superior in design to the one that was actually produced. But the design had been submitted to the War Office and was there pigeon-holed—until the war was over. There was also the promising idea contained in drawings submitted by a plumber of Nottingham. It also was unearthed after the war; the file bore the brief but decisive verdict: 'The man's mad.' Similar blindness marked the attitude of even the more thoughtful among leading soldiers to the possibilities of the air. When Foch watched the 1910

325

Would Another War End Civilization?

Circuit de l'Est, which proved the reliability of the new invention, he exclaimed: 'That is good sport, but for the Army the aeroplane is no use.'

A question that naturally arises to-day is whether the growth of dictatorship may overcome this resistance to novelty. A successful dictator is apt to be more of a realist than is the relatively cloistered member of a General Staff. Even if of military origin, he is less embedded in the professional grooves. By his circumstances, he is dealing every day in the fundamentals of strategy, instead of soaking in theory for most of a lifetime before he has a chance to practise against opponents. Also he is usually younger. A significant symptom is the marked increase of attention which has been given to military aviation and army mechanization in Italy since Mussolini, and in Germany since Hitler came to power. Under these dictators Balbo in the one country and Goering in the other have also been giving strategy a fresh direction—skywards. Here, certainly, is a warning of danger for democratic countries where military doctrines have been dictated by the heads of a professional class, autocratic within their own sphere and cut off from others.

Nevertheless, the case of Napoleon, the supreme example of military dictatorship, brings a measure of comfort. For with more power than any modern soldier has enjoyed, he made less use of it to develop new tactics and weapons. He was content to continue with the means that existed, merely developing their application. And even here it was mainly in imparting energy to a technique he had inherited that he excelled. Most astonishing of all incidents in his unevolving military career was his action in disbanding the French Balloon Corps, which in 1794 had made its first effective appearance in battle at Gosselies near

Would Another War End Civilization?

Waterloo. If Napoleon had not stifled this promising infant, on its twenty-first birthday in June 1815 it might have saved him from irretrievable disaster at that very spot.

Appreciating the gradualness of military evolution, it behoves us to enquire as to the main lines it has taken in the past century or so.

First, was the growth of size. From France under the Revolution and Napoleon, through America in the Civil War and Prussia under Moltke, the armies swelled to the millions of 1914. Yet back in the eighteenth century Marshal Saxe had foreseen the hindrances of size when he delivered his dictum: 'Multitudes serve only to perplex and embarrass.'

Second, came the growth of fire-power, beginning with the adoption of rifles and breech-loading weapons. This, imposed on size, conduced to a growing paralysis of warfare on land and sea.

Third was the growth of industrialization. The change from well-distributed agricultural communities to a concentration of population and an interdependence of areas, together with the more complex needs of such a civilization, gave more influence in war to economic objectives. By acting against those, even in the comparatively primitive South, Sherman decided the issue of the American Civil War. Soldiers in Europe, however, remained unable to see much beyond the opposing army. Their eyes were bloodshot. Yet in the end it was the economic pressure, mainly applied by the Navy, which decided the issue of the World War.

A fourth was the revolutionary growth of mobility, due in turn to the steam engine and the motor. Paradoxically, its chief effect when added to the other tendencies was to reduce the effective mobility of armies. The railway—which had speed but not flexibility, the other constituent of mobility—fostered the accumulation of masses, and these were hampered not only by their own bulk but by the growth of fire. The road-motor, a much later development, was neglected until the war came and was then at first applied merely to the service of mass. Not until it was embodied in the tank did it begin to assist the recovery of mobility—by making it possible for men to advance in face of bullets. The aeroplane likewise began as a mere auxiliary, and to this minor role it was still mainly confined as its numbers grew. Even in the greatest bombing raid on London only thirty-three machines were employed, although four thousand were in use for the narrower duties of army co-operation. But in the last phase of the war, aircraft showed their powers at the expense of armies by frustrating the escape of the defeated Bulgarian, Turkish and Austrian armies: they turned the ebbing tide into a stagnant shambles.

What were the outstanding lessons of the war along these lines of evolution? The first, certainly, was that the huge conscript armies tended to make war inevitable, just as, when war was engaged, they tended to make it immobile. 'Mobilization means war', the German ambassador threateningly said to the Russian Foreign Minister with more profound truth than he intended. For, once the mass of the people were summoned to arms from their normal occupation, an atmosphere was created in which peace-feelers were stifled. Moreover, these armies were so cumbrous, their movement so complex, that even direction could not be modified. Thus, when the Kaiser, clutching at a report that France might forsake Russia's side and remain neutral, said to Moltke, the Chief of the German General

Would Another War End Civilization?

Staff: 'We march, then, only towards the East?' Moltke replied that this was 'impossible. The advance of armies formed of millions of men was the result of years of intricate work. Once planned it could not possibly be changed.' Even when a twenty-four hour delay of the invasion of France was ordered, Moltke pathetically recorded: 'It was a great shock to me, as though something had struck at my heart.' So the millions went forward.

But when they reached the battlefield, they were stopped by the machine-guns, few as these were. Back in 1884, a military prophet had acclaimed the machine-gun as 'concentrated essence of infantry'. Military authorities had paid little attention to such prophecies—until the war came in 1914. Then it was shown that one man sitting behind a machine-gun was equal to ten, a hundred, even a thousand, who were rushing on him with the bayonet. The generals were puzzled. They had always counted strength by count of heads.

It was the machine-gun that made infantry advance hopeless and cavalry futile. The next four years were spent in trying to overcome this obstacle.

First, the generals, true to their theory of mass, tried masses of artillery. This method achieved poor results in proportion to the effort. It made a short advance possible but forbade a long one—by ploughing up the ground over which the advance had to be made.

A new method dawned in 1916—the use of tanks. Reluctantly accepted by authority, it did not receive a real opportunity in the field until the last year. Then it produced longer and quicker advances than had hitherto been made, and proved, by German confession, the decisive weapon. If the war had continued into 1919, the Allies, at a young colonel's instigation, were going to try a more

329

original way of using tanks—to pass straight through the front, neglecting the enemy's fighting men, and strike direct at his headquarters and communication centres, dislocating his fighting power at the source.

The Germans had also tried, in 1915, a new means to overcome the barrier. This was gas. Luckily for the Allies, the German soldiers thwarted the German chemists, and the best chance of a decisive result was forfeited. Still, by ringing the changes on various types, gas continued to play an important part. The most effective, by far, was mustard gas, which disabled by blistering the skin and took effect even after a long interval. The strategic effect, however, was more in hampering an enemy's attack than in assisting one's own. Thus it tended to increase the paralysis in which the war was already gripped.

One possibility of overcoming machine-guns was largely neglected—the advance in obscurity. Night attacks were rare, for fear of confusion—although this was a lesser risk than a daylight advance in face of defending machine-guns. Smoke screens were never fully developed. When first suggested in 1914, Kitchener had emphatically declared that they 'would be of no use for land operations'! Yet in 1918, it was under cover of fog—nature's smoke—that the Germans repeatedly broke through the Allied front. When fog was lacking, they failed. It is strange that neither side sought to produce artificial fog on a great scale.

At sea likewise the same lines of evolution led to the same conclusion—a state of general paralysis. The traditional purpose of destroying the enemy's main forces in battle was never fulfilled, and although the fleets were once within range of each other, at Jutland, analysis of that tactically ineffective encounter tends to emphasize the factors that made for paralysis.

Would Another War End Civilization?

Naval development had been marked by swelling as on land, although this elephantiasis at sea affected the size of individual ships rather than the numbers of a fleet. Battleships became so large, and hence so few compared with Nelson's day, that admirals became more reluctant to risk them. And the growth of fire-power tended to keep the fleets apart; fighting at long ranges made a decision more difficult. To this check was added that of a new weapon, the torpedo; if it did not attain the results in sea fighting that had been anticipated by the prophets, this was largely because the fear of it made the admirals shy of pursuing an offensive movement—and thereby exposed the ineffectiveness of a battle-fleet. The lighter craft, too, were in consequence diverted to the unprofitable duty of chaperoning their big sisters. The British official history candidly confesses: 'The Grand Fleet could only put to sea with an escort of nearly one hundred destroyers . . . the German U-boats had hampered our squadrons to an extent which the most expert and far-sighted naval officer had never foreseen.' A few months after the 'victory' of Jutland, the danger of a German invasion of Denmark loomed on the horizon of the British Government; after examination by the Admiralty, the conclusion was reached that 'for naval reasons it would be almost impossible to support the Danes at all'. What a humiliating confession of impotence! The shadow of the German submarine was longer than the shadow of Nelson's column.

Nor was that all. The growth of industrialization had made nations, Britain above all, more dependent on overseas supply. By multiplying commerce it had multiplied the targets for indirect attack. While British destroyers were chaperoning battleships, the German submarines were sinking British mercantile shipping—until Britain herself was

in sight of collapse. When part of the destroyers were
diverted to protect commerce, the Grand Fleet had to be
practically locked up for its own safety! It was history's
most ironical case of 'protective arrest'.

As for the growth of mobility, through the supersession
of sails by steam, its influence is to be traced throughout
the stalemate that prevailed. Its effect, as on land, was to
engender a fundamental immobility. In the case of the
outer and greater naval power this prevented it destroying
the enemy's fleet; in the case of the inner and weaker,
Germany, it ensured her ultimate collapse from pernicious
anæmia.

Here we have traced the evolution of the past that has
produced the present state of warfare. What of the future?
Unless the whole current of history be reversed, it will
be a prolongation of the past. It is not practical to deal
here with hypothetical influences that might revolutionize the situation. Electric waves and stratospheric rockets
may be left to the imaginative novelist until the scientist
has produced results that not only stand inspection but
provide ground for scientific military speculation. Meantime, we shall be wise to bear in mind that the pigeon-
holes of War Offices have proved an effective antidote to
any new poison—at least until its greatest menace has
passed.

So, on the basis of what exists and what reflection
shows, let us try to trace the outline of another great war
—the outline of the opening act, at least. And for reasons
better or worse, there may be no second act in the true
sense; only an epilogue.

By the very force of custom, and the natural desire to
justify their existence, it is likely that the armies may again
attempt to act as they did in 1914. We may even see the

Would Another War End Civilization?

many-headed columns of troops passing down the roads across the frontier. But it needs no small feat of imagination to see them going very far. They may be able to start if they get off before the starter's pistol as in 1914, and make their approach marches under cover of night; it is likely that the major part of the opponent's air force will be aiming at more important targets during this initial phase. But once across the frontier, they will meet brakes more severe than any in past experience. Chains of machine-guns ensconced in hidden concrete casemates or rushed up in motor vehicles; a cloud of tanks looming on their flanks; a darker cloud of aircraft overhead that will force them to disperse, besides assailing the long supply trains that cannot disperse. There has also been much advance since the last war in the art of stopping progress by demolitions. An invasion may soon become slow motion, and then a pitiful stagnation.

Motor vehicles abound not only in the establishment of armies but in the households of every town and village. Motor vehicles, even the humblest runabouts, can carry machine-guns; and machine-guns are movement-stoppers. They can be switched to any point, to block any threatening line of invasion, and will certainly impede the enemy's advance. By use of the motor, armed civilians may play a more formidable part in the future than ever in the past, while professional motor bandits may turn temporarily to patriotic employment like the freebooters of old.

If and when the opposing armies come in contact, the machine-gun obstacle, intensified by wire entanglements and land minefields, will still have to be overcome. Is there any more chance of success than in the last war? The contrary, rather. For the proportion of machine-gun-destroying weapons—artillery and tanks—is at present lower in all armies than it was in 1918. And, on the other hand, the proportion of machine-guns, heavy and light, has greatly increased. Thus, it is a matter of simple arithmetic to deduce that the advantage of the defensive is even greater than before. Realizing this, a clear-sighted commander-in-chief may elect to stay on the defensive and await his enemy's attack. His troops will thus suffer less physical damage and less shock to their confidence, but they will not achieve any positive result unless the enemy is rash enough to persist so long in his vain attempt to advance that he exhausts his troops so severely that they cannot withstand an attack in their turn. Another possibility is that both sides will be clear-sighted, and await attack—in which case they will merely produce stalemate without conflict.

If mustard gas be employed, early stalemate is still more probable. For an army will tend to spray mustard gas along the parts of its front where it intends to stay on the defensive, and to concentrate its forces on the parts more favourable for its own attack. As the favourable and unfavourable sectors will commonly be the opposite for the enemy army, we may even see a reduction to absurdity by which each army's would-be offensive sector is blocked by the enemy's mustard gas barrier—so that the two will sit facing each other helplessly, separated by a continuous mutual barrier which both have combined to raise!

Tanks offer a possible means of advance, both in face of machine-guns and across a gas-belt. But the proportion of them is so small, and the fear of them so great, that each side is likely to give its first attention to blocking and destroying the other's tank forces. So long as the tank forces are but a small fraction of the total forces, this effort

334

at cancellation has the chances in its favour. Moreover, until it does, the fear of the enemy's armoured troops will have a numbing effect on the movement of all unarmoured troops—and thus promise to aggravate the paralysis of the past.

The prospect for armies is a dull one. The gloomiest aspect is due to the cloud overhead. Air attack is not much of a menace to infantry who are deployed or entrenched. But long columns on the march are vulnerable. Their movement can easily be stopped—and if they cannot move they cannot reach the battlefield. Tanks and other cross-country vehicles, by contrast, offer a poor target to air bombers while on the move, especially when they move off the roads on a wide front. When they halt, voluntarily or involuntarily, they become vulnerable. Moreover, they are dependent, like all troops, on being supplied with fuel, food and ammunition. It is against the long and narrow arteries, as well as the concentrated sources of supply, that air attack has its greatest scope. There is no need to accept all the claims made by air enthusiasts for the present accuracy of bomb-dropping. The system of supply of a great army is so complex that it can easily be thrown out of gear. Dislocation will suffice, with little destruction, to cripple the power of movement. Every increase in the mobility—the speed and range—of aircraft threatens to increase the immobility of armies.

Thus the awe-inspiring advance of the armies may end in a general farce—although locally it may spell tragedy. For little imagination is needed to picture the mobs of unfed soldiery, breaking their ranks as hunger becomes acute and pillaging their own towns and countryside—to the quicker starvation of all in common, unless an armistice be speedily arranged so that communications may be restored. And the war may peter out in an atmosphere charged with the sense of futility.

A further deduction is unmistakable. The larger the army that a country maintains and tries to mobilize on the outbreak of war, the weaker that country may be. For, by the congestion of all the national arteries that large-scale mobilization entails, it will immensely increase its own difficulties and dangers in face of air attack, thus diminishing its own ability to withstand the sudden stresses of the first days of war.

It is possible that a would-be aggressor might be deterred by foresight from these old methods of invasion—although there is only a glimmer of the new idea in the present composition of the European armies. An inroad of mechanized forces, powerful but relatively small, would certainly be more difficult to check than the advance of marching millions—especially if it came without warning. Such a force might assemble many miles behind the frontier overnight and be across before morning. It might overwhelm the defender's frontier-covering troops before they realized that war had broken out, and pierce by surprise a chain of forts. The possibility might be the greater if such a stroke were launched by machines equipped with direction-finders under cover of artificial fog—this is a potential development which deserves serious attention.

But even if successful, it is difficult to picture these forces achieving more than to multiply the disorder in the interior of the country which would already have been created by air attack on the industrial centres and arteries of traffic. Unless the defender signified his immediate surrender, and this would be difficult for him in a state of chaos, it would be necessary to follow up the stroke with reinforcements and occupying troops. Here would lie the invader's hardest problem—harder than ever in the past, since the difficulty of maintaining communications is greater. It is conceivable that by extraordinary foresight, by gauging the trend of developments exactly, and by perfectly calculated measures to diminish his own vulnerability while maintaining his strength, an attacker might succeed in producing the internal collapse of his adversary without courting his own—but such foresight has never been shown by any makers of war. The greater probability is that the sequel to the attack would be a mutual breakdown on land.

At sea, a similar prospect prevails. To the paralytic power which the submarine exercised in 1914-1918, is now added the power of the faster surface light-craft, the new torpedo-armed 60 m.p.h. speedboat, and of the 200 m.p.h. aircraft—soon, by all signs, to be 300 m.p.h. even for a normal service machine. Here again, the effect can be measured without counting upon the possibility that the battle-fleets may be bombed out of existence. For practical effect, paralysis will suffice, without destruction. And when we reckon the new agents now added to the submarine, it needs a greater stretch of the imagination to see the battle-fleets being less paralysed than they were in 1914-1918 than to see them recovering their lost powers under greater impediments. The stagnation of the trade-routes, now that they are exposed over so many miles to attack from shore-based aircraft, is equally calculable. If the flow of commerce could barely continue under the pressure of a few score submarines, themselves slow and vulnerable, is it reasonable to assume that it can survive this multiplied menace of to-day and to-morrow?

Nations may still go to war in face of the warning. But

can they go on with it? The outcome seems more likely to be merely ridiculous than to be fatally decisive. Certainly, so far as the conflict of armed forces is concerned.

This reflection, however, does not banish the risk to the nations who go to war. That danger is two-fold; first, that they will not come to their senses in time to retrieve order from the chaos into which their communications will be plunged; second, that irreparable damage may be done by deliberate attack on the centres of population, ignoring the opponents' armed forces.

There is an almost universal assumption that any future war will open with a concentrated air attack on the enemy's capital. I see reasons, and have already indicated some, for doubting this popular certainty.

We should be rash to place unreserved trust in 'rules of war'. Recent history shows all too clearly that rules are broken as soon as they are felt as an endangering hindrance to a nation that thinks it is fighting for its life—a conviction that has taken root with the growth of 'democracy'. But it would be equally unhistorical to disregard altogether the restraining power of such rules—especially in the early stages of a war, before frustration or disaster had come to aggravate the sense of constraint.

It is more probable that direct injury to the population will come indirectly, through attack on military objectives —such as arsenals, aerodromes, and dockyards—which lie in a thickly populated area. The intermixture favours the least scrupulous combatant by offering him a good opportunity and excuse for achieving a coincident effect on the enemy people's will. The use of incendiary mingled with high-explosive bombs—a combination that is likely to be more effective and militarily economic than gas— will have more promise at such objectives of striking in-

flammable targets and thus spreading a conflagration out-
wards. Such fires, in turn, are likely to spread panic faster
and wider than by the destruction of comparatively isolated blocks of houses and business offices attained in the
promiscuous bombing of a city. This possibility emphasizes
the importance of separating military from civil objectives
as far as possible, by removing munition works and other
military establishments away from the cities.

I have already referred to the antidote which is latent
in War Offices. So long as the official military minds of
the world cling to the dogmas of Clausewitz, that the
main aim in war is the destruction of the enemy's armed
forces, so long may we count on the restraining power of a
military 'rule of war' that is far more potent than any of
the rules drawn up at Geneva. Professional indoctrination
goes deeper than humanitarianism. Moreover, although
the war-minded statesman may be free from this professional bias towards battle, he will be influenced by his
responsibility to the people in his cities, and perhaps
also by his own presence among them. Fear of instant
reprisals—all the stronger from being in this new case a
fear of the unknown—may well incline him to accept
the inherent military preference for an orthodox war-
plan, aimed mainly at the enemy's forces and their
bases.

Another influence, working to the same effect, is the
irrepressible optimism of the military mind. To the
scientific historian the way that the wish has fathered
the thought throughout the course of warfare, and led to
endless futilities, is apt to seem the most extraordinary of
military phenomena. Yet it must be realized that the
power of command is largely based on this confidence,
however often misplaced. Inherent in the military nature,

it has now recovered from the shocks of hard experience in 1914-1918, which were the less severely felt because of the resiliency of this optimism. Studying the military leaders of the various powers in Europe to-day, one finds that with rare exceptions they are inflated anew with the confidence in victory that their predecessors had in 1914. They are dreaming again of an irresistible offensive and of a rapid decision. Only a short time ago the Italian authorities exuberantly declared that 'trench-warfare was obsolete'—that 'the first onslaught of tanks and fast-moving detachments would break through trench-lines, force fighting into the open, and make movement so rapid that nothing would be gained by digging new trenches'. And the authorities of other armies echoed the opinion. To a cool observer it seemed the more curious since Italy, while admirably endowed with natural defences against an invader, is even more deficient in tanks for attack than some of the other countries.

If this soldierly optimism unhappily makes for war, by its tendency to delude governments as to the chances, it promises a compensation—that it will direct the initial war-effort along the customary military road, which appears to be a cul-de-sac. As the martial crowds pour down it, congestion and then stagnation are likely to come as soon as air attack on the communications takes effect. The armies may not even reach the battlefield before paralysis overtakes them from the tail up.

It is then that the danger of direct air attack on the cities may come to a head. The air forces, with the military side of their mission accomplished, may be concentrated on the civil. But modern air forces depend on a large ground organization, and this may hardly escape the prevailing chaos. Thus the air menace may be limited, if not crippled, at source—just when the menace would otherwise reach its peak.

Against a limited menace, adequate preparation for protection is possible—not so much by direct defence as by diminishing vulnerability. For this it is an urgent necessity to remove military targets from the neighbourhood of cities, and more feasible than the construction of innumerable shelters. Air raid precautions and emergency preparations of all kinds, will count for much. But of all the possible safeguards, education and understanding are likely to prove the greatest. And on these equally depend the answer to the question whether a state is prepared, mentally as well as practically, to cope with the state of chaos that war promises to produce at an early stage. The fate of the peoples is thus to a large extent in their own hands.

'If you wish for peace, prepare for war,' ran the old Roman maxim. It is still true, but in a different sense. The wiser course to-day is not to multiply forces, especially the massive type of forces that conduce to the chaos of communications, but to prepare indirect protection by diminishing the target and inoculating the system against susceptibility to chaos. True preparedness lies in understanding the trend of modern war.

The most reassuring symptom is, certainly, that the most military-minded peoples at present show a misunderstanding of modern war. The proof lies in their retention of huge conscript armies that must inevitably hamper their power of adaptability to modern war conditions. Fatness is not strength. It is clear that they have missed the meaning of mobility. This is natural. For thousands of years war has been waged at 3 m.p.h. In a generation we have sprung to the possibility of waging it at 300 m.p.h. Such a change baffles military comprehension. So the military-minded peoples strive to achieve the impossible feat of blending 3 m.p.h. forces with 300 m.p.h. The proverbial folly of putting new wine into old skins is nothing compared with that of putting aviation spirit into inflammable skins. Happily, the risk is greatest for the men who make the unthinking experiment. Thereby there is reasonable hope that another war may produce the collapse of the attack before the collapse of civilization. And that a sense of the ridiculous may bring the warring peoples to their senses before they can renew the war-effort.

Index

Index

Index

Index

SPECIAL FACTORS

346

Index

347

Index